Novel Shocks

Novel Shocks

Urban Renewal and the Origins of Neoliberalism

Myka Tucker-Abramson

FORDHAM UNIVERSITY PRESS

New York 2019

Visit us online at www.fordhampress.com.

Library of Congress Cataloging-in-Publication Data

Names: Tucker-Abramson, Myka, author.
Title: Novel shocks : urban renewal and the origins of neoliberalism / Myka Tucker-Abramson.
Other titles: Urban renewal and the origins of neoliberalism
Description: First edition. | New York : Fordham University Press, 2019. | Includes bibliographical references and index.
Identifiers: LCCN 2018024887 | ISBN 9780823282708 (cloth : alk. paper) | ISBN 9780823282692 (pbk. : alk. paper)
Subjects: LCSH: American fiction—20th century—History and criticism. | Urban renewal in literature. | Discrimination in literature. | Neoliberalism—United States—History—20th century.
Classification: LCC PS374.U74 T83 2018 | DDC 813/.54093581—dc23
LC record available at https://lccn.loc.gov/2018024887

Printed in the United States of America
21 20 19   5 4 3 2 1
First edition

CONTENTS

	Introduction	I
1.	Blueprints: *Invisible Man* and the Great Migration to White Flight	25
2.	The Price of Salt Is the City: Patricia Highsmith and the Queer Frontiers of Neoliberalism	46
3.	*Naked Lunch*, Or, the Last Snapshot of the Surrealists	63
4.	Shock Therapy: *Atlas Shrugged*, Urban Renewal, and the Making of the Entrepreneurial Subject	84
5.	Fallen Corpses and Rising Cities: *The Bell Jar* and the Making of the New Woman	104
	Conclusion: *The Siege of Harlem* and Its Commune	125
	Acknowledgments	139
	Notes	143
	Works Cited	163
	Index	185

NOVEL SHOCKS

Introduction

In James Baldwin's 1962 novel *Another Country*, Eric Jones returns to New York City after spending three years in Paris to find his city suddenly foreign. "It might," he muses, "for strange barbarity of manner and custom, for the sense of danger and horror barely sleeping beneath the rough, gregarious surface, have been some impenetrably exotic city of the East" (230). Eric's experience of the postwar city as foreign was a common one among New Yorkers in the early 1960s. In the preceding decade, New York had been ground zero for a nationwide experiment, later termed urban renewal, that aimed to respond to what planners, politicians, and downtown business interests worried was an irreversible urban decline resulting from the interconnected processes of a great migration of blacks, Latinos, and Puerto Ricans into the city and the flight of industry, commerce, and the white tax base into the suburbs. Empowered by the Housing Act of 1949, the first national policy designed to deal with overcrowding and urban blight, New York bulldozed its slums to make way for modern housing and cultural complexes, freeways, public and private housing projects, medical centers, and commercial skyscrapers, all of which promised to restore profitability and order to a decaying downtown core. Taken together, these processes transformed New York's metropolitan region in as dramatic and wrenching a fashion as Baron Haussmann's creative destruction of Paris a century before.[1]

While the Housing Act of 1949, the Federal Highway Act of 1956, and the urban renewal revolution they engendered were national, the effects especially of the former on Manhattan were particularly notable. Throughout the 1950s and 1960s, countless "blighted" areas in New York were cleared out, bulldozed, and replaced with the infrastructure that would become emblematic of a new urban modernity: the miles of glass-and-steel office buildings, the headquarters of the United Nations, the arts and cultural complexes of Lincoln Square, the countless middle-class modernist housing developments, new world-class medical centers, and expanded university campuses. Indeed, New York City secured more money for projects than all other American cities combined (Caro, 12). However, urban renewal's importance for the remaking of New York was not just physical but also ideological. Then head of New York City's Committee on Slum Clearance Robert Moses, in particular, saw in the act the potential to transform New York and like Haussmann before him, in the words of David Harvey, to "bludgeon [Paris] into modernity" (2003b, 2).[2] He was not alone. The Housing Act was part of a Cold War vision shared by city planners, politicians, architects, and even in some cases the city's left wing and union membership, which, as Samuel Zipp explains, sought to establish Manhattan as "an icon of global power, and make it, quite literally, the capital of international modernity" (2012, 5).

Like the writers, artists, and walkers of Paris, Eric, too, struggles to make sense of this new rationalized modernity that seems so unaccountably alien and so hostile to its inhabitants. "One was continually being jostled," Eric mourns, "yet longed, at the same time, for the sense of others, for a human touch; and if one was never—it was the general complaint—left alone in New York, one had, still, to fight very hard in order not to perish of loneliness" (230). For Eric, though, the real horror of the city is not just the foreignness of the landscape but how this landscape and this loneliness have created a "kind of plague" that has taken over and "blighted" the city's youth (231), literally altering the very subjectivity of its urban dwellers. New York, he argues, has forced men to become "at home with, accustomed to, brutality and indifference, and to be terrified of human affection" (231); it has become a city in which men become machines, walking with "a kind of anti-erotic, knee-action lope [. . . that] was a parody of locomotion and manhood" (231).

In this evocative description, we hear echoes of Walter Benjamin's famous depiction of the subject whose overexposure to the stimulus of urban modernity has deadened and automated him. In his famous essay on Paris after it had been modernized by Haussmann, "On Some Motifs in Baudelaire" (1939), Benjamin wonders what happens when the processes of urbanization transform the experience of "shock"—what Sigmund Freud described as the traumatic experience that occurs when the "protective shield" of the subject's conscious brain is unable to protect the unconscious from "the excessive energies of the outside world" (27)—into an experience of daily life. Benjamin speculates that in such a world, the "shield" grows ever-thicker and the subject is increasingly "cheated out of experience" (332): "Whereas Poe's passers-by cast glances in all directions, seemingly without cause, today's pedestrians are obliged to look about them so that they can be aware of traffic signals. Thus, technology has subjected the human sensorium to a complex kind of training" (328). The question that both Benjamin and Eric ask is, What is the possibility of experience, and thus of a politics, under such conditions? But where Benjamin's question is addressed to the monumentalism and centralization of nineteenth-century urbanization, which, as Benjamin insists, expressed the imperialist ambitions of Napoleon III (Buck Morss 1991, 89), Eric's question addresses a very different moment of urban modernity: one marked by the interconnected forces of urban renewal and decentralization alongside the new "informal empire" of US hegemony. This book argues that this question of the possibility of experience within the sensoria of urban renewal is central to the postwar novel. And through the novel's engagement with this question of experience, the postwar novel began to grapple with, and shape, the subjectivities and landscapes of prosperous, private, white suburbs and entrepreneurialism and poor, public, black cities and criminality that would nourish the roots of neoliberalism.

Baldwin was a well-known critic of urban renewal, famously quipping in a 1963 interview that urban renewal amounted to "negro removal" (Stanley and Pratt, 42). *Another Country* stages this process in particularly stark terms. While Eric's descriptions of New York—its exoticism, its barbarity, and its decay—echo the discourse of blight that became the staple of Moses's glossy slum-clearance brochures, Baldwin turns the language of slum clearance and urban renewal on its head. Whereas in the discourse of urban renewal, "blight" either referred to older, densely populated, industrial neighborhoods in economic decline or, more often, was a code word for what Eric Avila terms the "bodies and places of people of color"

(2004, 3), for Baldwin's Eric, "blight" refers to the massive modernization and renewal projects that he sees destroying the city and dehumanizing its residents.

Baldwin was not alone in using the language and imagery of shock to depict and critique the processes of urban renewal that were transforming the landscape and culture of New York City. Throughout the 1950s and early 1960s, a spate of New York novels such Ralph Ellison's *Invisible Man* (1952), Patricia Highsmith's *The Price of Salt* (1952), Ayn Rand's *Atlas Shrugged* (1957), William Burroughs's *Naked Lunch* (1959), and Sylvia Plath's *The Bell Jar* (1963) depicted and responded to these new urban spaces as forms of traumatic "shock" that required new aesthetic forms and political structures. These novels rejected older shock-based modernisms such as surrealism and naturalism and, like the urbanization projects they depicted, forged a new kind of modernism, one that transformed shock from a traumatic effect of urban modernity that disrupts the subject's psychic economy into a therapeutic force that helps strengthen and shape a more flexible, self-reliant, and resilient subject.

Often drawing on and revising the Western genre of the turn of the twentieth century to reimagine both the city and the human psyche as a frontier that can be retaken, these novels reveal the origins of the renewed frontier imaginary that shaped and nourished the gentrification of US cities in the 1970s and 1980s (N. Smith, 1996), and that played a crucial role in forging what Matthew Huber, following Michel Foucault, terms the "entrepreneurial subject" of neoliberalism: that is, the subject who sees life as a "coherent space of privatized freedom [. . .] entirely produced by and reducible to one's own life choices and entrepreneurial efforts" (xv). *Novel Shocks* argues that resituating the novel within the context of (sub) urban transformation and the rise of neoliberalism transforms both our understanding of the midcentury novel and its resonance for our contemporary moment, as well as our understanding of the "roots and routes" of neoliberalism's emergence.[3]

The Roots and Routes of Neoliberal Urbanism

Between the 1870s and the 1930s, American cities appeared to be expanding at a limitless rate. Cities were home to the factories producing the weapons and goods that provided the United States economic and military dominance, to the thousands of immigrants arriving every year from Europe, and to the internal migrants moving from the rural South to escape the economic and physical violence of Jim Crow. During the Great Depression, however, that growth screeched to a halt. Cities were no longer associated with growth, prosperity, and futurity but with population loss, declining land values, unemployment, and a foreclosed, industrial past.[4] Throughout the 1930s, proponents of what would come to be known as urban renewal began to speak of a "blight" that was plaguing the core of northeastern industrial cities. A Depression-era building freeze compounded by the influx of racial and ethnic populations created a housing shortage that empowered predatory landlords to cram more and more people into already densely packed inner-city areas, transforming these once prosperous urban neighborhoods into shantytowns and slums.

In the 1930s, business interests, charities, housing activists, and government officials all struggled to come up with solutions to this seemingly intractable housing problem and the problem of the inner-city slum. While most of these solutions were organized around a haphazard mix of charity, private initiative, and limited public housing, a new generation of European-inspired housing reformers and activists like Catherine Bauer and Lewis Mumford started organizing around the so-called Modern Housing movement, which called for the creation of a broad, noncommercial, and "universalistic" federal housing policy (Radford, 1).[5] Throughout the 1930s, these activists and reformers gained traction and influence in Franklin Roosevelt's New Deal administration, which began passing bills that recognized the need for federal planning and intervention: the experimental housing program of the Public Works Administration; the Housing Act of 1937; the first National Housing Act, which established standards for reasonable housing and provided (ultimately inadequate) federal assistance for the purpose of slum clearance and the "provision of decent, safe and sanitary dwellings for families of low income" (qtd. in Oberlander and Newbrun, 157); the Highway Act of 1944, which provided $125 million to improve urban roadways; and the 1944 Servicemen's Readjustment Act, which enabled veterans to borrow money for housing without a down payment.

However, the racist presuppositions behind and often explicitly within these bills did not create the system of Modern Housing that Bauer et al. envisioned but, instead, a two-tiered system in which the state provided support for the white middle- and upper-class segments of the population to resettle in relatively spacious and affluent suburbs, while relegating African Americans, Puerto Ricans, and other minorities to the slums, ghettoes, and, when available, poorly funded and demonized public housing projects of the city.[6] By the 1950s, the suburbs had become the Cold War showroom for what Elaine Tyler May termed "the American way of life as the triumph of capitalism allegedly available to all who believed in its values" (8). But the suburbs didn't just model the American way of life; they shaped it, carrying out what Henri Lefebvre and the Situationists would decry as "the colonization" and privatization "of everyday life" (qtd. in K. Ross 1996, 7). Suburbanization created a nation of homeowners instead of renters; it created a nation of privatized, nuclear families that contributed toward the breaking down of older, more communal forms of living that centered around urban spaces; it brought about a return to, and calcification of, those nineteenth-century gender ideologies that rested on separate spheres for men and women; and it ushered in a proliferation of new gadgets and machines—cars, washing machines, dryers, dishwashers—that turned the home into a factory and the homemaker into an entrepreneur in charge of organizing and managing their own household. But these same policies also created a nation of urban slums. Contrary to the hopes of the New Deal reformers, throughout the 1930s and 1940s cities became increasingly impoverished and overpopulated as wealth and business followed the construction boom and tax subsidies to the suburbs, effectively turning US industrial centers into economic backwaters while creating mass unemployment and concentrating racialized poverty in urban cores. This, in turn, set the stage for the urban policing policies that formed that other *ur* identity of neoliberalism: the figure of racialized criminality.[7]

The final blow to the Modern Housing movement came with the 1949 Housing Act, a sweeping piece of postwar legislation that created a legal framework and secured federal funds for what came to be known as urban renewal.[8] Aptly characterized by Jacob Levenson as "a bizarre alloy of New Deal public housing idealism and postwar business acumen" (198), the 1949 Housing Act became a key tool in the hands of city boosters and developers to staunch the flow of capital and white bodies out of the city by remaking cities in the prosperous image of the suburbs, and thus luring the white, middle-class, and largely female shopper downtown (Zipp 2012; Isenberg 2004). It did so by enabling municipalities, downtown business interests, neighborhood organizations, and urban planning agencies to clear vast sections of the city deemed to be "blighted" in order to create new urban spaces in line with the principles of modern planning: clean, spacious, and well-ordered, with separate spaces for living, working, and leisure.

In the United States, if not in Europe, this vision of separate living and working spaces was embedded in another kind of separation: a separation between races. Almost as soon as the 1949 Housing Act was drafted, Frank Horne, the head of the Housing and Home Finance Agency (HHFA) Race

Relations Service, warned that that the act would likely be used to reconsolidate practices of racial segregation through economic means. Writing to Raymond Foley, the head of the HHFA, Horne argued that this act lacked the necessary safeguards to "prevent the possibility of Federal funds and powers being utilized by localities to clear entire neighborhoods, change the location of entire population groups, and crystalize patterns of racial or nationalistic separation by allowing private developers—for whose benefit the legislation is primarily drawn—to prohibit occupancy in new developments merely on the basis of race" (qtd. in Hirsch 2000, 398–89). If this occurred, Horne warned, the HHFA would be guilty of using "Federal funds and powers to harden into brick and mortar the racially restrictive practices of private real estate and lending operations" (399).

Horne would be proved right. In the ensuing years, urban renewal contributed significantly toward a new ideological and spatial regime of segregation.[9] Ideologically, urban renewal allowed for seemingly race-neutral economic arguments about declining property values to replace older arguments based on biological difference (Freund, 12). Physically, urban renewal provided the legal framework and federal funds to respatialize and fracture the city into spacious, private, middle-class housing developments for whites and constrictive, public, and poor ghettoes for blacks. As Clarence Mitchell, civil rights activist and then staff of Roosevelt's Fair Employment Practices Committee, put it, "What the courts have forbidden state legislatures and city councils to do and what the Ku Klux Klan had not been able to accomplish by intimidation and violence, the present Federal Housing Policy is accomplishing through a monumental program of segregation" (qtd. in Hirsch 2000, 411). Race was now so thoroughly absorbed into the circuits of housing capital such that when suburban tax protestors in the 1970s called for cuts to taxes and to public service provisions, they no longer needed to talk about race; "public" already signified racialized, and "private," white.

This racialization of the real estate market was not merely a local issue; real estate and housing were central to the United States' bid to both restabilize and establish itself as the leader of the global capitalist system. Alongside suburbanization, urban renewal helped the United States restabilize global capitalism after World War II by absorbing the surpluses of capital and labor whose stagnation manifested itself in the global Great Depression of the 1930s (Harvey 2012, 8). While this accumulation strategy rested on the massive outpouring of state funds for the construction of highways, housing, hospitals, universities, and cultural centers, it also required transforming the city into a new frontier of capital through the creation of what Neil Smith has termed the "rent gap"—that is, the gap between actual and potential ground rent (1996, 65).[10] Thus, urbanization as a strategy for the restabilization of global capitalism rested on the underdevelopment of urban space, which in turn transformed the city into a new frontier and site for profit-making and development. It is this capitalization on the rent gap, often carried out through extreme mobilizations of local, national, and international state power and particularly violence, that is one of the defining features of gentrification and what Neil Smith terms "neoliberal urbanism" (2002, 427). Urban renewal, in other words, formed the basis for the long and soon to be global struggle over the displacement and dispossession of urban populations that has been a defining feature of neoliberalism. Urban renewal, however, was also entangled with the United States' aspirations to gain global hegemony and establish its legitimacy as the leader of the so-called free world, along with its attempts to win the patronage of the newly decolonizing countries. Renewal thus ended up playing a contradictory role. At the same time that urban renewal calcified patterns of segregation and heralded a new regime of urbanization based on racialized violence and displacement, it was also central to the United States' Cold War strategy of presenting itself as a racially harmonious and prosperous nation able to act as a champion for global freedom.

Whereas suburbia emblematized the fantasy of the white middle-class suburban household that underpinned the "American way of life," urban renewal allegorized what the road to such a way of life might look like for the Third World countries emerging from the nonage of colonialism. In the years following World War II, forty countries and 800 million people fought for and secured their independence from the old colonial powers (Von Eschen, 125). The support and patronage of these newly independent countries played a central role in the Cold War battles for hegemony as each superpower fought to establish itself as the best path to modernization (Medovoi, 11–12). Both the Soviet Union and the United States understood the importance of US cities in this larger battle. Not only were cities becoming home to an increasingly militant, anti-imperialist, and anticapitalist black power and black workerist movement, but throughout the 1950s the Soviet Union pointed to the endemic segregation, violence, and inequality that marked Jim Crow in the South and urban slums in the North as evidence of the United States' inability (and that of capitalism more broadly) to assume global power.[11] Within this context, the increasing poverty and segregation plaguing America's cities became a central concern for the US state, which sought both to quell dissent at home and to shore up what State Department officials regarded as the Achilles heel of Cold War foreign policy (Singh 2004, 7).

Urban renewal went hand in hand with what Melamed usefully terms "racial liberalism" to describe the twenty-year period of racial reforms that sought to counteract widespread, international criticism of US racism by creating an image of America as racially harmonious and inclusive, and thus formally enacting an alignment between decolonization, self-determination, and capitalist-democracy. Especially in New York, urban renewal was seen by liberal advocates such as the State Committee for Anti-Discrimination as an important tool in the campaign for urban interracialism (J. Schwartz, 169) and subsequently became a key strategy through which the United States attempted to demonstrate its ability to solve its own racial problems. African Americans were thus positioned simultaneously as a site of what Harvey terms "accumulation through dispossession" (2003a) and, through programs like the Goodwill Jazz Ambassadors, as the ideological symbol of America's racial democracy, used to paper over or provide ideological cover to the United States' often violent modernization and development programs that underwrote its hegemony.[12] This double bind of urban renewal's dispossession and selective inclusion lies at the center of *Another Country*. It is, most notably, focalized through Eric's friend and lover Rufus Scott, a jazz drummer whose suicide is the foundational trauma that at once fractures and catalyzes the novel. Through Rufus's status as a famous jazz musician, his bohemian and multiracial circle of friends, the parties he attends in skyscrapers overlooking the city, and his free and easy movements across the lushly described landscapes of New York City, Baldwin positions him and New York as symbols of the promise for a new, racially mixed, prosperous, free, and multiracial freedom that American freedom had on offer. And yet, as we saw, just beneath the city's vibrant, shiny exterior is a "murderous" (5), segregated, and highly policed city teeming with racially inflected hatred and rage. It is a city that ultimately destroys Rufus, driving him to a mental breakdown and finally to suicide, as he jumps off the George Washington Bridge and into the Hudson River, acting as a kind of final symbol of Baldwin's oft-quoted claim that urban renewal was simply "negro removal" (42).

But while Rufus's death illustrates Baldwin's incisive critiques of urban renewal, it also announces the demise of the hegemonic force of urban renewal and racial liberalism by staging the shattering of any kind of consensus. Read one way, Rufus's suicide demonstrates the utter failure of racial liberalism's laws and social policies to bring about an improvement in the conditions of African Americans. In doing so, the novel anticipates the critiques and anger that motivated the urban rebellions of 1964 and 1965, which marked the end of urban renewal and racial liberalism, and the ascension of the black power movement. But Rufus's death can also align with a very different kind of critique of urban renewal and racial liberalism. After all, the descriptions of Rufus's life—marked by alcohol abuse, queerness, sexual promiscuity across the color line and an eventually violent relationship with the white, southern woman Leona, and ultimate mental breakdown, institutionalization, and suicide—would not be antagonistic to the narrative visions of decaying and blighted cities, and black cultural and psychic poverty espoused by the movies, books, and imaginaries of what Eric Avila aptly terms white flight's *"new* 'new mass culture'"* (2004, 7). Read thusly, Rufus's death also anticipates the antistatist critiques of urban renewal and racial liberalism put forward by a burgeoning politics of white suburban conservatism, which would eventually focalize around a sustained struggle to withdraw suburban tax dollars from postwar cities, especially New York and Oakland, in the 1970s.[13]

In Rufus, *Another Country* captures the breakdown of urban renewal and racial liberalism as it shattered into two antistatist pieces: one primarily black, urban, and revolutionary, the other primarily white, suburban, and reactionary. These movements both announced the end of the so-called postwar deal but were also part of the larger political crises that neoliberalism would quell through a new regime of selective inclusion and economic exclusion: the crafting of a state premised on the private property, individualist, and antistatist politics of the suburban rebellion on the one hand and, on the other, on a dual-pronged strategy of criminalization and limited accommodation, appropriation, and rerouting of the more radical demands of social movements into institutional spaces, like the university.[14] In his depiction of the breakdown of racial liberalism, then, Baldwin provides us with a necessary prehistory of neoliberalism, one rooted not in the ideas or ideologies of protoneoliberal thinkers but in the built environment and urban sensoria of the postwar United States out of which the political, subjective, and ideological conjuncture of neoliberalism was forged.

The Neoliberal Novel and Novel Neoliberalism

In this book, I argue that the midcentury US novel was an important terrain on which the battles that result in neoliberal hegemony in the United States were forged. In so doing, I intervene in contemporary debates on neoliberalism within postwar US literary studies in two ways. First, by drawing on the research of urban historians and geographers who argue that the protoneoliberal suburban tax revolts of the 1970s emerged from implicitly, and often explicitly, racist postwar urban and suburban policies developed in the 1940s and 1950s,[15] I emphasize the role that cultural production played in the struggles out of which neoliberalism was forged. In doing so, I build on recent work that has considered the cultural, ideological, and affective effects and productions of a fully realized neoliberal system by both extending current discussions of neoliberalism and the American novel back to the midcentury and interrogating the material histories that produced these neoliberal forms of reason and affective structures.[16] I do so, however, by turning not to the ideas and forms of reason developed at a gathering in the mountains of Mont Pèlerin but rather to the lived struggles over urban and suburban space, within the larger context of decolonization and US-backed neocolonialism out of which, I contend, neoliberalism emerged.[17]

Just as urban historians and political economists have shown how Keynesian policies and institutions like those developed at Bretton Woods created the very markets, social relations, and subjectivities that nourished neoliberalism's roots, so I argue that an attention to 1950s culture, particularly novels, is crucial for our understanding of how the narratives of neoliberalism were developed and take hold.[18] In offering a cultural prehistory of neoliberalism, I also aim to offer a more materialist account of neoliberalism, one that forefronts the role of political and cultural struggles rooted within the built environment in shaping the affective, subjective, and ideological effects of neoliberalism.

Second, through this rehistoricization and respatialization of neoliberalism, I aim to refigure our thinking about the midcentury novel, particularly by challenging new historicism's subversion/containment framework that has, quite peculiarly, continued to govern our reading of the postwar and midcentury novel.[19] In 2002, Andrew Hoberek perceptively noted that, "while the Cold War culture framework has revolutionized the way we talk about the 50s . . . its dominance as a critical paradigm has produced a certain blindness as well. At its worst, it has become a routinized reading generator: take a 50s text that hasn't been discussed yet, explain how it reflects an ambivalent liberalism hostile to political extremes (or designates some group as subversive, or denigrates the radical legacy of the 30s), and publish" (146). Recent attempts to challenge what Hoberek has termed containment's "omnipresence and inevitability" (146) have largely been unable to escape the Cold War frame and often end up shifting from one side of the coin to other, from containment to subversion, asserting that the 1950s was oppositional (Dickstein) or at least more experimental and interesting (Castronovo 2004); that class remained a central concern (Hoberek 2005); or that the 1950s also produced the seeds of the global 1960s in all of its subversive and contained forms (Medovoi 2005).

These accounts—and the containment narratives that haunt so many of them—take the nation-state, and particularly the discourse of the state, as the horizon of their politics. This has become especially pronounced within the field of post-45 studies with the predominance of what Fredric Jameson diagnosed as Walter Benn Michaels's, and again new historicism's, revamped "homology" (1991, 187) method of literary criticism,[20] which has found its most celebrated examples in Michael Szalay's works on modernism and the New Deal state (2000) and on postwar cultures of hip and the Democratic Party Cold War liberalism (2012), as well as Sean McCann's work on the hard-boiled genre and American liberalism (2000). The problem with these homologous accounts is that they often end up treating political discourses, and particularly the official discourses of the state, as objective descriptions of reality instead of the very ideas and ideologies to be analyzed and questioned. It appears, one might say, that before surface reading rejected what Paul Ricoeur terms a "hermeneutics of suspicion" (71) with regard to literary texts, literary critics had already given up their suspicion of the state.

This new embrace of the "surfaces" and skins of not only texts but of political and especially state discourse has also limited our ability to think about the relationship between literature and the world in which it is made by beginning with spurious understandings of the historical context itself. For instance, while George Kennan's famous telegram calling for the "patient but firm and vigilant containment of Russian expansive tendencies" (qtd. in Nadel, 16) did take hold of the popular imagination, and while the state may have claimed a similar policy for the need to "contain" communism domestically, containment is not the most accurate way to describe the activities of the US state in the postwar period. From its construction of the Bretton Woods agreement that laid the basis for the global financial order of the present day, to its import of scientists and engineers into the Third World to create and develop market-based economies, to its use of CIA operatives to manipulate the affairs of foreign countries up to and including coups and assassinations, to its overdevelopment of white suburban areas and underdevelopment of urban space, and also to its use of programs like COINTELPRO to destroy black, queer, feminist, and class-based liberation movements—all of this suggests that "intervention," "invasion," "expansion," "penetration," "displacement," or "dispossession" might be more accurate terms around which to base a study. Indeed, even the National Security Council's own "master" on containment recognized its spurious nature, stating that the "overall policy at the present time may be described as one designed to foster a world environment in which the American system can survive and flourish . . . a policy which we would probably pursue even if there were no Soviet threat" (qtd. in Panitch and Gindin, 95). Given the state's own awareness of the surface nature of this policy, it is particularly bewildering that literary studies continued to traffic that concept as a viable framework well into the 2000s. *Novel Shocks* aims to move away from a homologous study of texts and discourses by instead considering how novels struggled to create, challenge, alter, and form narratives able to make sense of the interlined city-, nation-, and empire-making processes that were occurring around them.

"Always historicize!" Jameson famously wrote in *The Political Unconscious* (1981, 9), but with the caveat that we understand history itself as an absent cause, one "that can be approached only by way of prior (re)textualization" (82). The historicization of texts through the narrative of containment was one such (re)textualization, but one that has severely limited the horizons of interpretation of the postwar novel as well as reinscribing many of the myths or ideologies of American exceptionalism. In this book, I both rehistoricize, or (re)textualize, the postwar novel through its built environment, in order to bring into relief the double horizon of US global hegemony and the rise of neoliberalism, and to suggest that the postwar novel's own rehistoricization and (re)textualization of modernist narratives and tropes, particularly shock, provided the narrative shape of neoliberalism.

My goal here is not to argue that 1950s novels *are* neoliberal but rather that they gave narrative shape to the social and particularly urban struggles out of which neoliberalism emerged, and that they created the discourse and imaginary through which neoliberalism articulated its project. Part of this project, then, requires changing the geographical scope of our inquiry, and a shift away from US exceptionalist accounts of the 1950s that focus solely on the state, to the account recently offered by Leo Panitch and Sam Gindin, which conceives of the United States' role in the postwar world as the primary creator of a system of "globalized capital accumulation" through the "integrat[ion of] all the other capitalist powers into an effective system of coordination under its aegis" (8). Specifically, the global import of US domestic policy in the period immediately following World War II suggests we rethink US literature as "world literature" in the sense of the term recently proposed by the Warwick Research Collective, "as the literature of the [combined and uneven] world-system—of the modern

capitalist world-system, that is" (8). This is not to say that American literature is more worldly than other literatures but rather that the political
horizon of the US novel was not, and could not be, national. Instead, it
reflected the global empire it was attempting to consolidate. While such a
claim may seem peculiar in a book so committed to the local, I argue that
because of the importance of urbanization as both a site of accumulation
and a symbol of American modernity, novelistic engagements with urban
space—and particularly New York's role as both the US's metaphoric and
often economic capital—work to chart the shape, structure, and imaginary
of this new US-run global system.[21]

To track this engagement, I turn to the widespread tendency within the
midcentury novel to reenvision the metropolitan scene within the imaginary and mythos of the US West and the frontier, a revision that echoes a
broader cultural resurgence of the frontier. Writing about the gentrification of New York City in the 1970s and 1980s, Neil Smith (1996) has noted
the explosion of frontier images. Gentrification, he writes, became "associated with the forging of the 'national spirit' [. . .] in the most extreme sce-
nario, the new urban pioneers were expected to do for the flagging national
spirit what the old ones did: to lead the nation into a new world where the
problems of the old world are left behind" (17). While Smith's focus here is
on the 1970s and 1980s, the frontier also acted as a key metaphor for urban
redevelopment throughout the 1940s and 1950s. Initially, however, it was
not the city but the suburb that was envisioned as the frontier. In *The Last
Landscape*, American urbanist William Whyte argued that the great postwar expansion of suburbia in the 1940s and 1950s drew on the "romantic
veneration of the frontier tradition" by treating the metropolis "as though
we were in fact on the frontier" (1968, 1–2). But, as Catherine Jurca shows
in her pathbreaking study of suburban fiction, *White Diaspora: The Suburb
and the Twentieth-Century American Novel* (2011), very quickly this project
came up wanting. Perhaps aware of the depth of their dependence on state-
subsidized roads, buildings, and mortgages, suburbanites lacked the kind of
individualist triumphalism associated with the nineteenth-century frontier
projects. Instead, she argues, literary treatments of the suburbs—emblematized in midcentury novels such as Sloan Wilson's *The Man in the Gray
Flannel Suit* (1956)—tended to "reinvent white flight as the persecution
of those who flee" by turning their "material advantages into artefacts of
spiritual and cultural oppression and sympathetically treats affluent house
owners as the emotionally dispossessed" (9).

It was not just suburban homeowners who felt themselves to be dispossessed. Numerous sociologists, psychologists, feminists, urban planners,

and writers worried about the effect of the suburbs on the American character. In *The Lonely Crowd* (1950), for instance, sociologist David Riesman worried that housing developments like the suburbs, with their emphasis on conformity, accommodation, and community, were stripping the population of the frontier ethic on which America was founded. The American frontiersman, Riesman argued, "would cooperate "with his sparse neighbors in mutual self-help activities, such as house building or politics [. . . but was primarily] hard and self-reliant" (112). In contrast, Riesman saw the new American subject, what he identified as the "outer-directed" man of which the suburbanite was exemplary, as entirely dependent on the approval and respect of "an amorphous and shifting, though contemporary, jury of peers" (137).

If, as Jurca suggests, the suburbs were refigured as this space of "homelessness" (4) and anomie, a sense of home was ultimately to be found in the city. Thus, while in *The Price of Salt*, the lesbian love story must transform into a Western in which they escape from the city to the suburbs and then to the West, the love story's triumphant conclusion occurs within New York City. Similarly, in Ayn Rand's *ur* white-flight novel, *Atlas Shrugged* (1957), the "men of the mind" initially escape New York City for a suburban enclave in the midwestern mountains, but the novel concludes with their return to the city. In *Naked Lunch*, too, the protagonist's attempt to escape the narcotics agents moves him from New York to the West and then to the East but requires a return to Hard-boiled New York to succeed. And indeed, if we look closer, what we find in the 1950s, in other words, is rarely a suburban narrative but rather a narrative that refigures metropolitan space as a whole. While the suburbs, then, may have briefly taken on the imagery of the frontier, in the postwar period it is "the city," as radical urbanist Charles Abrams observed in his 1965 book of the same title, that "is the frontier." As the frontier shifts from the West to the city, the genre of the Western shifts to the road novel, recoding white flight and urban renewal within the older generic codes of western frontier narratives, and designating urban space as the ultimate space of conquest: a space in which man and, more importantly, as I'll soon argue, *woman* can conquer themselves.

While on the surface this return to the Western may appear regressive or nostalgic, it is anything but. Harvey has argued that capitalism requires new frontiers, spaces outside of it, that "overaccumulated capital can seize hold of [. . .] and immediately turn [. . .] to profitable use" (2003a, 149). These spaces can either be "discovered"—as with imperialist expansion or primitive accumulation—or created through underdevelopment and, as in the recent so-called War on Terror, through shock and awe. The resurgence of frontier imagery within the city thus reflects not a backwards nostalgia for the West but a prescient understanding of the resurgence of the city as an important space for renewed capitalist accumulation.

While the book therefore begins with Ralph Ellison's *Invisible Man*, a novel I argue is about the dual process of entrapment, ghettoization, and dispossession on the one hand, and cultural valorization on the other, the bulk of *Novel Shocks* turns to these new frontier narratives and tracks how these novels internalize the tropes of the Western, a process I argue culminates in Sylvia Plath's *The Bell Jar*, in which the frontier has been so thoroughly absorbed into processes of urbanization and nation-making that the actual space of the West ceases to be necessary.

Shock and the Cultural Front(ier)s of Neoliberalism

The mythos of the frontier, however, is important for another reason as well: it provides the language through which the postwar novel comes to imagine the self as a new frontier for capital. Like the Westerns on which they draw, the road trips of the midcentury novel constitute the "West Cures" prescribed by the famous nineteenth-century American nerve doctor Silas Weir Mitchell. In Mitchell's vision, the neurasthenic urban man goes west and engages in a "sturdy contest" with the environment in order to conquer both the anxious or unbalanced self and environment (Self, 294). Like the earlier Westerns, which were largely inspired by Mitchell, these characters' journeys out of, and back into, the city map onto a developmentalist narrative in which characters attempt to break out of the "organization man" or "outer-directed" traps that society had set for them and to conquer their own anxious, irrational, internally riven, or will-less subjectivities by becoming strong, stable, self-made, and independent figures.

The battle over the meaning of these processes of self-making becomes imagined, intriguingly, through a negotiation and refiguring of the modernist notion of shock. The novels I look at in this book are replete with the imagery of shock: from the literal shock therapy that Plath's protagonist Esther receives, to the sci-fi shock machines to which Rand's John Galt is strapped, to the numerous depictions of the industrial traumas of modernity (such as railway accidents, industrial accidents, and urbanization) that these novels describe as "shocks" to their protagonists. Moreover, shock provides a grammar through which to make sense of, and apprehend, the experience of urbanization that this book tracks. I say "intriguingly" because of the important role that shock has come to play in contemporary understandings of neoliberalism. Naomi Klein opens her best-selling book *The Shock Doctrine: The Rise of Disaster Capitalism* with an analogy between the psychological hypothesis that an array of shocks "could unmake and erase faulty minds, then rebuild new personalities on that ever-elusive clean slate" (29) and Milton Friedman's economic hypothesis that a course of painful policy shock treatment could similarly "depattern societies, [. . .] returning them to a state of pure capitalism, cleansed of all interruptions— government regulations, trade barriers and entrenched interests" (50). The premise in both cases, she argues, is that shock would intervene in a subject or market that had grown "sick" and return the subject or society to a salubrious state of nature. One of the questions that Klein's book raises but doesn't itself ask is, Why did shock form such a powerful and persuasive imagery under neoliberalism? How did it transform from a traumatic and potentially revolutionary force associated with the vagaries of the unconscious to become the dominant metaphor for economic rationalization and entrepreneurial subject formation throughout the second half of the twentieth century? The postwar novel fills in this gap, often literally narrating the shifting meaning of shock from rational subject unmaking into entrepreneurial, or neoliberal, subject making.

The theory of shock received its most substantial development in Freud's 1921 essay "Beyond the Pleasure Principle." Writing in the wake of World War I and drawing on his work with war veterans, Freud found himself troubled by his patients' compulsive repetition of traumatic events that seemed to contradict his theory of the pleasure principle, which assumed a rational subject who sought to maximize pleasure and minimize pain. Freud concluded that there was a human drive that exceeds the pleasure principle, the death drive, a conservative drive that seeks to keep external stimulus out and to return to an earlier, "inorganic" state (38). Imagining the unconscious as an internal space that is protected by the "outermost surface" of the "receptive, cortical layer," which has a "protective shield against stimuli [. . . and] functions as a special envelope or membrane resistant to stimuli" (27), Freud suggested that when certain external "excitations" arose that were "powerful enough to break through the protective shield" (29), the pleasure principle would be put "out of action" (29) and the death drive would take over. He termed these external excitations "shocks" and concluded that the compulsive repetition of traumatic events he witnessed in war veterans or industrial accident survivors was an effect of the unconscious trying to help the subject "master the stimulus retrospectively, by developing the anxiety whose omission was the cause of the traumatic neurosis" (32).

In 1940, Walter Benjamin suggested that within a context of urbanization and industrialization in which shock was the norm, the very structure
of "experience" (1999, 318) underwent a change. As stated earlier, for Benjamin, Paris under Haussmann was the laboratory for such conditions, and
the poetry of Baudelaire the greatest descriptor of how a world governed
by shock transformed the very possibility of experience. Baudelaire's poetry, Benjamin argued, revealed how the experience of the worker at the
machine or the individual in a crowd was one of shock, and thus that the
subject came to be in a perpetual state, not of perceiving but of limiting
perception: of absorbing, cushioning, and screening. Under these conditions, Benjamin suggested, the question of experience or perception itself
was under threat, and thus art's role became the restoration of perceptibil-
ity, of giving back to the crowds and masses the potential to see and interpret their surroundings and thus greater social truths.

Throughout the early twentieth century, shock and the possibility of
perception emerged as a crucial concept for understanding and interpret-
ing modern art. While they disagreed, often sharply, on its efficacy and potential, both Benjamin and Theodor Adorno argued that shock was at the
core of modern art—be it new technological forms like film and photo-
graphy, new aesthetic movements like surrealism, or new forms of narrative such as those produced by Kafka. For both, shock at once formed the
objective, material conditions of modernist art's production: that is, the
synesthetic environment of industrialization, urbanization, and mass culture that blinds, overwhelms, and deadens the subject and was the source of
art's potential. For Benjamin, modernist aesthetics of shock—particularly
surrealism—offered a form of "profane illumination," what he defined as
a "materialist anthropological inspiration" in which the subject is snapped
out of the reverie of reified life and is able to see the buried histories and
revolutionary potential in the mundane objects of their daily life (109).[22]
While for Adorno that potential was fraught and limited, always at risk of
becoming absorbed into the relentless reifying drive of mass culture, the
presence of shock within the modernist work of art still had the potential
to carry out "the explosion of their appearance" to shatter its reified exterior and reveal the historicity of its form (Adorno 1997, 84). For both Benjamin and Adorno, this shattering, this moment of vision, was a necessary
prerequisite for an apprehension of one's own objective social and class
position, and thus for even the possibility of a class-consciousness emerging (Buck-Morss 1979, 161).

At the same time that Benjamin and Adorno were considering the effects that industrialization, urbanization, and mass culture were having

on the European psyche, African American writers and activists across the Atlantic were making similar claims about the detrimental effects that urban policies and practices were having on the lives and psyches of the inhabitants of slums and tenements. In 1943, journalist Roi Ottley deployed the language of shell shock to critique what he saw as the deleterious effects of the slums, explaining that "Negroes become slum-shocked. They get distorted perspective, and become hardened or callous. War," he concludes, "is sometimes an intangible peril that is dwarfed by the stern realities of living" (2–3). Ottley's comparison made clear that these processes of urbanization—and the racial policies underpinning them— were as traumatic and psychically debilitating as those faced by war veterans and that this trauma similarly deadened, depoliticized, and numbed black subjects to their surroundings. In 1946 another journalist took up Ottley's language of "slum shock" when he wrote an article in support of Harlem's Lafargue Clinic, the first integrated mental health clinic in the United States. That article, "Harlem Is Nowhere," was written by Ralph Ellison. Likely influenced by the surrealist art he had encountered at the Museum of Modern Art (MoMA) exhibit *Fantastic Art, Data, Surrealism* (Fischer-Hornung, 249), Ellison deployed the aesthetic style of surrealism to capture the rhythm and realities of life in Harlem. "The most surreal fantasies are acted out upon the streets of Harlem" (297), Ellison writes, and his examples are surrealist to the letter. A man throws "imaginary grenades that actually exploded during World War I; a boy participates in the rape-robbery of his mother[, . . .] two men hold a third while a lesbian slashes him to death with a razor blade; boy gangsters wielding homemade pistols (which in the South of their origin are but toy symbols of adolescent yearning for manhood) shoot down their young rivals" (297).

The World War I ephemera that are both fetishes and weapons in a new race war, the oedipal violence of the boy, the lesbian murder fantasies, the refunctioning of a southern image in a northern context, all cast Harlem as the Paris of the United States, that most profane city in which the repressed histories, anxieties, and unconscious of the nation can be illuminated. Here, Ellison, like Benjamin, found in surrealism an aesthetic form capable of revealing how the most infernal aspects of urban life paradoxically contained the seeds for revelation and revolution. Thus, Ellison's Harlem is at once "the scene of the folk-Negro's death agony [. . . and] his transcendence" (296), a space of exploitation and despair that wears down and numbs the subject, and the one space in which revelation and transformation can occur.

However, as Adorno warned, "the most extreme shocks and gestures of alienation of contemporary art [. . .] are nearer than they appear to be by virtue of historical reification" (1997, 183). By the end of World War II, the shock-based aesthetics Ellison used to reveal and challenge the slum conditions of black urban life had become thoroughly absorbed into the rhetoric of this new coalition between government, downtown business interests, and developers who seized upon this comparison between the war and slums to push through slum clearance projects that would result in the mass clearance of largely black and Latino residents. In this new vision, both the old, slumified city and the bombed-out ruins of war were forms of shock, connected to the irrational policies of older forms of European imperialism, politics, art, and architecture, all of which needed to be cleared away.

Both the suburbs and the new Title 1 projects became refigured as a rational space of order in which the shocks and traumas of the war, of a decaying city, and of an old European order would be cleared away, and in which the process of rebuilding a new, modernist, and prosperous America could begin. This promise of the new American century was as much mental as it was spatial, promising to clear away not just the landscapes and power structures of the old European world but also its psychological structure.[23] For Freud, the structure of the human psyche was bounded by the principle of the death drive, and thus by the forces of traumatic shock, the uncanny, and the repetition compulsion, which together seemed to define the subject and modern experience. In the postwar era, however, the death drive was transformed from a limit point into a frontier, a space that, like its urban analogue, can and must be crossed by the principles of modern medicine and psychiatry. At the same time, the notion of "shock" too was refigured from a traumatic event to a therapeutic treatment that, while painful, would bring the city, the subject, and the nation through their frontiers and out the other end. Kristin Ross's notion of "evenness" (1996, 10) is crucial here for understanding the emerging new fantasy in which the self would become perfectly contiguous with the city and the nation: undifferentiated, unified, rational, free, and in control.

Where Benjamin and Adorno hoped that shock would be the precondition for a destabilization of the everyday and the emergence of a new revolutionary class-consciousness, in the 1950s a reparative fantasy forms that casts traumatic shocks as strategies of individuation and stabilization. These novels' refiguring of shock from an external force disrupting or traumatizing the natural ecosystem of a subject or market to a bitter but necessary medicine, or therapy, that will ultimately lead to a stronger, more flexible, resilient, and stable subject signals the deeper subsumption of the novel form into capitalism. With this transformation, shock became associated not with the eruption of an unconscious against the privatized and commodified logics of industrial capitalism but rather a tool in the privatization and colonization of the subject within these dominant market logics. One of my contentions, then, is that we can usefully understand Freud's theory of the unconscious as being premised on, and offering the reparative fantasy of, an unconscious as a private space not yet colonized by the economic logics of the market, a fantasy that can no longer withstand the pressures of modernization and suburbanization in the postwar period. In this reading, midcentury narratives of psychological development come to take on, and come into line with, the forces of modernization and creative destruction themselves, and they do so through their engagement with their built environment, or what Kanishka Goonewardena usefully terms the "urban sensorium" (49).

However, as often as novels are complicit in this process, they also offer powerful critiques. In the chapter on *The Bell Jar*, for instance, I argue that the novel makes palpable the larger and deeper respatializations and transformations of capital itself, and specifically the process of entrepreneurial subject making, by highlighting the profoundly ambivalent mode of freedom its protagonist, Esther, attains at the end of the novel as a suburban housewife totally divorced from the energies, politics, and desires associated with her earlier urban self. The psychological turn, then, should not be read as a turn away from the political but as a turn toward a new political ground, one through which the self becomes recoded as a market or neoliberal subject whose lot in life, to return to Huber, is determined by individual desires and decisions.

A Note on Structure

Novel Shocks moves between 1945 and 1965, that is, between the end of World War II and the consolidation of the idea of urban crisis. I argue that the emergence of "urban crisis" as a kind of national discourse consolidated a series of tropes—the divide between the public racialized space of chocolate cities and the private white space of vanilla suburbs; the gap separating the undeserving, and implicitly racialized, urban poor from deserving, and implicitly white, suburban affluence; and the consolidation of free market ideology, which assumes that social and economic position reflects skill and labor in a context free of external factors—that would come to underpin the revanchist policies of the US presidents Nixon, Ford, and Reagan. However, unlike Carlo Rotella, whose excellent survey of urban literature within this period traces the formation of a narrative of "urban crisis" as it emerges, I am less interested in the urban crisis per se than in how postwar thinking about metropolitan space across the period of suburbanization and urban renewal was crucial to forging the ideologies and geographies that would come to underpin neoliberalism as both an economic system and a political project of US global hegemony.

Thus, this book is organized both thematically and temporally. Thematically, it offers a series of case studies, with each novel illuminating a different aspect of urban renewal and how its transformation of the space and culture of Manhattan laid the groundwork for the neoliberal revolution of the 1970s. Chapter 1 argues that *Invisible Man*'s depiction of Harlem offers a clear-eyed account of how the racial politics of urban renewal and white flight worked to align public space with blackness and private individualism with whiteness. Chapter 2 reads *The Price of Salt* alongside a focus on the highway system that structures the novel itself as well as the transformation of both its protagonist and the city. Chapter 3 suggests that William Burroughs's *Naked Lunch* offers a critical examination of the relationship between decolonizing Third World and urban spaces as central sites in the formation of US global hegemony and the importance of both to the development of its ideologies of modernization and development that would shape the postwar period. Chapter 4 argues that *Atlas Shrugged* allegorizes the process through which suburbanization and urban renewal created a cultural realignment, as white suburban subjects came to identify with capital and against the welfare state. Finally, Chapter 5 turns to the importance of the United Nations Building, another Title 1 project, in Sylvia Plath's *The Bell Jar* in order to suggest how the novel tracks the often fraught relationship between urban renewal as a strategy to turn New York into the new cultural capital of the world, and the role of the white middle-class woman as the symbol of that power.

However, this book is also genealogical in its attempts to track the emergence and consolidation of the uneven landscapes of neoliberalism and the formation of the entrepreneurial and criminal selves that provided its subjective foundations. Like all books that attempt to track and explain the present, this book risks becoming determinist, of creating a narrative that there was no alternative. And there were many alternatives. Thus, this book concludes by turning from history to counterfactual futurity through Warren Miller's *Siege of Harlem* (1965), a novel that draws on the "internal colony" thesis of black power thinkers and imagines Harlem's secession from the United States. I argue that *Siege* can help us recover a different trajectory from the modernizing "evenness" of contiguous selves, cities, and nations, by reminding us of the radical urbanisms that were developed and nourished by black radicalism throughout the 1960s: urbanisms that disarticulated themselves from the national form and envisioned a militantly socialist, internationalist, and anti-imperialist lifeworld. Concluding here, I argue, offers a useful way to think about not just the roots and routes of neoliberalism but also the roots and routes of today's social movements: movements like Occupy, Black Lives Matter, No One Is Illegal, and anti-raids, which are creating new internationalisms, new urbanisms, and forefronting that old, and ever more relevant, call for the right to the city.

CHAPTER I

Blueprints:
Invisible Man and the Great
Migration to White Flight

Shortly after Ralph Ellison's protagonist arrives in New York, he encounters Peter Wheatstraw, a man in Charlie Chaplin pants, "pushing a cart piled high with rolls of blue paper" (172) and singing a blues song that reminds the protagonist of home. Often read as a carrier of blues and vernacular traditions within the novel, Wheatstraw is also a literal carrier of plans. When the protagonist asks him what is in his cart, Wheatstraw responds they are blueprints for "everything. Cities, towns, country clubs. Some just buildings and houses. [. . .] Every once in a while they have to throw 'em out to make place for new plans" (175). In Wheatstraw's description of the dizzying array of plans that aim to remake the city in its entirety, we hear echoes of the preeminent modernist architect Le Corbusier, who proclaimed that "the plan is the generator" (2007, 116), and also of the tradition of modern planning that culminated in the ascendancy of Robert Moses and his New York City Committee on Slum Clearance under the aegis of the Federal Housing Act of 1949. The emergence of postwar modern planning within a framework of urban renewal is an important context in which to consider *Invisible Man*. Plans and planning also generate and structure the novel's form. From college president Dr. A. Herbert Bledsoe's plan to "keep [the invisible man] running" (194), to those of the white philanthropist Mr. Norton, and of the industrialist's son, Mr. Emerson, and finally the parodic scientific socialism of the Brotherhood, *Invisible Man* is structured around, and generated by, the endless propagation of plans that serve to dispossess and repossess the strikingly naïve protagonist.

Invisible Man is most often read within the context of the Cold War, and Ellison's own later role as a central player in its cultural apparatus as a member of the Congress for Cultural Freedom (CCF).[1] While not always stated explicitly, these readings often parallel the protagonist's trajectory with Ellison's own political development from a fellow traveler and participant in the Popular Front to a Cold War cultural warrior (Purcell; Foley 2010; Wolfe). Deviating from this well-worn trajectory, this chapter asks the following: What if we read *Invisible Man* not as an exemplary novel of what Alan Nadel famously termed the "containment culture" of the Cold War (1995) but rather as an early critique of the regime of suburbanization and urban renewal that was only just emerging?

Kenneth Warren has argued that we deuniversalize Ellison by reading him as a great author who captured "a bit of American reality [. . .] as that reality was passing into history" (2). The reality Warren is speaking of is Jim Crow. This chapter makes the opposite claim, contending that what Ellison is doing is not capturing the racial regime of Jim Crow as it passes into history but rather trying to articulate the new race regime that emerges in its wake: one that seems to turn Jim Crow on its head. In its depiction of this new racial regime, the economic exploitation and political exclusion that marked Jim Crow is transformed into a regime of formal cultural and political inclusion and economic exclusion. It is within this new regime, I argue, that Ellison provides a genealogy for the entangled figures of racialized criminality and white entrepreneurialism that would mark neoliberalism's emergence.[2]

Ellison had a long-standing interest in questions of housing, segregation, and urban policy. In 1938 and 1939, Ellison worked for the Federal Writers' Project (FWP), conducting oral histories in Harlem. Recalling his methodology for conducting these interviews, Ellison explained: "I hung around playgrounds. I hung around the streets, the bars. I went into hundreds of apartment buildings and just knocked on doors. I would tell some stories to get people going and then I'd sit back and try to get it as accurately as I could" (qtd. in Banks and Siskind, 6). The Harlem of *Invisible Man* is the Harlem Ellison experienced through the playgrounds, streets, and bars of 1939. This Harlem was, as Ann Banks writes in the introduction to these reprinted interviews, published as *Harlem Document: Photographs, 1932–1940*, "a painful place" (8). The Great Depression cut short the social and cultural explosion of the Harlem Renaissance, halting the flow of white money into Harlem and leaving African Americans out of work as newly unemployed whites began taking historically black jobs. Unemployment mixed with New York's highly segregated housing policies and practices to hem African Americans into the increasingly cramped and expensive housing stock of Harlem's slums. Throughout Ellison's oral histories and his contemporaneous writings for the *New Masses*, Ellison emphasized the inordinate effect that the Great Depression had on black Americans' material and psychological states, while also showing how the violence and segregation in the northern United States was not only catastrophic for the lives of African Americans but for the democratic American project more broadly.[3]

Ellison's development as a writer occurred in tandem with the development of his analysis of segregation and housing. As his interest in the psychological impacts of segregation and racial violence increased, he began to shift away from the naturalistic style of his mentor, Richard Wright, and toward the aesthetic practices of surrealism, particularly a fascination with the marvelous, the uncanny, the repetition compulsion, and the return of the repressed.[4] In 1946, Ellison joined Richard Wright and other community organizers in Harlem to create the Lafargue Clinic. The first desegregated clinic in the United States, the Lafargue Clinic viewed mental health as a social issue, arguing that a "patient must be understood first and foremost as a member of a class, each patient positioned with a distinct social relation to the means of production, with specific concerns and problems based on this relation" (Mendes, 111). As part of his work on this clinic, Ellison published the essay "Harlem Is Nowhere," which made use of surrealist practices—both, as Shelley Eversley suggests, to treat "patients' symptomology [. . . as a] reasonable psychic response to the lunatic obsessions of US white supremacist culture" (447), and as a strategy to shock the reader into an awareness that lunacy was the social condition of segregation itself.

On the surface, *Invisible Man* appears to continue this trajectory, making use of a surrealist-infused aesthetics to reveal the deleterious effects that Bledsoe, Norton, Emerson, and the Brotherhood's planned exclusions and dispossessions have on the protagonist, the secondary characters, and, in turn, on society at large. But as is evidenced by the final riot, by the novel's end, even the most damning critiques of "the plan," along with the surrealist aesthetics Ellison uses to deliver those critiques, seem to have been subsumed into this new regime of urbanization. What *Invisible Man* tracks, then, is the failure of older, shock-based aesthetic strategies as "shock" itself transforms into a tool of neoliberal subject formation.

If we read the novel's famous ending with respect to the problem of urban renewal, the protagonist's famous realization that the riot was all part of "the plan" reflects Ellison's own growing awareness that the political and aesthetic critiques that emerged from the Great Depression era were becoming absorbed within the new political, spatial, and social regimes cohering around urban renewal and suburbanization. However, while *Invisible Man* may endorse the protagonist's critique, it does not endorse his response: that is, his turn to "personal responsibility" (463) and his broader embrace of Cold War liberalism. As with all of his previous positions, the protagonist's escape from the space of Harlem and his identification with, as Barbara Foley would have it, complexity (2010, 6), "existential ambivalence" (1), and "vital center patriotism" (1), turns out to be no solution at all. Instead, it articulates a still-nascent entrepreneurial subject position, and like every other position of identification he has occupied, his final identification, too, is misplaced. Such a position is not actually available to him because he has literally been barred from the preconditions of attaining such an identity and has instead been caught in its obverse: the position of surplus and of black urban criminality. Read thusly, the conclusion's seeming embrace of these postwar entrepreneurial values, like its aesthetic styles, should be read not as the novel's solution but rather as a new political problem that requires addressing.

The Surplus, the Preterite, and the Dispossessed

Walking through Harlem early in the novel, the protagonist "stumbles" across a crowd standing in front of a pile of "junk" on the sidewalk, "waiting to be hauled away" (267). This pile, he learns, is "actually worn household furnishings" (268) that belong to an old black couple being evicted from their home because they are unable to pay their rent. The protagonist stops and itemizes the objects, literally lifting them out of the rubble and bestowing narrative and sentimental value onto them. In his hands, these items come to constitute a kind of artifactual exhibit of African American history and struggles for freedom. Among the artifacts the protagonist itemizes are African "knocking bones" that function like "castanets" (271), and domestic objects such as gardening pots, a curling iron, baby booties, and a breast pump. There are the ephemera of various political struggles for freedom ranging from an "Ethiopian flag [and] a faded tintype of Abraham Lincoln," to a newspaper article about the deportation of Marcus Garvey, and free papers (272). There is also American cultural ephemera: an image "of a Hollywood star torn from a magazine" (271), a baseball "scoring card" (272), and a "plate celebrating the St. Louis World's Fair" (271). Discarded and ready for the dump, these objects parallel the evicted couple and all of the other surplus characters who fill the text. However, it is precisely through the dispossession of this couple and all of their belongings that these previously private and innocuous mementos are refigured as powerful and transformative documents of social history. Like Walter Benjamin and the surrealists who saw in obsolete and out-of-date objects the potential for "profane illumination" (2005, 209), the invisible man experiences these surplus objects as transformative. They both reveal to him the economic violence facing African Americans in Harlem, and they move him to begin fighting for the dispossessed. As he puts it, "with this sense of dispossession came a pang of vague recognition: this junk, these shabby chairs, these heavy old-fashioned pressing irons, zinc wash tubs with dented bottoms—all throbbed within me with more meaning than there should have been" (274).

It is here that the protagonist first encounters one of the novel's defining concepts: "dispossession." When he asks an angry member of the crowd what's happening, the heavyweight responds "they been dispossessed" (278). He is not being rhetorical here; throughout the Great Depression, landlords regularly applied to the city for "dispossess notices" so they could evict tenants who either refused to or were unable to pay their rent.[5] The protagonist, however, reads the term "dispossession" not as a legally or materially specific term but rather as "a good word" (279)—so good, in fact, that he decides to center his speech at the Brotherhood Rally on it:

> "Dispossession! *Dis*-possession is the word!" I went on. "They've tried to dispossess us of our manhood and womanhood! Of our childhood and adolescence [. . .] Why, they even tried to dispossess us of *our dislike of being dispossessed!* And I'll tell you something else—if we don't resist, pretty soon they'll succeed! These are the days of dispossession, the season of homelessness, the time of evictions. We'll be dispossessed of the very brains in our heads! And we're so *un*-common that we can't even see it [. . .] Think about it, they've dispossessed us each of one eye from the day we're born. So now we can only see in straight white lines." (343, emphasis in original)

While obliquely aware of its meaning within the specific context of grassroots struggles around evictions in New York, this remarkable speech recasts the entire novel within the terms of dispossession, anticipating what David Harvey terms "accumulation by dispossession" to emphasize the ways in which all processes of capitalist accumulation depend on continued processes of dispossession through processes of legalized violence, land appropriation, privatization, and labor commodification (2003a, 2).

The term "dispossession," the *Oxford English Dictionary* tells us, also has a second meaning: if the first meaning is material, the "deprivation of or ejection from a possession" (1a), the second is psychological or spiritual, "the casting out of an evil spirit; exorcism" (2). Ellison's focus on dispossession plays on both. It treats the legal dispossessions happening to African Americans in Harlem during the Great Depression as a metaphor for the broader systematic dispossession of African Americans of their material wealth, labor, and skills while also referencing the figuring of African Americans as a supernatural or, in psychological terms, a repressed threat that needs to be exorcised from the US state and imaginary. From the war veterans he encounters at the Golden Day bar, who have been removed from society and locked up in an asylum; to Brockway, who is confined and contained in the boiler room of the Liberty paint factory and who ultimately vanishes; to Tod Clifton, who is cast into the underground economy and then gunned down by the state, the minor characters are repeatedly excised. In this, the novel appears to continue in the vein of Ellison's prewar writing. These economically and socially dispossessed characters all take on the gothic role of the return of the repressed, haunting the society that excludes them and threatening the material and social fabric of that society. The veterans' riot both reveals the lie of the Negro college's ideological foundation of racial uplift and threatens its economic base by terrorizing Norton. Brockway reveals the impossible promise of both cross-racial union solidarity and hard work, and then literally blows up the paint factory; and Clifton's famous Sambo dance both unmasks the racialized power structures at present in the Brotherhood while also triggering a riot that sets Harlem aflame. Much like the discarded objects, these minor characters, too, come to act as a shock, a repressed unconscious that explodes the failed plans and promises in which the protagonist operates and that are meant to bring the reader to a similar understanding.

Ellison's use of shock draws on and refigures Sigmund Freud's understanding of the concept. Freud depicted shock as a psychological response to previously unimaginable traumas, often those caused by the new and unprecedented technologies of industrial modernization. In "Beyond the Pleasure Principle," he set out to explain why war veterans or survivors of traumatic events such as railway disasters relived those traumatic experiences either in dreams or in involuntary memories, when it so clearly violated the pleasure or reality principle. Freud theorized that such traumas created an "extensive breach" in the subject's "shield" (1955a, 25), which in turn created an anxiety in the subject about their "lack of any preparedness" for such an event (25). In response, Freud argued, the subject begins to compulsively repeat the traumatic event in either dreams or waking life in an attempt to "master the stimulus retrospectively, by developing the anxiety whose omission was the cause of the traumatic neurosis" (32). Whereas Freud understood shock as a consequence of specifically traumatic events like industrial warfare, Ellison depicts shock as a consequence of systemic and racialized violence. Thus, while many of Ellison's characters are exposed to the conventional traumas that Freud associated with shock—World War I, industrial explosions, and the urban experience in general—Ellison clearly attributes the shocked states of his surplus characters not to these traditional shocks but to the larger economic and psychic dispossessions they undergo.

Most notable in this regard are the World War I veterans-turned-inmates whom the protagonist and Norton encounter at the Golden Day. These veterans are based on the "Harlem Hellfighters," the elite black infantry unit that formed in 1916 at the urging of race leaders like W. E. B. Du Bois who saw African American enlistment as a strategy to achieve the double freedom of "freedom abroad; freedom at home" (Shack, 11).[6] Initially, they appear to embody the symptomology of the uncanny that Freud associates with shock: namely "an indistinction between the real and the imagined, [. . .] a confusion between the animate and the inanimate, [. . . and] a usurpation of the referent by the sign or of physical reality by psychic reality" (Foster, 7). Not only do the inmates confuse Norton for Thomas Jefferson, John D. Rockefeller, and the Messiah (78), confusing the real and the imagined and the animate and the inanimate (in this case the dead), but they also project their own internal compulsion to repeat onto history, describing it as a "roulette wheel. In the beginning, black is on top, in the middle epochs, white holds the odds, but soon Ethiopia shall stretch forth her noble wings!" (81). However, as he did in "Harlem Is Nowhere," Ellison resituates Freud's theory of shock into a critique of racial violence. Whereas for Freud this state would be reducible to their experience with the Great War, and while the Golden Day veterans are traumatized war survivors, the novel makes clear that the real source of their trauma lies not in the war itself but rather in the racist vigilante violence of disaffected southern whites who understand their desire for upward mobility all too well. One veteran, for instance, explains that he hoped to return to the

United States and work as a doctor, but when he tried, "[t]en men in masks drove [him] out from the city at midnight and beat [him] with whips for saving a human life" (93).

Moreover, the novel doesn't just suggest that racism, as opposed to war, is the real underlying cause of their collective state of shock; it also turns the veterans' shell-shocked state into an expression of the American psyche. After all, the veterans' seemingly traumatized and skewed vision of the world turns out to be far less unique or distorted than it might appear. The veterans' alignment of Norton with Jefferson and Rockefeller points to the entanglements of America's great men—be they the Founding Fathers, the great industrialists, or the new purveyors of racial uplift—in systemic racial violence and exploitation, while their theory of history turns out not to be strikingly similar to that of Jefferson himself, who offered an equally haunting and cyclical view of American history: "I tremble," he writes, in *Notes on the State of Virginia*, "for my country when I reflect that God is just: that his justice cannot sleep forever: that considering numbers, nature and natural means only, a revolution of the wheel of fortune, an exchange of situation is among possible events: that it may become probable by supernatural interference!" (qtd. in Greeson, 54). For Jefferson, slavery is the injustice that will catalyze the wheel of fortune's turn. The novel's deployment of both Jefferson and his haunted history similarly suggests that the Jim Crow regime of the South might also come to undermine the Cold War fantasy of the United States as global leader.

Ellison's refiguring of those made surplus as a shocked population who, in turn, haunt or shock the society that dispossessed them has a long tradition within modernist aesthetics. Geoffrey Jacques, for instance, draws a connection between what he terms the "African American imaginary" and the "colonial uncanny" (27), arguing that, like its colonial counterpart, African American culture "haunts" modernism (27), and numerous commentators have highlighted the connections between Surrealism and postcolonial struggles.[7] *Invisible Man*, however, marks a break from this trajectory of the haunted and repressed unconscious. The protagonist's opening gambit that he is not "a spook like those who haunted Edgar Allan Poe [. . . but] a man of flesh and bone" (3) suggests that his belief in the disruptive and transformative power of the figure of the dispossessed is just another faulty belief of his youth, another racist trap. Indeed, events such as the Golden Day riot, the factory explosion, and the concluding riot—which reveal the larger plan to "keep this nigger-boy running" (33), and which appear to disrupt those plans—turn out not to be disruptive at all, but often do the work of slum clearance, urban modernization, and psychological transformation.

The Golden Day riots, and the protagonist's unwilling participation within them, catalyze the series of events that lead to his expulsion from Tuskegee and his reluctant, if unwitting, participation in the Great Migration to the urban North. And once there, these surrealist sections of the narrative become even more ambivalent. These sections offer scathing critiques of the racist policies and assumptions inherent within white philanthropy, industrial unionism, and Communist Party politics (as well as the naturalist narrative impulses that uphold them). But these seemingly disruptive and explosive shocks have already been taken hold of by a new and equally nefarious racial regime. The material effects of these explosive scenes do the material work of urban renewal, carrying out slum clearance by often literally blowing up old buildings, alongside the aesthetic and affective work of crafting the fantasies, subjectivities, and narratives underpinning renewal.

The protagonist's rapid shift from the paint factory to the hospital, and specifically a mental hospital, is particularly instructive here. In addition to tenements, proponents of urban renewal regularly treated urban factories as blights that were driving middle-class shoppers to the cleaner and more pleasant suburban shopping centers. Part of urban redevelopment, and later renewal's strategy to clear out the vestiges of the nineteenth-century industrial cityscape was to replace these landscapes with new civic centers and other modernist urban complexes that were better suited to a new age. Hospitals were crucial to this process. As historian Joel Schwartz explains, in the postwar period, hospitals began to "stake their claims on" and work increasingly closely with what he terms the "city's redevelopment machinery" (210). The relationship was mutually beneficial. Hospitals took advantage of this new climate of redevelopment to expand both their facilities and programs in their aim to turn New York into "the medical capital of the world" (qtd. in J. Schwartz, 216). Meanwhile, hospitals—which had begun to transform from "from health-care facilities into modern complexes with social responsibilities" (216)—offered a veneer of social and public good to local developers, which gained them the public support necessary to carry out mass clearances and evictions.[8] Hospitals underwent this transformation in numerous ways, but one central strategy was to increase the construction of psychiatric facilities, which they claimed would offer medical solutions to juvenile delinquency, crime, and other social problems that emerged from these "blighted" neighborhoods (216).

While the violent exclusions that lead to Brockway and the protagonist's fight in the boiler room (and the boiler room's subsequent explosion) appear disruptive, this historical context suggests that their literally explosive response actually aids in the processes of creative destruction associated with urban redevelopment. Most pertinently, the protagonist's transition from the factory to the hospital enacts a temporally compressed allegory of both the hospital's role in the transformation of New York's urban fabric from low-density warehouses and factories to a glimmering postindustrial landscape, and also in the construction of a new racial ideology: specifically, the emergence of a new "medical solution" (J. Schwartz, 219) to the problems of racial antagonism and anger. Like Rip Van Winkle waking up into the post-Revolution world, Ellison's protagonist wakes up into a postplan world. Strapped to an "old, white, rigid chair" (231) in a factory hospital, he is immediately shocked for "therapeutic purposes" (231). These therapeutic purposes, however, are aimed not at helping him to deal with society but at protecting society *from* him. The goal of his therapy, the doctors explain, is to integrate the protagonist back into society by creating a new person who is unable to feel rage and thus will cause "society [to] suffer no trauma on his account" (236). The protagonist's rage is literally shocked out of him; he comments that he becomes unable to feel his rage because of the "pulse of the current smashing through [his] body" (237). Shock not only strips him of his anger but also turns him into an instrument as he is "pounded between crushing electrical pressures; pumped between live electrodes like an accordion between a player's hands" (232).

This scene marks a notable break in Ellison's focus and orientation. The Ellison of the Great Depression focuses primarily on the dispossession or exclusion of black men and African American culture from social institutions. In "Harlem Is Nowhere," for instance, he argues that "the negro cannot participate fully in the therapy that the white American achieves through patriotic ceremonies and by identifying himself with American power. Instead, he is thrown back upon his own 'slum-shocked' institutions" (300). In this hospital scene, however, Ellison is equally concerned with the violent practices that aim to *re-possess* and include black men into society. The role of the hospital in *Invisible Man* is thus twofold. In the hospital's attempt to reduce the protagonist's rage and integrate him back into society, the hospital appears as a key institution of what Jodi Melamed terms "racial liberalism" to describe the Cold War strategy to create an America that was, or at least appeared to be, a racially harmonious and integrated nation (2006, 4). At the same time, however, the hospital is also a key participant in the structural and racialized process of slum clearance. The impulse to be resisted here is to map the teleological beliefs of the protagonist onto Ellison. It is not that the Ellison of *Invisible Man* has overcome the faulty or naïve ideas of his earlier self, as represented by "Harlem Is Nowhere." Rather, what Ellison comes up against in *Invisible Man* is the failure of these older aesthetic strategies in confronting this new racial regime of official integration alongside economic exclusion and of-ten physical removal. Within this new regime, Ellison suggests that shock can't function as a resistant aesthetic strategy. It is no longer an effective way of registering the experience of the slum dweller who is excluded from society because it has been appropriated as a tool for the creative destruc-tion of urban space, and the neutralization, appropriation, and commodi-fication of black men.

Shocked States and States of Shock

The novel approaches this problem, somewhat peculiarly, through its myriad depictions of dolls. *Invisible Man* is filled both with dolls—piggy banks in the shape of Sambo dolls, dancing Sambo puppets, and lynched white mannequins—and with black men being shocked and turned into dolls. Its most emblematic doll, of course, belongs to Tod Clifton. Clifton, whose first name, Tod, is German for death, is the Brotherhood's most talented Harlem organizer and the figure most closely associated with the new black urban culture of hip. When the protagonist meets Clifton, he comments that "this Brother Tod Clifton, the young leader, looked somehow like a hipster, a zoot-suiter, a sharpie" (366). Clifton leaves both the Brotherhood and Harlem in what is ostensibly a protest against their exploitation of him and race issues more broadly for their own agenda. He becomes, notably, a puppeteer in midtown Manhattan, selling racial Sambo dolls. Clifton's puppeteer performance acts as a cipher through which we can read this new regime of commodification and criminaliza-tion. When the protagonist swerves off of Forty-Second Street to avoid a crowd, he encounters "A grinning doll of orange-and-black tissue paper with thin flat cardboard disks" (431). Both horrified and captivated, the protagonist watches as "some mysterious mechanism" causes it "to move up and down in a loose-jointed, shoulder-shaking, infuriatingly sensuous motion, a dance that was completely detached from the black, mask-like face" (431). The doll's "infuriatingly sensuous motion" and its "inanimate, boneless bounding" (431) always straddle the line between the sensuous-ness of human life, the inanimacy of the commodity, and the ghostly in-between spaces of the fetish form. Throughout this scene, the protagonist draws our attention to the doll's liminal position, and when Clifton drops the doll to escape the police, the protagonist picks it up, explaining that he half-expects "to feel it pulse with life" (434). Clifton is trying to show the protagonist that, like the doll whose movements might seem separate from both his blackness and from the mechanism pulling the strings, his movements, too, cannot be separated from either his race or those who are controlling and manipulating him.

Clifton's Sambo doll is not the only doll making this point in the novel. In the opening Battle Royale scene when the protagonist scrambles for coins on the electrified floor, he receives a shock and explains, "I tried frantically to remove my hand but could not let go. [. . .] My muscles jumped, my nerves jangled" (27). The protagonist here effectively transforms into a Sambo doll, moving mechanically under a force not his own, which the novel emphasizes through both the language of mechanization and the allusion to dance that occurs when one of the other boys slips and falls "upon the charged rug" and the protagonist sees him "literally *dance* upon his back; his elbows beating a frenzied tattoo upon the floor, his muscles twitching" (27, emphasis added). Similarly, in the factory hospital, Ellison describes the electric shocks that pulse through the protagonist's body as being "swift and staccato, increasing gradually until I fairly *danced* between the nodes" (237, emphasis added).

Why dolls? Hal Foster offers one solution, which emerges from his posing the same question about the surrealists and their fixation on dolls and mannequins. He suggests that this preoccupation is a result of the dolls' unique expression of the commodity fetish, giving human form to that "other yet not-other, strange yet familiar—'dead labor' come back to dominate the living" (129). The fetishistic power of these dolls as expressions of dead labor—or, in other words, as expressions of *capital*—is such that they begin to appear not as our creations but as our "demonic master" (129). Clifton's deft performance, which seems to literally bring the puppet to life, also offers a nod to Karl Marx's dancing table, that *ur* symbol of the commodity fetish, making clear that while he, like the protagonist, may appear to be lifelike and independent, they are just puppets of the brotherhood. In "The Fetishism of Commodities and the Secret Thereof," Marx argues that, under capitalism, commodities take on the peculiar appearance of having a reality independent of the work that created them. For him, the idea that a table has an inherent value outside of human labor is as irrational as the belief that a table can dance "of its own free will" (1977a, 82). Clifton wants the protagonist to understand that they, like the Sambo doll, are simply commodities, and the idea that they move independently of the Brotherhood is equally absurd. Clifton's critique, however, extends far beyond their specific roles in the Brotherhood to their role in US life. Clifton's dance enacts the much broader process through which seemingly independent and oppositional forms of black life, politics, and style have been captured and commodified.

The police's subsequent intervention into Clifton's dance enacts these precise relations by mimicking the shock-doll experiences that have marked the protagonist's development up to this point. While *Invisible Man* draws an analogy between the puppet's relationship to Clifton and Clifton's relationship to the police, the novel replaces the magical or hoodoo-inspired language of possession that suffuses Clifton's puppeteering with the jolting and mechanical language of industrialism. Where the puppet has the "sensuous" movements of a human body beneath Clifton's invisible strings, Clifton takes on the jagged movements of a machine beneath the police's highly visible force. The police "jolt him forward" (435) and push him, "sending him in a head-snapping forward stumble" (436). Even Clifton's attempts to resist the police become mechanized, as when he attacks the cop and his arm is described as swinging "like a dancer [. . . in a] short, jolting arc" (436). When the police finally murder him, the language returns to that of the puppet, with Clifton "suddenly crumpling" (436); but there is no magic here, only the "rapid explosion" (436) of gunfire. Where Clifton's Sambo dance reveals the figurative strings behind the puppet, highlighting the ways in which both he and the protagonist are mere commodities, the police's intervention reveals the material violence of that relationship. The police turn Clifton into a puppet, shaping his movements, and then killing him for those very movements. The point in both cases—Clifton as puppet master as well as Clifton as puppet—is that the problem is not exactly exclusion but rather the transformation of black men into what Marx identified as the "surplus population" (782): not a population outside of capitalist social relations but part of its "disposable industrial reserve army" (784).

In 1966, James and Grace Lee Boggs presciently argued that the major problem besetting US cities was deindustrialization, which they defined as labor becoming "more and more socially unnecessary" as a result of the "technological revolution" (163). This tendency, they argued, while ultimately national, first hit black, urban workers because they are "the ones who have been made most expendable" (163). Clifton's death dance dramatizes, quite precisely and with much foresight, the trajectory of black men in the postwar period as they are cast out of the realm of production and the wage relation, pushed into the underground economy, rendered criminal, and then subjected to the violence of state power, a fate that ultimately ends in death. But the protagonist cannot see what Clifton is trying to show him because his politics belong to a representative of an older moment, namely that of Booker T. Washington and a context in which black labor was necessary. The protagonist cannot see what Clifton can: namely, that black labor has become mechanized and thus that black men have become surplus and expendable.

Because the protagonist misses this economic or structural lesson, he makes two crucial mistakes. First, he believes himself to be an independent historical actor whose life and future is entirely of his own making instead of shaped by larger historical processes. Second, he doesn't actually escape the pseudohistorical science of the party so much as simply substitute a new locus of political salvation: this time the oppositional forms of black culture he encounters in Harlem. Immediately following Clifton's death, the protagonist returns to Harlem and, emerging from the subway, begins to notice the "crowds along 125th Street" (443). Like his encounter with the dispossessed objects of the blues couple, so here too the crowds come into focus. They are no longer the "bombardment of impressions" (159) that they were when he first arrived but are now a legible group he is able to discern. Ellison begins to describe them, the "men dressed like the boys, and of girls in dark exotic-colored stockings, their costumes surreal variations of downtown styles" (443). Staring at them, he realizes that "somehow I'd missed them. I'd missed them even when my work had been most successful. They were outside the groove of history, and it was my job to get them in, all of them" (443). Ignoring the warning of Clifton's trap, the protagonist immediately apes the Brotherhood's notion of history as a rational science of progress in which, as Robert O'Meally nicely puts it, "one dwells either 'inside' or 'outside'" and interpellates himself within their project by trying to get others "in" (177).

Importantly, it is this celebration of these stylish youths and his desire to bring them "into history" that motivates the protagonist to hold the funeral parade through Harlem, and to deliver his famous speech that turns on an analogy between Tod's coffin and a Harlem tenement building:

> He's in the box and we're in there with him. [. . .] It's dark in this box and it's crowded. It has a cracked ceiling and a clogged-up toilet in the hall. It has rats and roaches, and it's far, far too expensive a dwelling. The air is bad and it'll be cold this winter. Tod Clifton is crowded and he needs the room. "Tell them to get out of the box." That's what he would say if you could hear him. (458)

Both the coffin and the tenement become metaphors for being outside of history. Echoing the inside/outside logic of the Brotherhood's history, the novel twins the protagonist's call to get Clifton *out* of the coffin-tenement (where, the protagonist emphasizes, "we're in there with him") with the need to bring Clifton, and the crowds of hip Harlemites more broadly, into history.

Significantly, this is also the moment in which the protagonist changes his theoretical mind-set, moving from political to personal responsibility. Earlier, trying to make sense of Tod's death, the protagonist muses: "The incident was political. I looked at the doll, thinking. The political equivalent of such entertainment is death. But that's too broad a definition. Its economic meaning? That the life of a man is worth the sale of a two-bit paper doll. . . . But that didn't kill the idea that my anger helped speed him on to death" (447). The question of political versus personal responsibility underpins the protagonist's progression as he moves from the "social responsibility" that he calls for in the Battle Royale scene (30), to his Freudian slip into "social equality" (31), before settling on "personal responsibility" (463). Inasmuch as Clifton's funeral represents a moment when the Harlem of the author's past and future come together, it also represents a key transitional moment in which the protagonist of social responsibility, social equality, and personal responsibility intersect. For a brief moment, the protagonist fuses all three together, understanding his job, his *personal responsibility*, as politicizing Clifton's death, as bringing black people into history, and—significantly—of doing so through the project of housing reform. But, while the protagonist doesn't realize it, this alignment of personal responsibility and housing reform is already firmly entrenched within a broader shift from the model of widespread and accessible public housing called for by Depression-era planners like Catherine Bauer, Lewis Mumford, and Henry Wright to a new public-private regime of housing in which white families gained access to individual home ownership—and thus to the entrepreneurial fantasy of personal responsibility, self-sufficiency, and freedom—while African Americans were relegated to public housing and rentership, which became increasingly aligned with dependence, irresponsibility, and criminality.

While neither the protagonist nor the marchers could know this, attuned readers at the time of the novel's publication might have noticed two details about this scene. First, within the novel's setting, the protagonist's speech simply echoes the polemics and speeches issued by Depression-era civil rights activists such as Adam Clayton Powell who regularly decried the "dark, damp, cold dungeons" that passed for housing in Harlem and that *bred* "death and sickness" (qtd. in Heise, 132). By the 1950s, however, this kind of rhetoric was not coming from activists but from the coalition of Realtors, corporations, downtown merchants, banks, and other interests with significant economic interests in the downtown core who turned the language of housing reform into a tool for the uprooting and removal of largely black communities in the name of economic development. To qualify for Title 1 status, local authorities had to prove that the proposed neighborhood was a blighted slum, negatively affecting the health of both the residents and the city. Each plan proposed by Moses's New York City Committee on Slum Clearance thus contained a section entitled "Demonstration of Slum Conditions," in which authorities drew on the same language and imagery as housing activists before them to make the case for clearance and redevelopment.[9]

The second thing attuned readers would have noticed is that Clifton's funeral parade through the tenements plots a course through the very sections of Harlem that were about to be bulldozed under the auspices of the Harlem Title 1 project.[10] The problem, Ellison intimates, is that the protagonist's call to get African Americans "out of the box" and into history has already been captured by this new racial regime in which African American culture and style were "brought in" and made to stand for what Martin Luther King called the "amazing universalism" of the American project (qtd. in Singh 2004, 14), at the same time as they were being spatially and economically excluded. While this trap is only implicit in its positive, or acceptably liberal, instantiation—the funeral march and Harlem's stylish crowds—it becomes more explicit in its oppositional manifestation as the riot and Ras's African garb. Early in the riot, the protagonist encounters Scofield and Dupre as they try to burn down the "huge tenement building" where they live (545). At first, the protagonist is excited, thinking to himself "I couldn't believe it, couldn't believe they had the nerve" (545). But as Scofield and Dupre begin to carry out their "plan" (546), the protagonist begins to change his mind. As he's clearing out the building, an old woman approaches him and pleads, "*please.* You know my time's almost here . . . . you *know* it is. If you do it now, where am I going to go?" (547, emphasis in original). Dupre is unmoved. He continues his work, explaining: "Goddamn you rotten sonsabitches. You didn't think I'd do it but there it is. You wouldn't fix it up. Now see how you like it" (548). Like Brockway's blowing up of the factory, Dupre's burning of the tenements might seem to disrupt the process of urban modernization, but it is actually part of modernity's process of creative destruction: clearing the slums, evicting its residents, and making way for redevelopment.

It is finally at this moment that the protagonist learns Clifton's lesson. He realizes that "The committee had planned [the riot]. And I [. . .] had been a tool. A tool just at the very moment I had thought myself free" (553). He realizes, in other words, that his actions have never been autonomous but rather were shaped by larger historical processes and institutions. The protagonist tries to explain this when he encounters Ras the Exhorter who has become Ras the Destroyer by donning "the costume of an Abyssinian chieftain [. . . with] a cape made of the skin of some wild animal" (556). He calls out "They want a race riot. [. . .] The more of us who are killed the better they like" (557), but Ras does not listen, calling him an "Uncle Tom" who must be lynched. This commodification of black style—Tod Clifton's hipster chic, the Harlemites' colorful garb, Ras's Abyssinian costume, and, we could add, Rinehart's aesthetic, which, as Thomas Heise argues, turns out to be nothing but "a racial phantasm, a congealed set of social anxieties about [. . .] the black underworld" (154)—is in part Michael Szalay's point when he identifies the problem of reification as central to Ellison's creative process and its ultimate block. Szalay suggests that Ellison was unable to produce his second novel in part because he was unable to find "any self-consciously black style capable of escaping reification" (2012, 150). It is easy to see Szalay's point. By the time the protagonist has run through the horrors of the riot and the myriad instances of violence and commodification and fled down a manhole, it is difficult to find much potential anywhere outside the erudite mind of its protagonist.

Indeed, Szalay's point echoes Marshall Berman's argument that Ellison, like many of the postwar novelists of his generation, was unable "to imagine or engage the present, the life of the postwar cities and societies in which their books came out. [. . .] That poverty may have actually nourished the development of modernism by forcing artists and thinkers to fall back on their own resources and open up new depths of inner space. At the same time, it subtly ate away at the roots of modernism by sealing off its imaginative life from the everyday modern world in which actual men and women had to move and live." (310) This takes us to the most ideological reading of Ellison, the rejection of all models of social organizing, which comes to stand in for the Communist Party, or alternately any kind of socialist project as a metonym for the entire modernist project of planning. This is the Ellison we find in his own later work: the Ellison who explains that the protagonist's "movement vertically downward [. . .] is a process of *rising* to an understanding of his human condition" (1995b, 111), and the Ellison who argues that "In the epilogue the hero discovers what he had not discovered throughout the book: you have to make your own decisions; you have to think for yourself" (1995a, 220). This is the Ellison of individualism, self-reliance, and Cold War liberalism, the Ellison who lends himself so easily to what Foley has aptly termed "the circular practice of reading *Invisible Man* through the palimpsest supplied by Ellison's writings after 1952 and, more generally, by the cold war narrative that bindingly shapes most discussion of American writers on the left" (2010, 6).

And yet, this sealing is not as complete as Berman's and Szalay's comments—and even Ellison's own later assessment—might suggest. While *Invisible Man* offers an unceasingly scathing critique of the commodification of black men and black culture, and of the economic slumification in which Harlem comes to represent the most lascivious of American dreams and nightmares, the novel is deliberately ambiguous as to whose view of Harlem is being put forward in its final riot. At the same time as racial liberalism was trying to marshal African American culture as a symbol of a new racially inclusive America, cities were being conceived of as, in the words of Marshall Berman, "junkyards of substandard housing and decaying neighborhoods from which Americans"—specifically white Americans—"should be given every chance to escape": either through white flight, or through the destruction and recreation of the urban landscape itself (307). While the protagonist's tour of the riot replicates this process, turning all of Harlem into a horror-fantasy from which escape into suburban space is the only and necessary option, I want to insist, in spite of Ellison's own later explanations, that the novel advises us not to conflate the protagonist's belief in the triumphalism of this descent with Ellison's beliefs in this final scene.

Conclusion

By way of conclusion, I argue that *Invisible Man* distinguishes itself from the protagonist who, full of this anxiety about the reification of black style and culture, seals himself off from everyday life. Timothy Bewes has suggested that "reification, as a socio-political critique, co-exists with the anxiety towards reification" (247). In *Reification: Or the Anxiety of Late Capitalism* (2002), Bewes explains:

> An *obsession* with reification—meaning an overwhelming sense of
> the unreliability of language as a "technology" of modernity, of the
> corrosiveness of representation itself, a quasi-religious idealization of
> "timelessness" and the corresponding depreciation of "history"—is
> entirely congruent with a revulsion from civilization itself and a pessi-

mistic lapse into solitude and aestheticism. [The] attempt at a preservation of the self *against* the world masks, firstly, a nostalgic enchantment with the "primitive," and secondly, an idealist, undialectical conception of truth as located outside history, and outside the bounds of human communication. (20)

Bewes, in this passage, is describing the character of Marlow in Joseph Conrad's *Heart of Darkness* (1899) to elucidate his larger thesis about the nature of reification itself. The protagonist of *Invisible Man* also cites Conrad when he flees Harlem and escapes into the tunnels of the city, explaining, "Since then I've sometimes been overcome with a passion to return into that 'heart of darkness' across the Mason-Dixon line, but then I remind myself that the true darkness lies within my own mind" (579).

It is here, in this heart of darkness, that we receive the final pronouncements that seem to solidify *Invisible Man* as the great Cold War text. Thinking back to his grandfather, the protagonist begins to interpret and reinterpret the meaning of his advice to "agree 'em to death" (575), asking: "Could he have meant [. . .] that we were to affirm the principle on which the country was built and not the men, or at least not the men who did the violence. [. . .] Or did he mean we had to take the responsibility for all of it, for the men as well as the principle. [. . .] Or was it, did he mean that we should affirm the principle because we, through no fault of our own, were linked to all the others in the loud, clamouring semi-visible world" (574). By the end of this list, the grandfather's words mean everything, which is to say they mean nothing. It is here that the protagonist spins fully around, moving from a desire to politicize everything to a complete evacuation from the political. Sitting in his manhole, he muses: "You go along for years knowing something is wrong, then suddenly you discover that you're as transparent as air. At first you tell yourself that it's all a dirty joke, or that it's due to the 'political situation.' But deep down you come to suspect that you're yourself to blame" (575). In this final pronouncement, the protagonist severs the link between the personal and the social, and abandons the struggle from social equality—it is the move from political struggles for social equality to the rhetoric of personal responsibility.

He takes up, in short, the position of Conrad's Marlow: a retreat from civilization and history into the underground, his own private heart of darkness. This transformation of the heart of darkness from the geographical space of the South—what Houston Baker and Dana Nelson aptly term "the abjected regional Other" (236)—to the psychological space of the African American mind is another of the compulsive repetitions that structure the novel in which the protagonist unwittingly comes to exemplify the new racial ideologies forming under an era of urban renewal and white flight.[11] In *White Flight: Atlanta and the Making of Modern Conservatism* (2013), Kevin Kruse argues that the "court-ordered 'desegregation' of public spaces brought about not actual racial integration, but instead a new division in which the public world was increasingly abandoned to blacks and a new private one was created for whites" (106). When the protagonist pronounces in the novel's final pages that, "I lived a public life and attempted to function under the assumption that the world was solid and all the relationships therein. Now I know men are different and that all life is divided and that only in division is there true health" (576), he articulates the logic of this de facto segregation by reifying and even celebrating the distinctions between public and private and the racial divisions underpinning that distinction.

The ideology he is here embracing is an ideology of segregation from which he is, as he has been throughout the novel, implicitly excluded. Just like his celebration of the values of Booker T. Washington and racial uplift in the South, and also his celebration of the values of Fordism in the North, so too his celebration of this new private life is equally absurd: he is as barred from this private life and its entrepreneurial subjectivity as he has been from all other positions he has identified with from the College to the Communist Party. The protagonist's final position is not the position with which the reader is meant to identify but the position to be critiqued. The protagonist's retreat is not, then, the novel's triumphant solution, but its final problem, a problem to which Ellison would return more than twenty years later in his 1978 essay "The Little Man at Chehaw Station." The essay closes with a story of Ellison's time as a worker for the Federal Writers' Project in the 1930s. He recounts approaching a tenement in San Juan Hill, which he explains was a predominantly black and Puerto Rican neighborhood that would eventually be cleared for the "coming of Lincoln Center" (515). Following the protagonist's ascension through descent, Ellison recounts how he walked into the tenement and worked his way from the top floor to the bottom trying to collect signatures for a petition supporting "some now long-forgotten social justice issue" (515). Having reached the bottom of the tenement, he realizes he has one more room to visit, which is in the cellar. As he approaches the last room, he overhears the "profane" and "angry" voices of two black men "in violent argument" (515). Gathering his courage, he enters the room and finds four black workers heaving coal, and "locked in verbal combat over which of the two celebrated Metropolitan Opera divas were the superior soprano!" (516). In response to

Ellison's surprise, one of them explains that they worked as extras at the Met: "Strip us fellows down and give us some costumes and we make about the finest damn bunch of Egyptians you ever seen. Hell, we been down there wearing leopard skins and carrying spears or waving things like palm leafs and ostrich tail fans for years!" (519).

These men, he argues, are "products of both past *and present*; were both coal heavers *and* Met extras; were both working men *and* opera buffs. Seen in the clear, pluralistic, melting-pot light of American cultural possibility, there was no contradiction" (520). Richard Purcell has argued that this passage offers the integrative vision of American vernacular culture that, for Ellison, could stand against the "phantasmagorical black separatists, who seem to stand in for vanguardism, anticapitalism, and bebop" that motivated the writing of his essay (926–27). And yet the essay also undoes this integrative promise. Lurking beneath the integrated cultural pluralism embodied in each of these men are the material conditions that prohibit this integrative vision and that are fuelling the black separatism that Ellison is writing against. Stripped of Ellison's soaring prose, the story Ellison is telling us is of four men who could access the Met only as badly paid and exploited workers who are now heaving coal while housed in the basement of a tenement (reflections of *Invisible Man* here abound) that, Ellison makes a point of telling us, will soon be destroyed to make way for middle-class housing projects, an elite art school, and a world-class cultural center. What to make, then, of his plea for integration through a story about the underdevelopment of urban black space and the clearance and removal of African Americans?

In "Little Man," the Cold War liberal Ellison collides with the Ellison who was a keen observer of urban transformation. And while the essay papers over this collision, optimistically proclaiming that "there was no contradiction" (520), its anecdote reveals nothing if not the tensions inherent in the Cold War liberal project that at once seized blackness as symbols of cultural Americanness at the same moment in which African Americans, and particularly African American neighborhoods, were bulldozed and transformed into frontiers of capital. It is this contradiction that would underwrite the long 1950s becoming a central focus of, and problem for, the postwar novel.

CHAPTER 2

The Price of Salt Is the City: Patricia Highsmith and the Queer Frontiers of Neoliberalism

In 2009, the group Queer Kids of Queer Parents Against Gay Marriage issued a statement:

> It's hard for us to believe what we're hearing these days. Thousands are losing their homes, and gays want a day named after Harvey Milk. The U.S. military is continuing its path of destruction, and gays want to be allowed to fight. Cops are still killing unarmed black men and bashing queers, and gays want more policing. More and more Americans are suffering and dying because they can't get decent health care, and gays want weddings. What happened to us? (n.p.)

This statement is part of a larger critical reconsideration of how queer theory and politics have been appropriated by what Lisa Duggan and others have identified as "neoliberal 'equality' politics" (xii): that is, a politics both "designed for global consumption during the twenty-first century, and compatible with continued upward redistribution of resources" (xii), and also a politics that has helped to secure liberal consent for the expansion and intensification of US imperial violence through the "War on Terror" abroad and the prison industrial complex at home.[1] This chapter argues that Patricia Highsmith's 1952 novel *The Price of Salt* provides an answer to this opening question—"what happened to us?"—by rooting the intertwined emergence of neoliberalism and homosexual respectability politics, or "homonormativity" (Agathangelou, Bassichis, and Spira, 122), in the interlinked processes of suburbanization, white flight, urban renewal, and the expansion and consolidation of US global hegemony through the Cold War.

The Price of Salt narrates a love story between the department-store shopgirl Therese Belivet and her customer, the suburban housewife Carol Aird, as they fight both the law and social conventions to be together. But the novel also narrates two other transformations: Therese's transformation from a poor, anxious, shopgirl to a strong, successful, television set designer, and New York City's transformation from an overcrowded and blighted industrial city associated with poverty, racial mixing, and perversion to a spacious, modern, and prosperous city associated with affluent white women. The novel, in other words, links Therese's "coming out" narrative (and its lesbian love story more broadly) with a narrative of personal uplift and urban renewal. In so doing, *The Price of Salt* brings together two Cold War concerns: the Lavender Scare, in which sexual "perversion" or homosexuality became a sign of subversive or communist behavior, and an urban panic that viewed the slumification (and implicit racialization) of American cities as a breeding ground for sexual and political perversion, and thus a threat to the national character and national security.[2]

Not only does Therese and Carol's love story play out within the segregated landscape of impoverished cities and prosperous suburbs, but its two characters embody the subjectivities and social problems associated with their respective spaces. Read through Therese, the city is a naturalist space of overcrowding, decay, poverty, and ceaseless wage work that she seeks to escape through her connection to Carol and Carol's suburban lifestyle. Read through Carol, the suburbs are a space of confinement, boredom, and surveillance that she attempts to escape through what Victoria Hesford identifies as the urban space of "sex and freedom from the demands of marriage and family" (2003, 120) represented by Therese. Taken together, the novel stages the broader crisis in the postwar period that centered around the relationship between the suburbs and the city. At the same time that the prosperous suburbs were becoming Cold War showrooms of American values (Tyler May, 9)—often in stark contrast to the blighted, heterogeneous, and lascivious city—there was also a growing anxiety that it was not decaying cities but in fact the suburbs that posed the greatest threat to the American way of life. Fears abounded that the suburbs were making women bored, unfulfilled, and unsatisfied (Breines) and were feminizing and softening men (Breines; Ehrenreich and English; Geidel), stripping them of their frontier spirits and turning them into "organization men" (Riesman, Glazer, and Denney) or "outward-directed" conformers (Whyte 1956). Through Therese and Carol's relationship, the novel moves beyond the suburb/city dichotomy that marked the policy debates and cultural narratives of the time and reconceptualizes the metropolitan region as an interconnected whole, suffusing the suburbs with the energy of the city and the city with the domestic femininity of the suburbs.[3]

Where *Invisible Man* is a narrative about black entrapment, both economically and physically, within the decaying space of the city, *The Price of Salt* is a narrative of white female mobility and the recuperation of the city. This difference is enacted both spatially and generically. If *Invisible Man*'s narrative follows the increasing foreclosure of its protagonist's movement until he finds himself literally trapped within the city, *The Price of Salt*'s narrative tracks the increasing mobility and freedom of its protagonist as she moves from the metropolis to the West and back. Similarly, while *Invisible Man* ends in the surrealist landscape of the protagonist's mind, *The Price of Salt* enacts a generic shift from naturalist lesbian pulp to the Western, which it reconfigures as a lesbian road novel. Barbara Will has noted that, from its inception, the Western has operated as a "problem solving" genre for the subjects and space of the urban East, which have "dominated the arenas of commerce and industry but at the cost of neurasthenic strain" (296).[4] The Western as we know it has its origins in Silas Weir Mitchell's "camp cure," or "West Cure," and Owen Wister's literary response to it, *The Virginian* (1902). In his 1871 work, Mitchell called for "professional men, merchants of all kinds, dealers in money, and manufacturers" (40) suffering from nervous strain to undergo a "camp cure," where their "close communion with Nature" (55) would provide a "capital of vitality" (8) and an "elastic sense of strength" (8). This, too, was the promise of the Western genre, which offered imaginative visions of a new national hero—the urban merchant, manufacturer, or professional suffering from neurasthenic strain—who, through a brief encounter with the outdoors, would be cured of his strain and return to both master himself and continue his work of national mastery and domination. In *The Price of Salt*, Highsmith both draws on and refigures the Western genre. Her characters follow the Western's arc, in which the neurasthenic urban subject goes west, encounters a danger that cures and strengthens her, and ultimately returns home prepared to do the work of nation-building. However, Highsmith changes the protagonist from a professional man into a working-class, homosexual woman, and she expands the Western's scope from the urban core to the metropolitan region as a whole.

Through the novel's radical revision of the Western and its narration of Therese and the city's transformation, *The Price of Salt* cleaves apart the Lavender Scare from the Red Scare and constructs a Red Scare *defense* of lesbianism in which lesbianism becomes a tool for subjective, urban, and national renewal—and, in turn, the attainment of sexual rights and freedoms becomes linked with the construction of a thoroughly capitalist subjectivity organized around individual freedom, private property, and entrepreneurialism. In this respect, the novel creates a remarkable space within the national imaginary for the homosexual subject while simultaneously narrating the routing of queer politics from a revolutionary or redistributive project into a politics of state recognition, bourgeois ascension, and privatization, a politics that would become identical with, and catalytic of, neoliberalism.

Naturally Bohemian

The Price of Salt opens with Therese at a crossroads. Having been fired from a small press, she starts a new job in the doll section of a downtown department store, Frankenberg's. This fall from artisan to shopgirl terrifies Therese. As she puts it, "the store intensified things that had always bothered her, as long as she could remember" (13). Therese goes on to enumerate those things:

> the pointless actions, the meaningless chores that seemed to keep
> her from doing what she wanted to do, might have done—and here
> it was the complicated procedures with moneybags, coat checkings,
> and time clocks that might keep people even from serving the store as
> efficiently as they might—the sense that everyone was incommunicado
> with everyone else and living on an entirely wrong plane, so that the
> meaning, the message, to love, or whatever it was that each life con-
> tained, never could find its expression. It reminded her of conversations
> at tables, on sofas, with people whose words seemed to cover dead,
> unstirrable things, who never touched a string that played. (13)

Therese's description of her surroundings—and particularly its brutal vision of the dehumanizing and deadening effect of her job—echoes numerous other early twentieth-century fictional accounts of the alienation experienced by young women entering the job market. As she moves through her day at Frankenberg's, she watches as her fellow workers—with their "fifty-year-old faces [. . . of] exhaustion and terror" (14)—are reduced from people to a pair of "chapped" and "dirty [. . .] aging hands" (14).

Karl Marx famously argued that one of capitalism's brutal ironies was that the more of herself the worker put into her work, the more her alienation increased: that "the more the worker spends himself, the more powerful becomes the alien world of objects which he creates over and against himself, the poorer he himself—his inner world—becomes, the less belongs to him as his own" (272). In both of the above quotes, Therese limns precisely this process, offering a brutal vision of the dehumanizing and deadening effect of work in the form of these older women who are not only exhausted by their job but become themselves exhausted of life.

However, while Therese's critique of the dehumanizing nature of this work has many of the markings of left-wing, proletarian, and Popular Front fiction, her response breaks away from this impulse in crucial ways.[5] Most notably, she distances herself from these women by reminding herself that, unlike them, she possesses artisanal skills; by recalling her boyfriend Richard's assurances that he has "an absolute conviction [she]'ll be out of it in a few weeks" (12) while the others will not; and by comparing the department store to a Mondrian painting (12), proving that she, unlike her coworkers, is sophisticated and educated. Therese, in short, separates herself from her coworkers by identifying with the aesthetic ethos of modernism and the lifestyle of bohemianism: an identity the novel underscores through her Czech roots and the artistic ambitions and femininity of her father. Therese initially appears to be following in his trajectory. She lives alone, has a boyfriend she has no interest in marrying, and aspires to be a set designer. But Therese's relationship with bohemia is ambivalent. Where Richard passionately embraces bohemia with his love of modernist novels, working-class bars, Village life, and anti-establishment politics, Therese remains quite critical. She notes that, in his rants, Richard "mingles war and big business and congressional witch hunts and finally certain people he knew into one grand enemy, whose only collective label was hate" (131). She critiques Richard's friend Phil, who owns a "stock company" and thinks he can get Therese "a show in the Village" (26), for being like "any of the people one saw in Village bars, young people who were supposed to be writers or actors, and who really did nothing" (32). And she dislikes the bars to which Richard brings her, which, she notes disapprovingly, are filled with people like "the clunky figures of the two Italian workmen [. . . and] the two girls at the end of the bar [. . .] in slacks" (146).

The scattershot and often contradictory nature of Therese's numerous critiques masks what the novel suggests might be the deeper reason for

Therese's aversion to bohemia: it fails to be a viable alternative to Frankenberg's. In *American Pulp: How Paperbacks Brought Modernism to Main Street* (2014), Paula Rabinowitz argues that within the lesbian pulp novel both the department store and bohemia functioned as sites in which "the limits of legitimate middle-class and proper working-class behavior" could be transgressed: particularly because the activities associated with them—namely, "shopping and art making"—allowed women to meet and disrobe (184).[6] But while the department store and bohemia represented spaces of potential for art making, consumption, and lesbian encounters—all things Therese wants—they are also spaces of cross-racial and cross-class mixing.

In short, the problem with bohemia is ultimately that it is not an alternative to, but instead a double of, the department store. And this means that the very attributes that Therese hopes will distinguish her from the women at Frankenberg's—her artisanal skill, appreciation of art, and connection to Europe—are the very attributes that connect her to the Frankenberg's women: their sexual and racial ambiguities, the deskilling of their labor, and thus their downward economic trajectory. This dance of distancing and identification comes to the fore most clearly in Therese's initial encounter with her new coworker, Mrs. Ruby Robichek. On first meeting her in the cafeteria, Therese feels a connection to Mrs. Robichek, whose kindness makes her heart beat "as if it had come to life" (15). This meeting is one of the rare moments in which the Frankenberg's women move from hands to people, a connection that comes from Therese's sense that Mrs. Robichek is like her, or an older version of her. This connection deepens when she goes to Mrs. Robichek's house for dinner and discovers that, like herself, Mrs. Robichek is an artisan, a dressmaker who used to have a "fine big" dress shop in Queens (21) before her dress styles were copied by other stores that, presumably able to sell them cheaper, drove her out of business and into her job in the sweater department at Frankenberg's.

Almost immediately, however, Therese's sense of connection is replaced by one of repulsion and horror, culminating in her refiguring of Mrs. Robichek as a supernatural hunchback who has taken control of, and imprisoned, her. This refiguring occurs, peculiarly, as a result of Mrs. Robichek's dresses. On entering Mrs. Robichek's house, Therese is initially excited by the beautiful fabrics and rich colors of her dresses, and, encouraged by Mrs. Robichek, she excitedly selects a dress "of queens in fairy tales, of a red deeper than blood" (22). Putting the dress on, she turns to the mirror and comes to admire "herself meeting herself," remarking that "this was she, not the girl in the dull plaid skirt and the beige sweater, not the girl who worked in the doll department at Frankenberg's" (22), but a truer version of herself. Very quickly, however, the meaning of the dress changes from something freeing to something suffocating. Like the department store that Therese earlier compared to a "prison" (12), this dress, too, becomes a source of entrapment, which she compares to "chains" that are about to "fall around her and lock" (23). She feels "as if she were being strangled" (23) by the dress and finds herself "unable to move" (23) and "out of control" (23), entirely overtaken by both the dress and Mrs. Robichek. From here, Therese's thoughts spin out. "What was she doing here?" she wonders, "How did she happen to have put on a dress like this? Suddenly Mrs. Robichek and her apartment become a horrible dream in which Mrs. Robichek is the hunchback keeper of the dungeon" (23).

What do we make of this peculiar vision in which Therese envisions herself becoming a lifeless automaton and Mrs. Robichek a dungeon keeper with supernatural powers? Hal Foster's turn to dolls is once again informative. Drawing on Marx's theory of commodity fetishism—that under capitalism, relations between people "the fantastic form of a relation between things" and things (namely commodities) come to "appear as independent beings endowed with life" (48)—Foster argues that these figures come to symbolize the uncanny experience of being a worker within industrial capitalism. "The modern machine," Foster argues, "emerges not only as an uncanny double but as a demonic master. Like the commodity, it is uncanny both because it assumes our human vitality and because we take on its deathly facticity" (129). And indeed, Therese's anxiety that she has become an automaton with no will of her own mirrors her description of the mechanical objects in the toy department that seem to spontaneously "come to life. [. . .] Mechanical toys began to toss balls into the air and catch them, shooting galleries popped and their targets rotated. The table of barnyard animals squawked, cackled, and brayed [. . . and] the giant tin soldier who militantly faced the elevators [. . .] drummed all day" (6). Therese becomes a lifeless commodity and commodities come to life.

While largely eschewed by Foster's account of the uncanny mannequin, the commodified female body is tied up with both the entrance of working-class women into industrial work and mass production, and also with what Rita Felski identifies as the subsequent erosion and "destabilization [of] the notion of an essential, God-given femaleness" (20). While Therese gets the nature of the relationship wrong—Mrs. Robichek is certainly not the supernatural keeper of the mythical dungeon—her sense that there is a relationship between the commodification of her body and wage labor is prescient. Her real horror regarding Mrs. Robichek is not that

Mrs. Robichek can *do* anything to her but that she will *become* Mrs. Robichek, that, as Therese puts it, she will "be one with the hunchback" (24): a queer, ethnic, working-class woman whose artisanal skills and love of beauty will serve only to entrap her into a lifetime of wage drudgery in a department store.[7] Therese's identification of Mrs. Robichek as the demonic master is a bizarre and backwards iteration of commodity fetishism in which Therese turns the grotesque and racialized working-class body into the demonic master.

Even as she casts Mrs. Robichek as a demonic master whose dress has magical powers, she also recognizes the psychological displacement she is carrying out, acknowledging that it "was the terror of this hopelessness," represented by Mrs. Robichek, "that made her want to shed the dress and flee before it was too late, before the chains fell around her and locked" (23). The chains of the dress locking around her are at once the magical chains of fantasy and the chains of wage labor, but they are also the chains of the naturalist genre, perhaps best represented by Lawrence Selden's observation that Lily Bart's bracelet in Edith Wharton's *House of Mirth* (1905) "seemed like manacles chaining her to her fate" (9). Jennifer Fleissner has noted naturalism's tendency to adopt the repetitive and compulsive logic of Sigmund Freud's death drive and its symptomology of shock, "an ongoing, nonlinear, repetitive motion—back and forth, around and around, on and on—that has the distinctive effects of seeming also like a stuckness in place" (11). However, this stuckness, she argues, is linked not to the often-assumed male protagonists of naturalism but instead to its female heroines, and more broadly to the "figure of the modern woman" (11) that naturalism represents: that is, to the women who moved "to the cities in droves in the 1880s and 1890s in search of new forms of wage work" (17).

What happens in Mrs. Robichek's apartment, and what Therese depicts in supernatural terms, is that she comes to embody this naturalist position of stuckness and compulsion. She gets lightheaded and has to sit down before passing out—she is "out of control" (24), she "struggles against the chair, knowing she was going to succumb to it" (24), and even once she forces herself to stand, she finds herself "unable to move" (24). Back and forth, stuck in place, unable to move: Therese seems to belong to the list of naturalist heroines like Lily Bart and Trina McTeague whose compulsive striving is fated to bring about their downfall. And yet, the novel emphasizes, Therese is not actually trapped; she just needs to change her strategy of escape. The underlying message of her encounter is that neither the artisanal aesthetic of bohemianism nor its cross-class solidarity will offer a meaningful way out.

But this rejection of bohemianism, as Tom Perrin points out, is also a rejection of the modernist aesthetics it was often linked to. And through the bohemian characters of the novel, bohemianism's culture and politics become indistinguishable from its aesthetics. Most prominent here is Richard, who is at once a symbol of bohemianism and associated with the modernist culture he endlessly consumes. Richard is both marked by his love of modernist novels—"How anyone could have read Gertrude Stein without reading any Joyce, Richard said, he didn't know" (38)—and by his radical politics. Recall Therese's observation that Richard "mingles war and big business and congressional witch hunts and finally certain people he knew into one grand enemy, whose only collective label was hate" (131). Perrin argues that the novel's critique of Richard—who ends up "selling out" to work as a general manager in his father's bottled-gas company— concretizes the novel's larger critique of modernism's claims to "constitute a radically new aesthetic paradigm, appropriate to the task of representing the world in a condition of modernity" (382). This is partially true. Therese's critique of Richard does offer a scathing indictment of the politics of slumming, and of the large gap between the romanticization of poverty and being a poor, working-class woman. Indeed, Therese's critique of Richard as a "little boy playing truant" (148) echoes the appraisal that communist, writer, and editor Joseph Freeman put forth in *New Masses* in the mid-1930s, wherein he denounced the bohemians as "confused adolescents" (qtd. in Levin, 355). And yet, this critique's signification is altogether different in the 1950s than it was in the 1930s. Freeman was concerned that bohemianism was losing its shock value and thus its socially transformative potential, becoming another commodity for the consumption of a bored elite. Therese's critique of the bohemians and modernism, however, is a wholesale rejection of the modernist impulse toward what Susan Buck-Morss terms "revolutionary cognition"—that is, the kind of cognition required to awaken from the narcotic of the reified historical present (1986, 109). Therese's critique of Richard is ultimately not that he is betraying a radical cause but rather that he, like Mrs. Robichek, will not be able to transcend his working-class roots and will end up being wage slave—a somewhat well-off wage slave but a wage slave nonetheless. Therese's misrecognition, her turning of Mrs. Robichek into a dungeon master, serves to shift the problem from a critique of wage work, alienation, commodification, and capitalism more broadly, to the problem of Mrs. Robichek's—and ultimately Richard's—grotesque and racialized working-class body. The goal, Therese makes clear, is not to challenge the system but to change herself, her genre, and thus her lot in life.

A Breath of Air

This transformation, both personal and generic, occurs through Therese's love interest: the pointedly named Carol *Air*d. Initially, Therese's encounter with Carol repeats her encounter with Mrs. Robichek. Like her, Carol is an older woman whom Therese meets in the heterogeneous space of the department store, and also like Mrs. Robichek, Carol takes her home, feeds her, and clothes her like a "doll" (50)—all typical tropes of the lesbian pulp genre (Rabinowitz, 155–56). But it is a repetition with a difference. Most notably, the uncanny sense of doubling associated with Therese being turned into a doll is stripped of its shocking and traumatic valence and transformed into a positive encounter of subject making. This shift occurs in large part because of who Carol is and what she represents. Carol is everything that Mrs. Robichek is not. Where Mrs. Robichek's body is "short," "heavy," and "shockin[ly] ugly" (20), and her voice alternately "dull" (19) and "shrill" (15), Carol is "tall and fair" with a "graceful [. . .] long figure" (39) and a "soft, distinct voice" (41). Where Mrs. Robichek's name is foreign and heavy, Carol's last name literally signifies lightness and air. Where Mrs. Robichek is associated with the slowness and drudgery of labor, Carol is associated with the speed and sleekness of consumption, as when they drive to Chinatown to "look at things and buy things" (110) before racing "uptown for a late supper in a restaurant where a harp played" (110). Where Therese and Mrs. Robichek take public transportation to her home, becoming part of the "sluggish mob at the entrance of the subway" and getting "sucked gradually and inevitable down the stairs, like bits of floating waste down a drain" (12), Carol takes Therese home in her car, which feels like "riding inside a rolling mountain that could sweep anything before it, yet was absolutely obedient" (60).

Even more profound is the difference in their housing. Mrs. Robichek's apartment is a tenement in an overcrowded area of Manhattan; it is dark and gloomy, the rooms unclean and cramped, and the bed unmade. Meanwhile, Carol's house in suburban New Jersey is a clean and new "white two-story house" with "projecting side wings like the paws of a resting lion" (61), a "big shining brass mailbox," and a "white garage" (62). Where Mrs. Robichek's house smells "of garlic and the gustiness of old age, of medicines, and of the peculiar metallic smell that was Mrs. Robichek's own" (24), Carol's house smells nicely of "some spice" (62). In short, Mrs. Robichek and her apartment embody Lavender Scare concerns that suture together queerness with fears of social unrest, national vulnerability, and anxieties about overcrowded cities and the sexual, racial, and class mingling that such overcrowding facilitates, while Carol and her home embody the Cold War vision of the modern, prosperous, domestic, and secure suburban way of life that would be, or at least so the United States proclaimed, available to all under its leadership of the free world (Tyler May, 8).

However, If Carol's appeal for Therese is an escape from her urban life, Therese's appeal for Carol is the very working-class bohemianism from which Therese seeks to abscond. Carol sees in Therese's life an alternative to the suburban anomie of a husband, child, and two cars. Trying to make sense of the novel's complicated relationship to urban space, Victoria Hesford has suggested we understand the city as an ideal space, arguing that it "suggests the possibility of sex, and freedom from the demands of marriage and family, [while] New Jersey becomes symbolic of the oppressive claims of heterosexual middle-class convention" (120). Accordingly, she argues that, while the suburban house provides "a modicum of privacy" in which their sexual encounter can occur, "The threat of exposure is always present" (121). But this "modicum of privacy" is crucial. While they can meet in the city, there is literally no space in the city for them. It is only in the modicum of privacy offered by the suburbs that their relationship can develop because it is there that Therese can finally escape her old life. The suburbs need the energy of the city as much as the city needs the lactification and class ascension of the suburbs. And it's this double movement that suggests we can't exactly read the novel as privileging one space over the other. Rather, what makes *The Price of Salt* a remarkable novel for its time is its attempt to reconceptualize the entire metropolitan region, a process the novel enacts by repurposing the genre of the Western.

The Price of Salt belongs to a series of novels—such as Vladimir Nabokov's *Lolita* (1958), Jack Kerouac's *On the Road* (1956), and Flannery O'Connor's *Wise Blood* (1952)—that shifted the frontier tales of the Western genre into road narratives. These narratives are both made possible by, and register, a larger transformation wrought by the national highway system that was consolidating in the United States at the time.[8] Throughout the 1930s and 1940s, politicians, planners, and downtown business and real-estate interests began to conceptualize urban expressways as an important tool for slum clearance. While the expressway system was initially designed to offer ways to bypass the city in its entirety, urban planners began to consider how these expressways could be used to facilitate (private) transportation between city centers and the suburbs surrounding them, and thus lure suburban shoppers back downtown in order to revitalize declining urban cores (Mohl; Biles, Mohl, and Rose). In *The Price of Salt*, too, the highway becomes a crucial site for Carol and Therese's relationship, and allegorically for the transformation and revitalization of the metropolitan scene; the highway both links Therese's home with Carol's and allegorically brings both these spaces into contact with the West.

This contact is at once geographic and generic. That is, Carol and Therese's literal movement west is accompanied by a generic shift from the naturalism of the lesbian pulp novel—with its cramped polluted poverty, neurasthenic shopgirls, and stuckness—to the Western, with its outdoor spaces, rugged individualism, and freedom. This shift happens almost as soon as their car turns west—as Carol, the suburban housewife, suddenly produces a gun, proclaiming that while she is "no Annie Oakley," she "can use it" (182). Moreover, the novel itself pivots as they hit the road, turning from a tragic and salacious story of the lascivious life of the city to a Western adventure narrative with a clear enemy: the private investigator who has been paid to prove they are engaging in a lesbian relationship. While the private investigator is not a cowboy per se, he looks an awful lot like one, with his "cigar" and his "broad-brimmed hat, with Western boots" (191). Even the device he uses to catch them in the act, the listening "spike" that was driven "into the wall" (277), evinces the railway-built West.

This generic shift—from naturalism to the Western—is crucial for understanding the novel's ability to reconceptualize the entire metropolitan region of New York and carry out its own form of slum clearance and renewal. From its inception, the Western was intimately connected to the city and particularly the East Coast city and its dual role as the seat of American empire and the cause of death of the American frontier spirit. Thus, as Will puts it, while on the surface, the West Cure and its narrative instantiation in the Western appeared to be an anti-urban or anti-eastern genre in which the cowboy "rides West into the sunset, rejecting the neurasthenic logic of the East" (309), the Western actually turns out to be a thoroughly *urban* genre in which the "Western world [. . .] functions less as the antidote to neurasthenic modernity than as its better half, a world that exhibits the East's strenuous thirst for economic and military 'triumph' while avoiding its 'effeminate' pathologies" (296). The Western thus acted as a West Cure for the cities of the East by shoring up its archetypal subject and, through him, its own military and economic might, as well as that of the nation.

In *The Price of Salt*, a similar process is at work, only it is not men who are at risk of becoming "nervous women" (300) but rather those nervous women themselves who must undergo the West Cure to become the striving and triumphant figures responsible for the saving of the urban East. Furthermore, it is not the city but the metropolitan region as a whole. This transformation reflects the important but contradictory role that women, and particularly suburban female shoppers, came to play in the redevelopment dramas then unfolding across the United States. Alison Isenberg has argued that, throughout the 1950s, the growing urban crisis was often imagined as a crisis of shopping and shoppers and the question of who was downtown shopping. Renewal efforts, she argued, explicitly "pursued 'suburban homemakers' and 'housewives,' rather than working women or women of color living downtown" (176). And yet, as Rabinowitz points out, the downtown department store was also the space "where women of differing classes meet and interact, linking downtown to midtown and beyond" (202). Urban renewal's constant struggle to lure white middle-class women downtown, in other words, created a contradiction. While suburban women were tasked with the urgent role of redomesticating urban centers and returning them to an earlier period of prosperity and profitability, their very contact with the racialized and working-class denizens of America's inner-city spaces threatened their role as maintainers of a domestic white femininity.

In *The Price of Salt*, this problem is resolved through the redeployment of the West as a safe third space wherein this drama could unfold—a resolution made possible because of the association of the West, however inaccurately, with classlessness and whiteness.[9] The suburban housewife receives the scintillation of the bohemian excitement provided by working-class women, and the bohemian working-class women are suburbanized and made middle-class—all in an environment safe from the dangers of interracial and interclass fraternizing. In other words, Highsmith's "West Cure" is twofold: the suburban subject experiences the danger and excitement they're seeking in urban space, but in a deracinated and declassed setting, while the working-class urban dweller is able to suburbanize.

The danger of Carol's West Cure takes the form of the detective tracking her down: a danger that forces her back into the metropolitan area to fight him. Therese's West Cure begins only once Carol has left. Free of both Richard and Carol, Therese now has to make it on her own, learning to become an independent and self-sufficient woman. And as with Silas Weir Mitchell's West Cure, outdoor physical labor is necessary to Therese's revitalization as well. Specifically, Therese goes to work in a lumberyard, a job that stands in marked difference from her job as a sales girl. While the work is no more complex than that she performed at Frankenberg's—her job consists "simply in checking the mill shipments to the yard against the orders received, and in writing letters of confirmation" (264)—it stands in stark contrast to the "pointless" and "meaningless" labor she performed there (13). Similarly, while she is certainly not a lumberman, "the smell" of lumber, the novel emphasizes, "was in the air, fresh as if the saws had just exposed the surface of the white pine boards" (264), and she is surrounded by "lumberjacks and truckdrivers who came into the office to warm their hands at the fire" (264). It is through this process of work, and her proximity to the "barbarity" of the great outdoors, that Therese completes her West Cure, a process that is signaled by the arrival of her friend Dannie. "You look all grown up," he comments when he comes out to visit her, noting further that "you don't look frightened anymore" (268). She is not—and so, like many neurasthenic men or tenderfoots before her, she returns home to retake and revitalize the city.

The New Western Front

The novel ends with Therese's return to New York and her looking at "the familiar hodgepodge of restaurant and bar signs, awnings, front steps and windows, that reddish brown confusion of the side street that was like hundreds of streets in New York" (273). But her journey west, her West Cure, has changed Therese and her perspective on the city. Where before she recalls "the sense of oppression" (271) she felt wandering around one of these streets in "the West Eighties" (271), now she comments that "the same kind of street filled her with a tense excitement, made her want to plunge headlong into it, down the sidewalk with all the signs and theater marquees and rushing, bumping people" (271). Therese, in short, has refigured her relationship to the city as that of the cowboy excitedly heading west into the frontier.

But it's not just Therese that has changed. New York, too, has transformed. Before, Therese's New York was a city of wage labor and poverty, of bohemian theater and queer masculine women in working-class bars. Upon her return, Therese's New York is a city of skyscrapers, cocktail parties, important directors, television producers, and elegant and established actresses. *The Price of Salt* erases Therese's past and the past of New York, establishing a new vision for a postindustrial and pointedly white urban future. And it is within this position—her subjectivity secured, and a new kind of vision restored—that she is able to see Carol again. They arrange to meet in the bar of the Ritz Tower, where Carol immediately comments how "grown up" Therese looks (274). Therese announces that she's "learned a few things" (275), but when she tries to remember what these things are, her mind is "obstructed suddenly by the memory of the portrait in Sioux Falls" (275). This portrait, which she saw hanging in the library at

Sioux Falls, is almost identical to one that hung in the hall near the music room when she was a child. She identifies it immediately as a portrait of Carol, but a Carol whose gaze is that of "mockery and gloating, the splendid satisfaction of the betrayal accomplished" (277). Here, we return again to both the uncanny and the doubling we encountered at the novel's start. But once more, there is a difference. Unlike in Sioux Falls when Carol left, this time she does not "betray" her for her family; Carol chooses Therese, and the novel ends with their presumed reunion. Through Carol, Therese has freed herself from the chains of naturalism and its symptomology of the uncanny, compulsive repetitions, and déclassement—and Carol has freed herself from the chains of suburbia and the anomie of her life therein.

What do we make of this ending? On the one hand, it is triumphant, often being read as "the first lesbian novel with a happy ending" (Esteve, n.p.). As Highsmith herself explained in her afterword to the 2004 edition of the novel: "The appeal of *The Price of Salt* was that it had a happy ending for its two main characters, or at least they were going to try to have a future together. Prior to this book, homosexuals male and female in American novels had had to pay for their deviation by cutting their wrists, drowning themselves in a swimming pool, or by switching to heterosexuality" (292). But it seems worth considering how happy their ending actually is—or what it actually means to consider the novel's ending to be a happy one. Yes, they are able to be together, and in so doing, have both become freed of their past. Carol has broken away from the suburbs and Harge— they are selling their suburban house; she is living in her own apartment on Madison Avenue—and has taken up a job as a buyer for a furniture house (278), while Therese has broken free of her boyfriend and the poverty associated with her wage labor at Frankenberg's for a job in the creative economy of television. Both of them have achieved a model of freedom; they are completely independent subjects, free of their past attachments.

And yet, the sacrifices they make for this happiness in a new, postindustrial and shiny city—"the price of salt," as it were—are not inconsequential. Most dramatically, Carol must give up her child. As she explains, "I refused to live by a list of silly promises they'd made up like a list of misdemeanours—even if it did mean that they'd lock Rindy away from me. [. . .] And it did mean that" (277). And it's not just her child. She has to give up motherhood itself and thus her entire past subjectivity as the valorized figure of suburban white domesticity. On the surface, Therese's sacrifices are smaller and in fact the central aim of her personal development. She must give up her bohemianism, her roots in a working-class and ethnically diverse culture, and her more artistic desires. Her work as a theater designer, she notes, "wouldn't pay enough to live on," but she could find other sources, "television, for instance" (271).

This happy ending, the implicit "I do" between Carol and Therese, requires a different kind of "social contract" (22) and compromise than that which Franco Moretti found in the nineteenth-century bildungsroman. In *The Price of Salt*, both bohemian urban life and suburban white domesticity are given up for the attainment of white middle-class respectability within a lesbian love story. The end of bohemia for the end of Betty Friedan's problem that has no name. This "I do," however, fractures the text into two. The novel's wholesale rejection of suburban domesticity presages the much more radical feminism and gay liberation movement of the 1970s. It not only offers a critique of McCarthyism and the Lavender Scare through its rejection of the tragic lesbian narrative that marked the pulp tradition of the 1950s, but, more remarkably, it imagines a satisfying and happy narrative solution that explicitly rejects the nuclear family. This is a queer politics in line with Lee Edelman's recent provocation that "queerness" names the politics "of those *not* 'fighting for the children,' the side outside the consensus by which all politics confirms the absolute value of reproductive futurism" (3). Read in this way, *The Price of Salt* is indeed a remarkably radical novel: one that challenges the entire basis of not just the Lavender Scare but also the suburban politics of Cold War domesticity that provided the fuel—in senses both ideological and literal—for the expansion and consolidation of global capitalism under US hegemony.[10]

And yet, *The Price of Salt*'s resistance to, and critique of, the Lavender Scare is carried out not against the American Dream, and certainly not against the Cold War project. Rather, it disarticulates what Elaine Tyler May identifies as the persistent linking of sexual "perversion" to "national weakness" (94). Within the novel, it is Carol's very deviation from her nuclear family—her lesbianism—that rescues Therese from being swallowed up by the blight of the tenement and the department store; that breaks her attachments to the other ethnic characters of the novel who often represent a more critical politics; and that stands for the revitalization of the city and the national subject. Read thusly, *The Price of Salt* offers an equally remarkable early iteration of what Jasbir Puar terms "homonationalism": the US nation-state's "recognition and incorporation" of a very narrow kind of homosexuality (2). But this homonationalism, the "fleeting sanctioning of a national homosexual subject," Puar argues, always occurs "through the simultaneous engendering and disavowal of *populations* of sexual-racial-others who need not apply" (2, emphasis in original). In *The Price of Salt*, Carol and Therese become exalted homonational and entrepreneurial subjects, and they do so in marked contrast to the "masculine" women in the working-class bar, Mrs. Robichek, and the numerous other queer, effeminate, or otherwise deviant ethnic, working-class subjects who fill the book, all of whom are effaced from the text—and, allegorically, from the city.

The point, however, is not that this novel is, in Eve Kosofsky Sedgwick's marvelous phrase, "kinda subversive, kinda hegemonic" (15), or that, as Perrin suggests, the novel invites us to have our critique and eat it too. Instead, the point is that *The Price of Salt* narrates the process through which the United States' reorganization of global capitalism in the postwar period effectively deployed and monopolized certain "kinda subversive" demands for inclusion and integration, while casting out, clearing, and criminalizing so many others. And, it demonstrates the process through which the remaking of the subject occurs alongside and through the remaking of metropolitan space. Accordingly, the novel suggests that we locate the political and ideational origins of neoliberalism not in the annals of the Mount Pelerin Society but rather in the cultural and political struggles over the remaking of urban and suburban space domestically, and—as will be broached in the next chapter—in the struggles over decolonization abroad.

CHAPTER 3

Naked Lunch, Or, the Last
Snapshot of the Surrealists

Naked Lunch opens in the register of the noir and its typical visions of a once-grand US urban core in decay:

> I can feel the heat closing in, feel them out there making their moves, setting up their devil doll stool pigeons, crooning over my spoon and dropper I throw away at Washington Square Station, vault a turnstile and two flights down the iron stairs, catch an uptown A train . . . Young, good looking, crew cut, Ivy League, advertising exec type fruit holds the door back for me. I am evidently his idea of a character. You know the type: comes on with bartenders and cab drivers, talking about right hooks and the Dodgers, calls the counterman in Nedick's by his first name. A real asshole. And right on time this narcotics dick in a white trench coat (imagine tailing somebody in a white trench coat. Trying to pass as a fag I guess) hit the platform. I can hear the way he would say it holding my outfit in his left hand, right hand on his piece: "I think you dropped something fella." (3)[1]

The Brooklyn Dodgers. The fast-food chain, Nedick's. Men in Brooks Brothers shirts. L'il Abner. The *News,* and the *Saturday Evening Post.* These are the vestiges of what Eric Avila terms the new public "heterosocial" but implicitly white "world of urban strangers" (2004, 3) that emerged at the turn of the twentieth century around the public spaces of the streetcar, baseball parks, department stores, and parks, such as Washington Square Park. This is the world that the new urban underclass of drug addicts is seen to be destroying. Not only is this "world network of junkys" (7) transforming an old vision of urban America into a set piece for their drug habits, but these vestiges of an older and imagined Americana are squeezed out of the paragraph itself by the drama of the junkys that comes to dominate.

However, on closer inspection, what this passage delineates is less the erosion or blighting of the city, particularly the area around Washington Square Park, but rather its recently announced renewal as both the narcs and the "good looking, crew cut, Ivy League, advertising exec" begin to move in and penetrate the area. The context here, of course, is the now infamous decade-long "Battle of Washington Square." While the apex of this fight—the final showdown between Robert Moses and Jane Jacobs—wouldn't take place until after the novel was completed, struggles over the renewal of the park and Greenwich Village more broadly started far earlier. In August 1953, Robert Moses and his New York City Committee on Slum Clearance announced plans for the removal and renewal of Washington Square Southeast. In the plan, Moses called for the clearance of huge swaths of light commercial and industrial areas to make way for nine fourteen-story buildings, which would contain 2,184 middle-class apartments, subsidize four acres of land for NYU, and create a new roadway through Washington Square (J. Schwartz, 262).[2] As with many of the other proposed sites for urban renewal initiatives in New York City, community resistance in the densely populated area formed quickly. Inspired by the scathing critiques of urbanists like Charles Abrams who denounced Moses's antihuman vision of "a cluster of tall buildings [. . .] rimmed by parking lots" (qtd. in J. Schwartz, 263), groups like the Americans for Democratic Action and even the Italian pinochle clubs began to urge for a slower renewal that would respect the diversity of their neighborhood. But, as Joel Schwartz argues, while these groups' defense of "a gradual renewal and respect for urban diversity anticipated the views of another Village critic, Jane Jacobs [. . .] lurking behind the appeal for tolerance was a racist populism" (263). As one flyer warned, "'Slum clearance' here [. . .] would mean clearing *out* of crowded slums in Harlem and elsewhere *into* the Village projects" (264).

It is this new urban order—marked by the double-bind of the modernist bulldozer and a more ostensibly community-oriented vision of gentrification—that threatens to entrap the novel's protagonist, William Lee. Caught between the threat of being criminalized and cleared out by the narcotics officers in order to make room for Moses's Title 1 project, and turned into a "character"—a little bit of "local color" for the new "advertising exec" type seeking some excitement—Lee attempts to escape in what by now might seem a familiar way: namely, he "buy[s] a secondhand Studebaker" and "start[s] west" (8). Except that he doesn't move west. Or rather, while he starts west, heading across the United States and down into Mexico, he ends up in the East: specifically, in the "International Zone," or "Interzone," of Tangier.

Burroughs's choice of the International Zone is an important one. Between August 1945 and the victory of the Istiqlal movement, and the return of Tangier to Morocco in 1956, the United States gained primary control of the International Zone, which consisted of Tangier and its surrounding ports.[3] The International Zone had long been a unique experiment in European imperialist cooperation, orchestrated by various groupings of the major imperialist powers of the nineteenth century. The United States' assumption of control after World War II both marked a break with and continued this pattern. While the United States was seen as playing an important role in the decolonization of Morocco, the United States in action (if not in name) also operated as an imperial power, maintaining Tangier as a free-trade zone that was amenable to the interests of US capital.[4] The United States' contradictory position in Tangier reflected larger shifts in the structure of coloniality that would emerge as the United States gained global hegemony: namely a shift from the formal imperialism of direct-territorial control exemplified by Britain to what Leo Panitch and Sam Gindin term the deterritorial and "informal global empire" of the United States (6), an empire organized through expanded investment and under the banner of "anti-imperialism" and "self-determination" (Arrighi, 70).[5]

Burroughs was not alone in plotting out narratives of escape from a rationalizing and modernizing New York into spaces that were increasingly coming under the control of this new informal empire. Throughout the 1950s, a spate of novels emerged in which alienated men attempted to escape the liquefying commodity culture of postwar New York in search of the more authentic cultures of the South, East, or West. In Alejo Carpentier's *The Lost Steps* (1953), an anthropologist/composer flees his job making music for a fisheries association "whose sole objective was to [. . .] stimulate the daily consumption of fish" (27), along with his relationship to a vapid actress, to go in search of a musical instrument belonging to a South American tribe not yet touched by civilization. In Paul Bowles's *The*

Sheltering Sky (1949) and *Let It Come Down* (1952), New Yorkers flee the vapidity of the city in search of authentic experience in the decommodified desert of the Maghreb. And in Jack Kerouac's *On the Road* (1957), it is Mexico that becomes the locus of escape and salvation from the cramped tedium of New York.

This body of work drew on a longer tradition of American writers and journalists who often identified the Maghreb Desert with the frontier space of the American Southwest (Edwards; Ngô; Walonen) as a space of free markets and moral permissiveness.[6] Within this vision, Tangier, like the American West before it, became reimagined as the frontier space outside of law and regulation where capital and men could go to shore up the American subject and its economic might. *Naked Lunch*, however, breaks from this longer tradition of twinning the frontier West with the East in that Burroughs's Tangier has less in common with the frontier West than it does with New York City itself. In its shift from the twinning of the desert and the West to its twinning of a newly renewed New York and a decolonized Tangier, *Naked Lunch* helps elucidate the process through which US cities and decolonizing countries became refigured as the new frontiers of this emergent informal empire.

Naked Lunch maps this twinning in two ways. Formally, the novel brings together two imperialist genres: the domestic imperialism of the Western and the foreign imperialism of the drug-induced travelogue-cum-Romanticist reverie. Narratively, it brings together the domestic and international faces of a newly revised US imperialism through its focus on the role of drugs and drug control in both the expansion of US economic might and the establishment of the United States as what Loïc Wacquant termed the "self-proclaimed policeman of the planet" (2009b, 120). Not only are drugs an important focus of the novel, appearing throughout in myriad guises—from the opening standoff between the world network of junkys to which the protagonist belongs and the narcotics agents, to the Cold War psychiatrist and Dr. Benway's constant experimentation—but drugs also configure, shape, and transform the generic structure of the novel, which, depending on how you read it, is a drug-induced hallucination, or an "irrealist" exploration of the role drugs played in controlling and shaping urban and Third World spaces and subjectivities during the Cold War.[7]

It is no great claim to argue that drugs and genre are important to *Naked Lunch*. Often read as one of the *ur* texts of Beat counterculture, *Naked Lunch* is known for both its postmodern and idiosyncratic style, as well as its scenes of shocking and lascivious sex and violence, alongside its aforementioned focus on drugs. Avital Ronell and Frederick Whitting have gone so far as to argue that it was the novel's formal management of intoxication and addiction that led it to the center of one of the most important obscenity trials in twentieth-century US history.[8] In this chapter, however, I suggest a different interpretation. Specifically, I argue that drugs aren't just a vehicle of shock but that they also provide a lens through which *Naked Lunch* focalizes the nascent political, economic, aesthetic, and psychological transformations that occur as a new system of US global hegemony begins to emerge, as well as a means to map the interconnection between the domestic and foreign aspects of this new model of US anti-imperialist imperialism.

The World Network of Drug Capital

While numerous drugs populate the pages of *Naked Lunch*, cocaine and morphine, which Burroughs suggestively shortens to C and M, are privileged. I say that it is suggestive because Burroughs's cycle of drug addiction has an unexpected resonance with Marx's general formula of capital, MCM', which traces the circuit of money (or capital), through commodity production, on its way to becoming an increased sum. Burroughs explicitly connects morphine to money. In his "Deposition: Testimony Concerning a Sickness," Burroughs argues that, unlike hashish or mushroom cults, "no one ever suggested that junk is sacred. There are no opium cults. Opium is profane and quantitative like money" (201).[9] Cocaine, on the other hand, is a drug of content. For Burroughs, while cocaine creates a sensation of "exhilaration" and "euphoria" (223), it is not in and of itself addicting because it "leads to nervousness, depression, [and] sometimes drug psychosis with paranoid hallucinations" (224) that require, not more cocaine, but an antidote. Unlike morphine, where the problem is addiction to the drug and not the drug itself, the negative symptoms of cocaine "are not alleviated by more cocaine [. . . but] by morphine. [. . .] The use of cocaine by a morphine addict always leads to larger and more frequent injections of morphine" (224). In short, C—commodities or cocaine—creates an overproduction, an excess of what can be absorbed, and thus requires a return to an expanding field of M—money or morphine—which then drives the cycle forward.

This resonance between Burroughs's description of cocaine and morphine and Marx's description of the circuit of capital is even more suggestive when considered within the context of Giovanni Arrighi's attempt at periodizing Marx's cycle of accumulation. In *The Long Twentieth Century,*

Arrighi argues that Marx's general formula is not simply a description of how an individual capitalist investment works, but it also describes "a recurrent pattern of historical capitalism as world system" (6) in which capitalism moves through a series of ever-expanding "systemic cycle[s] of accumulation," each of which is underpinned by a world hegemonic state power (6). In Arrighi's formulation, the history of capital has unfolded across four distinct, yet overlapping cycles: an Italian or Genoese cycle lasting roughly from 1350 to 1625; a Dutch cycle lasting roughly from 1460 to 1800; a British cycle lasting from 1750 to 1945; and a US cycle lasting from 1880 until its present decline. Each of these cycles of accumulation, he argues, moves through a period of material expansion in which production is dominant (MC), which is then followed by a period in which finance comes to dominate (CM'). While the relationship between Marx's economic cycle of accumulation and Burroughs's psychoactive cycle of intoxication is associative or metaphorical, the historical connections between cycles of accumulation, revolutions in psychoactive use and production, and imperialist policy is thoroughly material.[10]

Opium's importance to British imperialism has been well documented.[11] Primarily grown in British-held India, opium was an integral commodity for the financing and expansion of the British Empire. Beginning in the early nineteenth century, Britain began to export opium en masse to China, which solved the former's balance-of-payments problem (resulting from Britain's dependence on China for tea, silk, and porcelain) and financed both its imperialist expansion on the Indian subcontinent as well as its import of cotton from the United States—which, in turn, underpinned the Industrial Revolution (M. Davis, 2000). Moreover, drugs such as opium and cocaine played a significant role in the reproduction and pacification of the working classes, who were fuelling the Industrial Revolution. In his now infamous booster tract "Über Coca" ([1884] 1974), Sigmund Freud boasted that cocaine reduced workers' needs for food and sleep, thus allowing them to perform "Long-lasting, intensive mental or physical work [. . .] without fatigue" (60). Opium, on the other hand, reduced their need for food and, as in the case of the Chinese "Coolies," numbed the pain, boredom, and loneliness associated with migrant labor (Courtwright 1982). Finally, cocaine and opium weren't used just by the working classes. They were also the chief narcotics used throughout the nineteenth century to treat the middle and upper classes who were suffering from shock disorders such as nervous exhaustion (Gootenberg; Courtwright 1982). Where opium was understood to be "'the chief' of all drugs used for 'nervous exhaustion'" because of its perceived ability to bring the

"brain-cells" into a "state of tranquility" (qtd. in Oppenheimer, 115), cocaine was heralded for its unique ability to "increase the reduced function-
ing of the nerve centers" (Freud [1884] 1974, 64) and thus would act as a
prophylactic against nervous exhaustion.[12]

In *Naked Lunch*, however, these drugs seem to play a very different role.
They are not associated with the upper, middle, or even working class but
with a growing urban surplus population of vagabonds who compose the
landscape of a blighted and decaying New York City. Here, drugs are attached to a population who have been unable to withstand or harness the
shocks of urban modernity; who have been cast out of society and the
wage relation; and who have ultimately been rendered surplus. Burroughs's
adoption of the Freudian language of shock here is informative. Most notable are the characters Pantopon Rose and Willy the Disk, whose addicted
bodies embody the two sides of the Freudian theory of shock and the death
drive. Pantopon Rose ("pantopon" is a mixture of various opium alkaloids)
exemplifies the extreme openness of the shocked subject whose "protective
shield" has been unable to keep external stimulus out. Her entire body is
a gaping wound. She is covered in "splintered glass" (10), her thighs are
"ravaged [. . .] looking rather like a poster on soil erosion" (10), and she has
a "great hole in her leg which seemed to hang open like an obscene, fester-
ing mouth" (10). Willy the Disk, on the other hand, has so fully inhabited
his "protective shield against stimuli" (Freud 1955a, 27) that his entire
being has ceased "to have the structure proper to living matter, [and] has
become to some degree inorganic" (27). He "is blind from shooting in the
eyeball, his nose and palate eaten away sniffing H, his body a mass of scar
tissue hard and dry as wood" (7). In short, where Pantopon Rose is on the
verge of death from shock, Willy appears on the verge of death as a result
of the body's defense against shock. In both cases, cocaine and morphine
become associated with the surplus body that has been criminalized and
cast out from both the formal economy and the state.

As with the Golden Day vets in *Invisible Man*, these figures of surplus
are refigured as a shocked population that in turn comes to haunt or shock
the society that dispossessed them. In the case of *Naked Lunch*, this is quite
literal. These drug-addled surplus figures are often constituted as ghosts,
ghouls, and the undead. In addition to Pantopon and Willy, there is, for
instance, Bradley the Buyer, who is both a narcotics agent and an addict,
and who takes on an "ominous grey-green color" (15) before addiction
drives him to literally eat his way up the career ladder. And even more
pointedly there is the drug addict simply named Vigilante, who is being
prosecuted "in Federal Court under a lynch bill" (9) for possessing drugs,

and uses schizophrenia as a defense, explaining: "I was standing outside myself trying to stop those hangings with ghost fingers . . . I am a ghost wanting what every ghost wants—a body" (8). The way the novel connects the prosecution of drug crime with a lynching bill, and its consonant transformation of the drug addict into the figure of the haunting ghost, draws a direct line between the bodies of lynched black men in the South and the figure of the surplus urban drug addict, both of which become refigured as colonized populations returning to haunt the text.[13]

As cocaine and opium become almost entirely associated with this new and implicitly racialized criminal underclass, the novel begins to chart the emergence of an innovative class of drugs—synthetic and chemical narcotics such as amphetamines, barbiturates, hallucinogens, and steroids—that are associated with the psychiatrist, Dr. Benway, and metonymically with the emergence of a new US Empire.[14] Dr. Benway is both a psychiatrist and an operative for the corporation "Islam Inc.," whom the narrator meets when he arrives in the Reconditioning Center. The development of these new forms of synthetic drugs, we learn, is part of Dr. Benway's larger project, which is to revolutionize how states control their populations. Specifically, Benway is working to replace blunt techniques of control such as "torture" and "concentration camps" (22) with more sophisticated modes of subject-shaping (22). Benway explains that concentration camps and torture fail because they "locate the opponent and mobilize resistance" (21). To rectify this failing, he develops a series of other technologies of psychological control. In addition to his development of a shock-therapy machine he calls "the Switchboard," in which "electric drills [. . .] are clamped against the subject's teeth" and used to break down the subject "like an overloaded thinking machine" (21–22), Benway also makes use of drugs and psychoanalysis, which he uses to break down and rebuild his subjects' identities.

Burroughs's depictions of Benway are often cited as a prescient evocation of what Gilles Deleuze—himself drawing on Burroughs—diagnosed as the shift from Michel Foucault's "disciplinary societies" of the eighteenth and nineteenth centuries, which were based on creating "spaces of enclosure" like the factory and the prison, to the "control societies" of the mid-twentieth century, which are instead based on "free-floating control" that takes place through "pharmaceutical productions, molecular engineering, [and] genetic manipulation" (4). While the focus on technologies of control is undoubtedly important, we lose much of Burroughs's insight if we don't dig a bit deeper and ask, Exactly what kind of state is carrying out this new form of control, and what kind of society (and subject) is being created? The answer to the first question arrives in the form of Dr. Benway and his dual role as both a stand-in for the Cold War psychiatric state, as well as for the rise of the multinational corporation "Islam Inc." (19). The answer to the second question can be gleaned from Benway's *pièce de résistance*, Freeland. Freeland is the realization of all of Benway's plans. It is a place "given over to free love and continual bathing" where "the citizens are well adjusted, cooperative, honest, tolerant and above all clean" (19). It is also a place that requires no policing or control because the citizens' very notion of freedom is already aligned with that of Benway.

But the above description is still quite vague; there is no clear articulation of what, for instance, these notions of freedom are that underpin Freeland. While Burroughs is never explicit, he leaves us some clues. One of the more striking aspects of his description of Freeland is the focus on hygiene and continual bathing. Why this relationship between freedom and hygiene? Kristin Ross provides one answer in her 1996 work on post–World War II French culture when she argues that an obsessive turn to hygiene accompanied its intensive, state-led drive toward modernization. This turn toward hygiene, she argues, served to create a social and racial distinction between France and the French citizenry, and its former colonies in the wake of decolonization.[15] If French superiority could no longer be built on whiteness, it could be based on character: on cleanliness and modernness. And yet, the turn away from the biological hierarchies of race underpinning colonialism to development was not unique to fallen empires. Rather, it was symptomatic of the expansion of global capitalism under the aegis of this new regime of US coloniality and its governing ideology of modernization and development.[16]

In 1949, President Harry Truman launched his "bold new program" (Truman 1949a) called Point Four, a technical-assistance version of the Marshall Plan that targeted the Global South by providing training and supplies for economic development. Truman claimed this bold program would move beyond "the old imperialism of exploitation for foreign profit" (Truman 1949a) by offering scientific and technical training assistance to underdeveloped countries deemed susceptible to communism. Truman wasn't lying; this was not the same old imperialism. The United States eschewed extraterritoriality and interimperialist rivalry in favor of the creation and implementation of universal laws around trade, and it facilitated and developed its industrial rivals in order to stimulate and expand the global economy (Panitch and Gindin, 68). But it was imperialism nonetheless. As Aimé Césaire astutely observed in *Discourse on Colonialism* (1950), while Truman may declare "Aid to the disinherited countries" and that "the time of the old colonialism has passed," this simply meant that American high-finance considers that the time has come to raid every colony in the world (77). What Césaire here grasped was the new form of imperialism that Truman's Point Four platform announced: one based on the raiding of colonies not through the old technologies and ideologies of imperialism but instead by the penetration of US corporations in the form of foreign direct investment and—as Molly Geidel's recent book *Peace Corp Fantasies: How Development Shaped the Global Sixties* (2015) forcefully argues—through the development of markets and the ostensibly "anticolonial" and "anti-imperialist" ideological imaginary of modernization and development.

While never stated, "well adjusted, cooperative, honest, [or] tolerant" seems to mean the fully developed and modernized subject integrated into the US-led global marketplace. This becomes particularly evident if we read Freeland through its obverse: namely, the subjects in the Reconditioning Center who are presumably the opposite of well-adjusted and hygienic, and who need to be modernized and developed. The Reconditioning Center is peopled by matriarchs, homosexuals, drug addicts, religious fanatics, leopard men, a coprophage, all manner of indigenous tribes, queers, and both racialized and colonial populations—in other words, the very characters we find first in New York City and then again in the Interzone. The relationship between Burroughs's depictions of the Interzone and the ideologies of modernization and development are brought further into view if we think about the Reconditioning Center in relation to its historical equivalent.

At the time Burroughs was writing, the US Public Health Service (USPHS) was operating the US Narcotic Farm/Prison in Lexington, Kentucky, that used "military personnel, prisoners, asylum populations, committed 'narcotics addicts,' and poor people in need of medical assistance or cash" to carry out extensive drug testing (Reiss, 159). While the primary goal of the farm was to do research on what an addict was in order to develop nondangerous and nonaddictive drug substitutes (primarily to replace opiates and cocaine), it also served a second purpose. As Reiss notes, it served to make addicts and other "people deemed 'antiproductive' threats to the community" valuable (163) by turning them into test subjects. Benway's Reconditioning Center appears to play a similar role. It is both a laboratory and testing ground for the development of pharmaceuticals, and a prison for those deemed antiproductive, sick, criminal, or rebellious—all of which begin to collapse together. The measure of a clean and healthy body became an economically productive one—one that is actively contributing to a healthy, and implicitly capitalist, market-based society—while a sick or unhealthy body is accordingly unproductive. It is in this sense, then, that we should consider the Reconditioning Center as an allegory for the laboratory of Cold War American dominance: as a nucleus for the production of the forms of psychological, social, and economic control that would come to mark US imperialism. That is, the Reconditioning Center doesn't just come to stand in for the new systems of control that were being implemented but also models the specific kinds of subjects being shaped and controlled, and the relationship between these forms of subject-control and the larger horizons of capitalist expansion.

The Interzone: Or, a Vision in a Dream?

On the surface, the Interzone stands as the obverse to both Freeland and the project of the Reconditioning Center. Like the Golden Day in *Invisible Man*, the Interzone is a world in which the inmates have taken over, and in which their often-drug-induced dreams and desires have been let loose into existence. It is the very world that the Reconditioning Center is aimed at wiping out. Indeed, the Interzone even takes the form of, or rather, as we'll see, the appearance of, a dream. While often read alongside Burroughs's claim that *Naked Lunch* is a "cut-up" novel organized in an "entirely arbitrary sequence" (Sheehan, n.p.), *Naked Lunch* in fact has a quite precise dream structure in which the objects, people, and events that occur in both the New York and road trip West sections of the novel transmogrify into the characters and scenes that comprise the Interzone section.[17] The Madam from Peoria named Pantopon Rose, who is a customer of Lee's (5), becomes the figure that an old junky repeatedly asks for in the Interzone. This request also becomes the title of an Interzone episode, "have you seen pantopon rose." The police hanging of a minor character, Chapin, in the first episode (6) forms the model of power underlying the highly sexualized hangings that occur throughout the Interzone section, from the "mugwumps" who hang "Exquisite Balinese and Malays, Mexican Indians [. . .] Negroes [. . .] Japanese boys [. . .] Americans with blond or black curls [. . .] sulky blond Polacks [. . .] by the hundred" (67), to the actress, Mary, who begs Mark and John—whose names signify the labels of the "mark" (target of a drug scam) and the "john" (someone who patronizes prostitutes)—to let her hang them, and lynchings occur repeatedly. And the scene in which the Vigilante loses his mouth and eyes and is consumed by "one organ that leaps forward to snap with transparent teeth" (9) becomes the famous talking asshole episode.

Burroughs further emphasizes the dreamlike nature of these episodes through his numerous allusions to Freud. Drawing on Freud's association between dreams of sexual excitement and "the dreamer taking a tooth out of his mouth" (Freud 1994, 72), Burroughs continually deploys images of loosening teeth in the Interzone. The teeth that in the first two sections either "fall out" because of drug addiction (14), or become conduits for shock in Benway's "Switchboard" machine (21) reappear in the Interzone sections: the professor's students chase him with "switchblades clicking like teeth" (72), and teeth—also associated with genitals in the novel—are constantly spilling out, whether it is the teeth that "fly" from an old man's mouth (80) or the "vaginal teeth [that] flow out" of Mary (84).

Here, Burroughs belongs to a long trajectory of gothic, Romantic, and particularly surrealist writers who saw within the mind of the dreamer, and particularly the madman, a unique intimacy with the unconscious processes whose "eruption," André Breton believed, would be the death of "bourgeois society" (1969a, 232). *Naked Lunch* is often read as part of a Romanticist trajectory stretching from the gothic to the surreal. For instance, Fiona Paton argues that the "execratory excesses of the novel" (49) form a gothic or "monstrous" response to "the official discourses surrounding communism, homosexuality, and national security at this time" (49); editors of an essay collection released to celebrate the novel's fiftieth anniversary have boasted that "the desire to shock, to rub one's face in human ordure, is the book's strategic, perpetual motor" (xii); while others such as Andrew Hussey, R. B. Morris, and Davis Schneiderman have traced the "cut up" method of Burroughs's text back to surrealist aesthetic strategies. These readings certainly resonate with initial reviews of the novel that pointed to the "shock value of its surrealistic prose" (qtd. in Whiting, 159–60) and that even led some scholars to accuse Burroughs of "exploding" the novel outright, "leav[ing] only twisted fragments of experience and the miasma of death" (Fiedler 1971, 170).[18]

It is pertinent that we briefly consider *Naked Lunch* in relation to its Romantic and surrealist forebearers because Burroughs's highly conscious negotiation of these earlier genres is key for understanding the political and generic interventions the novel is making. The relationship between drugs, Romanticism, and imperialism has been written about at length.[19] The consumption of drugs and particularly opium by Romantic authors, the hallucinatory reveries induced by opium, and even the structure of Romantic texts that assumed the form of an opium-induced hallucination—these depended on the imperial networks underpinning the opium trade and produced imperialist fantasies of an essentialized Orient to be explored and conquered. This entwining has led some critics to conclude that "the extensive literature of drug-induced hallucination, while appearing to be a culture counter to Enlightenment modernity, actually neatly reinscribes its gendered and racial antinomie" (Zieger, 1533), while others have argued that while drug-induced literature is entwined with imperialist orientalisms, it also became a tool for imagining a new and revolutionary world. Katherine Singer in her work on Shelley, for instance, argues that "drugs act like an emetic, forcing their users to regurgitate the poisonous status quo they have swallowed, insisting they contemplate social and linguistic change from the self-critical vacancy of an empty stomach" (688). Thus, she argues that, for Shelley, "drugs can help usher in political and social change" (706).

This tension between drug-induced Romanticism's revolutionary and reactionary impulses reached its apex with the surrealists, who pushed both the revolutionary potentials and the orientalist primitivism of intoxication and Romanticism to its limits. As Amanda Stansell points out, the surrealists' "critique of 'reason'" was the site of both their radical "anti-racism" and their complicity in racist and colonial tropes of "the 'primitive'" (112). This history is particularly connected to Morocco. In 1926 the surrealists, inspired by the anticolonial Riff Rebellion in Morocco, joined the Communist Party in supporting the rebellion, and in 1931 they protested against the Colonial Exhibition in Paris by hosting a counterexhibit called *The Truth about the Colonies* that featured "a black child with a begging bowl" as one of their "European fetishes" (Richardson and Fijałkowski, 4).

Burroughs's locating of the dream-space of the Interzone in Tangier is particularly relevant in this regard. Brian Edwards argues that, at the time Burroughs was writing, Tangier was often positioned as a challenge to "key tenets of cold war domestic America," particularly what he terms "the developing dialectic of heteronormative domestic arrangements, namely the concept of the procreative couple as family unit, and the primacy of the nation form within the postwar world order" (150). Not only was Tangier literally a space where gay or countercultural Americans would go to escape the containment culture of Cold War America, but Tangier occupied a particular space in the American imagination. As Edwards explains, Tangier's location in Africa, alongside its proximity to Europe, "magnified the threat" it posed as "the deep structural racism of cold war culture allied Tangier's queerness—as excess—and the cold war figure of 'blackness'" (150).

The question as to whether the Interzone's excesses are utopic or dystopic has long occupied critics. But wherever critics fall on this question, it is quite evident that its reputation as a space of excess is tied to the exotic location of the Interzone. Timothy Yu has offered the most perceptive diagnosis in his consideration of both the utopic and dystopic aspects of *Naked Lunch*. The novel's vision "of the rhythms of (interracial) sex integrated into the everyday activities of 'people eating talking bathing'" (52), Yu argues, represents the "utopian" aspect of the Interzone: an "ecstatic, borderless, postmodern utopia existing at the height of intoxication and orgasm" (51). But, he warns, it is a utopia that occurs "under an oriental eye" (51) and is always "linked to grotesqueries and death" (51). In its dance of attraction and revulsion with the Interzone, Yu concludes, "*Naked Lunch* broadens the reach of 'Orientalism' from the Middle Eastern fantasies of Joyce's Bloom to include East Asia and a polyglot, mongrelized America" (52).

Read as a dream, *Naked Lunch* seems to continue, deepen, and expand the orientalism of the Romantics and surrealists. And yet, *Naked Lunch* also seems to consciously refute such an alignment by contesting its very relationship with the Romanticist trajectory and its dreamlike structure. This refutation occurs most clearly in the vignette "Campus of Interzone University," in which a professor with multiple personality disorder tries to teach his students Samuel Coleridge's "Rime of the Ancient Mariner." Ignoring the story of the albatross, the professor instead focuses on the relationship between the Mariner and the Wedding Guest, and the Mariner's attempt to intoxicate the Wedding Guest with his story. The professor asks his students to "consider the Ancient Mariner without curare, lasso, bulbocapnine or straitjacket, albeit able to capture and hold a live audience" (73). The professor's reading of the poem implicitly connects the persuasive power of Romantic literature with that of drugs in its ability to "capture," or intoxicate, the subject.

In the professor's interpretation, the power of Romantic literature is akin to the controlling power of narcotics. In the actual poem by Coleridge, the Wedding Guest is intoxicated by the power of the Mariner's story, a power that is connected to the intoxicating powers of opium. The professor, however, is not in the realm of opiates or intoxication but rather in the realm of control. The professor's call to imagine the Mariner "without curare, lasso, [or] bulbocapnine" echoes Benway's earlier claim that "bulbocapnine potentiated with curare—give[s] the highest yield of automatic obedience" (73). For the professor, the Mariner is a master druggist, able to take control over passersby. The professor, on the other hand, is not. He is the Mariner without curare, and without the intoxicating powers of this new arsenal of drugs, both he and the Romantic literature he uses to try to capture his students' attention fail miserably.[20] The professor's students are entirely uninterested in the poem and attack him as soon as he starts discussing it, demanding instead that he return to the Americana of "Old Ma Lottie" stories. Compared to the tropes of narcotics and possession that serve to disrupt early episodes like "Vigilante," here drugs and the Romantic aesthetic tradition attached to them are stripped of their subversive or marvelous potential. They fail to possess their readers.

While part of the point Burroughs is making is that Romanticism has lost its ability to shock and that "Rime" has become one more tired canonical text, the students' revolt against Coleridge and the professor is also important to understanding both Burroughs's and the novel's own revolt against the Romantics. To read the Interzone as a drug-induced hallucinatory dream space, and thus as a repressed unconscious exploding out into reality in order to illuminate the "chamber of horrors" (Fiedler 1960, 116) lurking beneath the bourgeoisie's "smugly regarded world" (116), is to assume that there is an unconscious that can be shocked and exposed. In *Naked Lunch*, this is not the case. Thus, while the structure of the book draws on the older form of the dream novel or psychomachia, the content of the dream is no longer some hidden or repressed unconscious that the novel brings to the surface but instead a constructed fantasy. Dr. Benway, the protagonist tells us, is a "manipulator and coordinator of symbol systems, [and] an expert on all phases of interrogation, brainwashing and control" (19). Benway's methods are so successful that he can boast of how he once targeted an undercover "female agent" by inverting her real identity with her covert one. Bragging, he explains: "An agent is trained to deny his agent identity by asserting his cover story. So why not use psychic jujitsu and go along with him? Suggest that his cover story is his identity and that he has no other. His agent identity becomes unconscious, that is out of his control; and you can dig it with drugs and hypnosis" (24). As with the female agent whose identity is hollowed out and replaced with a new one, so too is the Interzone dream a fantasy imposed on the protagonist, William Lee. It is a space created by Benway's laboratory, or "Reconditioning Center" (15)—the place where Benway has been tasked with using psychoactive drugs, shock, and other forms of sexual and psychological manipulation to achieve "all phases of interrogation, brainwashing and control" (19)—and it is structured as an experiment in psychological and pharmacological manipulation.

This suggests we think about the Interzone not as the space of the unconscious dream let loose on the world but rather as a crafted fantasy of the spaces and subjects in need of modernization. And here we get at one of the clearest ways in which *Naked Lunch* breaks away from its surrealist and Romantic forebearers: the drug-induced hallucination is no longer the product of an individual unconscious but rather a conspiracy in which the state, or its corporate proxy, seizes onto specific desires for freedom and brutally constrains and shapes them to its purposes. What is at stake here is not just a wider Cold War paranoia about "shadow governments" working towards "mass social and political control," which Timothy Melley has usefully identified as a driving force of post–World War II US culture and discourse (2000, 178). Assuredly, anxieties about an overbearing Cold War state are at play here, but the psychological forms of penetration carried out at the Reconditioning Center also echo, in a decidedly less paranoid form, the new style of imperialism deployed by the United States as it emerges as a new global hegemon.

What Burroughs is tracing, then, is the exhaustion of the return of the repressed that accompanies the decline of traditional European imperialism. Because of the shifting form that imperialism takes, Burroughs seems to be suggesting, the Interzone cannot function as the return of the repressed or an unleashing of revolutionary energies. But if the novel's role can no longer be to "shock," what it can do is map the paranoid Cold War fantasies and visions of these underdeveloped spaces and subjects, and the forms of control the US state carries out in order to develop and modernize these spaces. Yu has pointed out that in the scenes of miscegenation that mark the novel, "it is always the white boys who are penetrated by Orientals and blacks" (51). Thus, in "hassan's rumpus room," a crowd watches as "A Javanese dancer [. . .] pulls an American boy [. . .] down onto his cock" (66) while nearby "Exquisite Balinese and Malays, Mexican Indians [. . .] Negroes [. . .] Japanese Boys [. . .] Venetian lads, Americans with blond or black curls [etc.]" all hang at the end of ropes ready to be taken (67). And in another incident, the protagonist watches as "On a ruined straw mattress the Mexican pulled him up on all fours—Negro boy dance [*sic*] around them beating out the strokes" (98). This perhaps explains why so many of these scenes, which are often read as utopic transgressions of Cold War social mores,[21] are also, as Yu points out, so horrifically violent. Almost every encounter ends in death, sometimes repeated deaths, as in the case of Mark, Johnny, and Mary, who take turns hanging each other and coming back to life in a series of B films. Moreover, ejaculation corresponds with hangings, such as the mugwumps who "snap the boy's neck [. . .] and he ejaculates immediately" (64), or the Aztec princes who take a Latahs[22] youth and secure him before "a waterfall pours over the skull snapping the boy's neck. He ejaculates in a rainbow" (68).

The rapidity with which queer Arab men's penetrations of whites becomes violent and deadly registers nothing so clearly as a deep horror and fear of the penetration of white, American boys by queer Arabs, and thus the queering of white Americans by Arabs. But this grotesquery also takes on an explicitly geopolitical frame. In one particularly telling episode, "ordinary men and women," an ostensible satire of the Istiqlal, the Party Leader himself is described as a "successful gangster in drag" (102), stalking around a "street boy [. . .] like an aroused tom cat" (102). There is here an implicit connection being drawn between the queer Arab figures penetrating white boys and the nationalist Party Leader's rebellion against the control of the United States and its enforcement of free trade. The Party's rebellion against the natural and open US market here is related to their queerness.

It is this twinned queerness and desire for a form of freedom that exceeds or differs from the freedoms promised by the United States that is both the justification for, and the ostensible object of, Benway's study—and, metonymically, for the United States' intervention into, and indeed penetration of, their movement and country. When one the upper cadres of the Nationalist Party attempts to talk to a "street boy" by asking, "You hate the French, don't you?" (103), the boy responds: "I hate everybody. Doctor Benway says it's metabolic, I got this condition of the blood . . . Arabs and Americans got it special . . . Doctor Benway is concocting this serum" (103). Similarly, when the nationalist leader drops dead, "poisoned by hate" (119), after trying to import "Latahs from Indochina" to start a riot (118), Benway rushes up and takes a blood sample. In each instance of rebellion, Benway appears, carrying out bizarre drug experiments on subjects, claiming "disinterested research" (110) while he often "slash[es] his patient to shreds" (118).

Drawing on the work of María Josefina Saldaña-Portillo, Geidel argues that modernization was able to "incorporate the liberatory desires of revolutionary struggles [. . .] through its appeals to Third World masculinity" (xv). This appeal, Geidel argues, had both a positive and a negative valence. On the one hand, the achievement of modernization and independence was continuously equated with the achievement of "full masculinity" (xv) and thus the promise of membership in "this US-controlled global brotherhood" (xv). On the other hand, US-led development drew on this "gendered logic of penetration and humiliation" (xv) by threatening to intervene in countries refusing to modernize, thus undercutting the autonomy of national leaders and inducing "the leaders of these 'developing' countries to destroy the 'traditional' forms of social organization that development discourse characterized as passive and feminine" (xv).

What *Naked Lunch* depicts is the way in which this new form of US imperialism is cast into a sexual drama. Not only is it the intertwined queerness and refusal of the tenets of economic modernization that becomes the implicit justification for Benway's thorough penetration of the Interzone at both the bodily and national level, but Benway's intervention into the Interzone also implicitly casts Benway (and thus the United States) as active and masculine and the Tangerinos as passive and feminine.[23] And this sexual drama is not unique to the Interzone within *Naked Lunch*. The same dynamic plays out domestically, particularly through the criminalization of drugs. Just as it is the National Party's queerness and resistance to US-style development that becomes a justification for Benway's intervention, so it is Lee's status—as a drug addict, as queer, as criminal, and as a threat to urban renewal—that justifies Benway's penetration of his mind in the Reconditioning Center: the very penetration that creates the novel's form.

Hard-Boiled Fantasy

What, then, to make of the novel's ending: namely, its return to its original urban setting and Lee's subsequent escape? In 1956, the Istiqlal movement succeeded in gaining independence and the International Zone of Tangier was shut down. With the loss of US control, US capital fled too: taking with it the pleasure- and freedom-seeking tourists of Europe and America. Tangier itself came to resemble the decayed and hollowed-out cores of many Depression-era US cities. And so too in *Naked Lunch*, the world of the Interzone ends as Lee is finally able to escape both the Interzone and Benway and return to the city.

Lee's return echoes the Western's movement from the frontier back to the city, and thus suggests a reading of Lee as becoming the Western hero that has achieved his "full masculinity," to return to Geidel and Saldaña-Portillo's formulation. But Lee's adventures do not provide the vitality and strength necessary for him to dominate the city, and accordingly the novel doesn't generically return to the Western. Rather, it turns to the cadence and style of the noir and hard-boiled genres that excelled at both exciting and containing all the anxieties that the Interzone raised—miscegenation, emasculating women, the erosion of borders at once national, sexual, racial, and psychological, and a looming socialist threat—through the figure of the lone, white male protagonist who would restore order to the dangerous city.[24]

In the final episode, "hauser and o'brien," the eponymous narcotics agents who have been ostensibly chasing Lee throughout the narrative finally catch up with him at the Hotel Lamprey. Lee hoodwinks them with a violent flair that Mickey Spillane's detective Mike Hammer would admire and begins to plot his escape. Running out of the hotel and into the "beautiful Indian summer day," Lee muses to himself, "I didn't have much chance, but any chance is better than none, better than being a subject for experiments with ST(6) or whatever the initials are" (178). He concocts a plan to call Hauser and O'Brien and give them a tip about a massive drug shipment in an attempt to switch sides from criminal to narc in order to free himself. In enacting this shift, Lee comes to resemble the ideal subject of development: shedding himself of his queer and criminal background, and taking on the subjectivity of the hypermasculine, hard-boiled hero able to maneuver between the overbearing nanny state and the urban underworld.[25]

And yet, for all of this, the protagonist's escape and transformation—and in many ways the genre of the hard-boiled itself—is not quite successful. When Lee calls the Narcotics Department and asks for Hauser and O'Brien, the department responds that there is "no Hauser no O'Brien in this department" (181). Lee realizes that either he has imagined the entire Interzone or that reality itself has shifted and he is no longer being pursued by the Narcotics Department. He comments: "I had been occluded from space-time [. . .]. Locked out . . . Never again would I have a Key, a point of Intersection . . . The heat was off me" (181). Lee's awakening pulls him back from the Interzone and both its libidinal horrors and the excess of state violence enacted there. Lee escapes, but not through the masculinist codes of the hard-boiled. It is, after all, not Lee's actions that save him; he doesn't succeed in outflanking the narcotics agents and, indeed, it seems unlikely that Lee would have been able to. Instead, in order to save Lee, the novel intervenes with another twist in genre by trying to reconstruct the psychomachic structure it already rejected: namely, by turning the entire preceding narrative into a dream.

Unlike the Western-inflected *Price of Salt*, in which Therese is able to upwardly ascend and escape the violence of the state, Lee's hard-boiled narrative cannot do the same, in large part because of the limits of the hard-boiled novel in doing for men what this new form of Western could now do for women. This failure of the hard-boiled to achieve the same uplift as the Western is connected to the decline of the hard-boiled itself at the moment in which Burroughs was writing. Sean McCann has explained this decline thusly: the hard-boiled detective story was both a product of New Deal liberalism and a genre that took up, and formally modeled, its attempt to negotiate the "paradoxes of liberal democracy" (85), namely "the competing needs of the public and the economic and political elite" (200). The genre, thus operated, through its formal ability to negotiate between "literary art and popular expression" (198), creating in effect a reading public, a "public" that McCann aligns with "the urban, ethnic, working class" of the Popular Front (200).

In McCann's account, the genre buckles in the postwar period because the "public" of the New Deal and the hard-boiled respectively becomes absorbed into the postwar Deal and its model of "state-fueled, but privately managed, economic growth" (200). In other words, McCann suggests that as the very tensions that created the hard-boiled were resolved in the postwar period, the genre declined. While McCann accurately diagnoses the erosion of the popular, he misdiagnoses exactly how the so-called "postwar deal" fractured the popular. As we have seen, there was no unified transformation of the ethnically diverse urban "people" of the Popular Front to suburban Americans. Rather, there was a sharp division that saw postwar state privatize the white middle class and a certain stratum of the white working class by turning them into a relatively affluent, home-owning class able to claim independence from the public sphere (through, somewhat ironically, their state-backed and subsidized mortgages in private suburbs), while simultaneously forging a class of racialized, and often criminalized, renters trapped within the public sphere of the city. In other words, the popular wasn't absorbed so much as it was (further) split and divided.

While the hard-boiled novel was imbricated within these processes— forging the idea of the private, individual, white male subject who stands in relation to a criminal, feminized, and racialized urban underclass—it was also a victim of them: as its democratic promise was unable to hold up within the sharply divided cityscapes of public chocolate cities and private vanilla suburbs. At the same time, the promise of the lone, white, male, individual savior itself fell apart, as the city—increasingly imbricated in the spheres of global capital and expanding through the network of highways—became impossible to individually map.[26] As the divisions between the city and the suburb began to grow, the line between the private eye and the criminal began to erode. It was increasingly difficult to live within, but apart from, the city; to be within the city and its streets was to be connected to criminality itself.

While the hard-boiled might borrow from the frontier imagery of the Western, then, the hard-boiled is no Western; the protagonist is neither able to escape nor master the criminal underworld. The hard-boiled detective can never achieve the demands of the entrepreneurial or fully developed subject because he is always the other of the criminal and of the concomitant urban underclass. This is certainly the case for Lee, who remains on the verge of criminality and embroiled in the decaying city. And indeed, in the novel's concluding paragraphs, this hard-boiled ending falls apart:

> The Heat was off me from here on out . . . relegated with Hauser and O'Brien to a landlocked junk past where heroin is always twenty-eight dollars an ounce and you can score for yen pox in the Chink laundry of Sioux Falls . . . Far side of the world's mirror, moving into the past with Hauser and O'Brien . . . . clawing at a not-yet of Telepathic Bureaucracies, Time Monopolies, Control Drugs, Heavy Fluid Addicts. (181)

In this final paragraph, the clean, cool, and sleek hard-boiled language of the episode breaks apart and returns to the associative and messy language of the Interzone. Here, the hard-boiled has been relegated into the past, its fantasy of white, male, individual objectivity and freedom unable to hold. It cannot stand up against the "not-yet" of the "Telepathic Bureaucracies, Time Monopolies, Control Drugs" and "Heavy Fluid Addicts" (181), all imaginative rehashings of the well-trod anxieties about the expansion of capitalism, state and organizational power, and the rise of mass culture and mass communication that were creating "organization men" instead of "outstanding men" (Whyte 1956, 5), and "outer-directed man" instead of "well-shod cowboys" and "inner-directed subjects" (Riesman, lxvi).

It is not just that the genre of the hard-boiled fails. Rather, as the novel suggests, the vision of masculinity put forward by the hard-boiled—a vision that also draws on the imaginary of the "well-shod cowboy" or "the inner-directed subject"—is not adequate for the new kind of state emerging and ceases to be able to manage the contradictions of its moment. *This* is the revelation that one of the hard-boiled's big fans will come up against as she realizes that she must abandon the hard-boiled for the Western in order to realize its vision. The fan in question is, of course, Ayn Rand— and it is to her that we will turn in the next chapter.

CHAPTER 4

Shock Therapy: *Atlas Shrugged,* Urban Renewal, and the Making of the Entrepreneurial Subject

Atlas Shrugged opens with Eddie Willers, the assistant of the railway magnate and protagonist Dagny Taggart, strolling through a seemingly war-torn New York City, its streets, houses, stores, and factories all empty, abandoned, or destroyed. Eddie makes three ostensibly disconnected observations about his surroundings: first, that the skyscrapers look "like an old painting in oil" (12); second, that he hates the new electronic calendar, which "the mayor of New York had erected last year" (12); and third, that the plenitude of commodities in the store windows on Fifth Avenue comfort him as "he liked to see [. . .] objects made by men, to be used by men" (12). These full windows, however, also arouse a feeling of the uncanny in him, triggering an uncomfortable childhood memory of an oak tree struck by lightning. He recalls the childhood "shock [that] came when [he] stood very quietly, looking into the black hole of the trunk" (13). What is this shock and why does his stroll through the streets of New York City trigger this memory? Furthermore, why is this intrusion—a memory of nature's awesome and destructive power—into the urban landscape of department stores and skyscrapers so deeply troubling for Eddie? Why is this single "shock" able to disturb his otherwise "sunlight"-filled (13) memories of childhood and his love of New York?

The blasted oak tree of Eddie's childhood recalls the opening scene of Mary Wollstonecraft Shelley's classic novel of modernity, *Frankenstein: or, the Modern Prometheus* (1818), wherein Doctor Frankenstein recalls his childhood experience of witnessing a storm that reduced "an old and beautiful oak" to a "blasted stump" (33). He explains: "we found the tree shattered in a singular manner. It was not splintered by the shock, but entirely reduced to thin ribands of wood. I never beheld anything so utterly destroyed" (57). When he asks his uncle, in awe, what force had just reduced a magnificent tree to ribands, his uncle responds, "Electricity!" (57). This story of creative destruction both marks the "primal scene" of Doctor Frankenstein's obsession with technology and progress, and—like Karl Marx's sorcerer who "is no longer able to control the powers [. . .] he has called up" (226)—foreshadows Frankenstein's downfall: his inability to harness the forces of nature he has conjured. *Atlas Shrugged*, however, is no *Frankenstein*. Where *Frankenstein* projects the horrific consequences of modernity, *Atlas Shrugged* celebrates modernity and refigures these Promethean shocks as necessary for the cleansing of the postwar Keynesian state (called "the looters" in the novel) and the production of a new, utopic, market-driven society. In doing so, the novel transforms modernity's metaphor from Prometheus to Atlas: from a model of modernity rooted in traumatic shock, deadly compulsion, and ultimate destruction, to one rooted in strength, stability, and domination.

Atlas, in *Atlas Shrugged*, is the *ur* capitalist figure of John Galt: a low-level employee for Dagny's railway company who is at once building and destroying the infrastructure underpinning New York City's economy, and ultimately a US-driven capitalist world system. When the novel begins, Dagny is trying to save the city and her family's railway, Taggart Transcontinental, from two threats: the looter state and an elusive figure she calls the "destroyer," who is disappearing the country's most innovative and competent industrialists, artists, and thinkers (whom the novel terms the "men of the mind"), thus exacerbating the looters' large-scale economic crisis. As the novel develops, Dagny must learn that the destroyer is actually Galt and the disappeared are on strike against the looters. These men do not seek to destroy capitalism but rather to save it. The novel follows Dagny as she realizes that the "destroyer" is actually the "redeemer" and that she must join the men of the mind and give up her attachments to her railway company and city in order to save the city and transform herself into one of them.

Atlas Shrugged emerges out of, and participates in, the debates surrounding the future of America's cities at a time when the often opposing forces of urban sprawl, suburbanization, urban decay, and urban renewal were making that future increasingly uncertain. What Rand calls a "strike" turns out to be an enactment of the twinned processes of residential and industrial white flight to the suburbs, while Eddie and Dagny's traumatic encounter with the decaying city simply rehearses the myriad white-flight narratives that cast the postwar city as a war zone that shocks and traumatizes the working- and middle-class white subject who needs to flee. Where the previous three chapters focus on the inhabitants of urban space that were the focus of housing reformers—specifically, the ghettoized black subject, the ethnic working-class woman, and the junky—this chapter turns to the white middle-class subject for whom the suburbs are being built and the city is being remade.

Read as a novel about the white middle-class subject's traumatic encounter with the decaying city, *Atlas Shrugged* belongs to the category of what Catherine Jurca terms the "white diaspora" novel: that is, a novel of white middle-class *ressentiment* that promotes "a fantasy of victimization that reinvents white flight as the persecution of those who flee" (9). However, *Atlas Shrugged* ultimately refuses a position of victimization as a form of looter ideology. Instead, it reimagines the shocks and traumas of a decaying urban core as a therapeutic force that purges both the characters and the reader of their neurotic, anxious, and compulsive drives: facilitating the creation of—or, in this case, a return to—the natural, self-reliant, and resilient entrepreneurial subject. Ultimately, this transformation is not just about the nature of the city or the subject but also about the experience of shock therapy, which becomes, within the novel, a positive force of subject formation. Through this transformation, I argue, *Atlas Shrugged* simultaneously acts as an origin story for the emergence of the entrepreneurial subject and reveals the racialized and revanchist urban processes that helped create and shape these seemingly objective economic narratives and subjectivities.

Shocked Cities

By the mid-1950s, *Frankenstein* was an apt analogy for the vertiginous rise and fall of the United States' great industrial cities, which had seemingly overnight gone from representing the American promise of endless growth, prosperity, and futurity, to serving as a symbol of decline, unemployment, and a foreclosed, industrial past.[1] Throughout the 1930s, proponents of what would become urban renewal started speaking of a "blight" that was plaguing the core of US cities as industrial and commercial enterprises closed up shop and moved to the suburbs, alongside the white middle class who, induced by government incentives, were moving into their newly built and subsidized suburban homes (Fogelson, 57–62). By the 1940s, a consensus emerged across US cities that an urban crisis was brewing, which, without large-scale government intervention, would result in a national catastrophe. While Eddie might not be able to find the words in the "empty shape" of his mind" (12) to connect the "shock" he experiences staring at the hollowed-out oak tree and the hollowed-out city, the novel itself does. Eddie's anxious and uneasy observations that the setting sun's reflection off the skyscrapers makes it look like a fire that "is too late to stop" (12); that even the "prosperous" streets are filled with "dark and empty" windows (12); and that the skyscrapers themselves are "brown" and "soot-eaten" like "the color of a fading masterpiece" (12) all make clear that, for Eddie, New York City *is* that oak tree, struck down and dying out. New York is the blighted city that must be saved.

The term "blight" was first used by the Chicago school of urban sociology in the 1920s, which introduced an "ecological approach" to processes of urban change (Pritchett, 16). According to their point of view, "blight" itself was an amorphous term, and "blighted" areas were not necessarily dangerous or unsanitary places to live, work, or shop like slums were. Instead, they were areas considered old, obsolete, in need of repair, poorly planned, or whose property values were declining (generally as a result of the movement of industry and white shoppers to the suburbs).[2] In short, as Marc Weiss put it, where "A 'slum' was a social concept: low-income people living in generally crowded, unsanitary, and crime-ridden conditions," blight "was an economic concept. Basically, it meant declining property values" (255). While the slums had been a longtime concern of urban reformers, blight did not discursively emerge as a widespread social concern until the late 1930s.[3] The term's prominence reflected a discursive shift surrounding urban policy from the moral economy of Jacob Riis, Edith Elmer Wood, and Mary Simkhovitch—and later, Catherine Bauer, Lewis Mumford, and Henry Wright—to those of economic development.

As this ecological language became appropriated by the coalition of downtown merchants, banks, Realtors, and developers who made up what Joel Schwartz has usefully termed the "redevelopment front" (61), the language of blight became a tool used to naturalize the urban economy and reconceptualize factors that were perceived to harm that economy into unnatural diseases that had to be removed. As numerous scholars have argued, however, both these economic factors, and the language of blight, which appeared neutral and natural, were always political and invariably racialized.[4] In 1943, for instance, the National Association of Real Estate Boards' *Fundamentals of Real Estate Practice* added the category "colored man of means" to its list of factors that would create blight in residential neighborhoods (qtd. in Avila 2004, 80). Technically speaking, they were not wrong. Because federal housing policy discriminated against, and effectively condemned, neighborhoods that were densely populated, aging, or had what one Federal Housing Authority manual described as an "infiltration of inharmonious racial and national groups" (qtd. in Abrams, 61), the arrival of African Americans or other ethnic groups *did*, in fact, reduce property values.[5] As a result, while "blight" was ostensibly an economic term used to describe neighborhoods that were either in decline or simply not growing in accordance with the wishes of specific downtown business interests, the term provided a race-neutral sheen for the thoroughly racist assumptions underpinning urban redevelopment and renewal.

The objects to which Eddie attaches himself in defense against the decay and blight that he sees as taking over his city are, in this respect, particularly revealing. Eddie lists three objects that inexplicably "reassure" him: a vegetable pushcart with "bright gold carrots and fresh green onions," a "clean white curtain blowing at an open window," and a "bus turning a corner, expertly steered" (12). These objects implicitly articulate a vision of the unblighted, or "natural," city: prosperous, healthy, well-ordered, spacious, white, and clean. While Eddie never explicitly uses the term "blight," his sudden desire that "these things [. . . not be] left in the open, unprotected against the empty space above" (12) frames the city within the ecological imaginary of blighted versus healthy. The problem that Eddie faces is that he feels unable to protect these enclaves of prosperity against the creep of blight. Dagny, however, is confident that she can protect these spaces. At least initially, the solution she offers—both politically and aesthetically— is remarkably in line with the modernist principles of urban renewal. Not only does Dagny live on the top floor of a large, glass-sheeted skyscraper (68)—the de facto modernist treatment for crumbling and blighted older neighborhoods—but she tries to work (albeit grudgingly) with the state, investing her private capital in large infrastructure projects to rescue a city floundering from the flight of industry, capital, and skilled labor. She soon realizes, however, that her efforts are in vain. No matter how hard she works to save the city from blight, the blighted city instead consumes her. Just as she finds herself increasingly unable to overcome the chronic mismanagement, bad government policy, and industrial decline that threaten to destroy her business, so she finds herself physically swallowed up and lost in the city's maze of abandoned parks, dilapidated houses, and other ruins. In one particularly notable instance, Dagny finds herself in a neighborhood near the East River that has become a jungle, to use the term Rand often returns to when describing a blighted New York. She spots "the black shape of a ruin" (167) that she realizes "had been an office building, long ago; she saw the sky through the naked steel skeleton and the angular remnants of the bricks that had crumbled" (167). As with Eddie, so Dagny's experience of the city, too, becomes one of blight, decay, and decline.

In contrast to this decayed and rotten city, the novel offers us Atlantis, the "private property" enclave (650) constructed by the men of the mind in the midwestern mountains. Rand's comparison of New York and Atlantis reads like any number of modernist architectural and urban planning tracts expressing visions for an alternative to the industrial city. Like these tracts, Rand's Atlantis, too, is perfectly in line with the 1933 Athens Charter of the highly influential International Congress for Modern Architecture, which called for, among other things, the rational organization of urban space, a focus on air and sun to ensure healthy living, and "segregating the four functions of work, residence, transportation, and leisure" (qtd. in Klemek, 11). Whereas in New York, directionless and chaotic citizens stumble around a poorly designed and crumbling downtown, in Atlantis, the buildings are new, well-designed, spacious, and maintained; the healthy inhabitants walk the streets with orderly purpose; and the factories and businesses are open and prospering. And while New York City is a tangled mass of industrial, residential, and commercial neighborhoods, in Atlantis, these uses are separated into discrete "districts" (667) and connected by a system of well-planned roads and rail lines. Atlantis, in short, is an exemplar of the modernist garden city. Except that Atlantis is not a city but a planned, private, and homogeneous development located in an enclave outside of the city. In other words, Atlantis is the model suburb.

Stripped bare, *Atlas Shrugged* is a white-flight novel—a novel about the processes of suburbanization, urban decay, and urban renewal. What makes this context difficult to see is a twofold operation that also explains *Atlas Shrugged*'s efficacy. First is the novel's complete erasure of race, save for a one-sentence description of the oil baron Ellis Wyatt's servant as "an elderly Indian with a stony face and a courteous manner" (233). Second is its coding of white flight within the imagery of the frontier. The two are related. Not only is the Indian servant the only racialized character in the novel, but, as Andrew Hoberek has noted, the frontier mythos he evinces plays a crucial role in the larger narrative operation of *Atlas Shrugged* (36).

Hoberek persuasively reads the novel's "celebration of frontier individualism" as an "ahistorical fantasy" that serves "as a site for the conservation of
middle-class agency" (36) at a moment when that agency was eroding. The
frontier, however, is also a far more timely metaphor than Hoberek suggests. It reflects the reconfiguration of first suburban and then urban space
into the new frontiers of capital.

Rand captures this fusing of nineteenth-century frontier imagery and
twentieth-century modernist architecture and urban planning within the
built environment of Atlantis. On the one hand, as Hoberek points out,
Galt lives in a cabin that has the "'primitive simplicity of a frontiersman's
cabin [. . .] while one of his lieutenants lives in a home 'like a frontiersman's
shanty'" (37). On the other hand, both of these buildings are thoroughly
modern. Galt's cabin, for instance, has both this "primitive simplicity"
(655) and all of the attributes of suburban modernity such as the "chro-
mium glittering on an electric stove" (655). Similarly, while Francisco
d'Anconia's house is a "log cabin beaten in dark streaks by the tears of
many rains," it also has "great windows withstanding the storms with the
smooth, shining, untouched serenity of glass" (672–73). Rand's refiguring
of Atlantis as both a frontier and a suburban enclave offers a remarkably
clear-eyed enactment of the suburb's role during the Cold War as a factory
of, and showcase for, what historian Elaine Tyler May terms "the American way of life as the triumph of capitalism allegedly available to all who
believed in its values" (8).

But the mythos of the frontier also points to the racial politics embedded within *Atlas Shrugged*. Like the Westerns from which it draws, the
novel's use of the frontier serves to efface the role of race in these processes of spatial redevelopment. In *The Frontier Club: Popular Westerns and
Cultural Power, 1880–1924*, Christine Bold traces how the "frontier clubmen" (2)—her shorthand for turn-of-the-century eastern aristocrats such
as Teddy Roosevelt, Owen Wister, and Frederic Remington—bleached
the West of Mexican, Indigenous, Jewish, eastern European, and African American inhabitants in order to reimagine the frontier as a space of
Anglo-American dominance. Writing within a context of Jim Crow, Bold
argues, these frontier clubmen "produced segregationist stories—not so
much arguing the case against African Americans as pushing them to the
margins of the western scene or out of the picture altogether" (131). Rand's
recasting of white flight into the terms of the frontier-Western participates in a larger cultural shift that produced a new segregationist rhetoric
for the post–Jim Crow era—one that, as David Freund documents, saw
whites shifting from arguments based on biological difference to economic

arguments that "racial-minorities simply threatened white-owned property" (12).[6] Put in slightly different terms, *Atlas Shrugged* doesn't need to mention race because Rand's depiction of the decaying and economically blighted urban core—contrasted with the well-organized and affluent suburban development that Atlantis represents—is already coded within the new segregationist language of white flight.

In this context, Rand's articulation of the main strategy of the men of the mind—the withdrawal of capital from public space and into the enclave of Atlantis—becomes all the more nefarious. At the end of the novel, Dagny tracks Galt down to his home in New York City, which she discovers is located in a slum. Surveying her surroundings, Dagny describes the "crumbling plaster, peeling paint, the fading signboards of failing shops with unwanted goods in unwashed windows, the sagging steps unsafe to climb, the clotheslines of garments unfit to wear" (1000). When a shocked Dagny asks Galt about his choice of abode, he explains that "no money earned in [Atlantis] is ever to be spent outside" (1005), and so he must work as a track laborer in order to pay his rent and buy food in New York. This conversation at once reveals the actual state policies that created a system of economic and racial segregation between the wealthy suburbs and impoverished central cities: namely, the subsidizing and expansion of home ownership and industry in the former and the underdevelopment and concentrating of poverty in the latter. And yet, paradoxically, it does so while giving voice to the moralizing fantasy of white-flighters that government interventions were helping only the urban poor, whereas the deserving suburban homesteaders had earned their houses through independent hard work.

Moreover, this scene reveals the deeper importance that the ideological fantasies underpinning white flight and suburbanization have in the forging of neoliberalism. Galt's identity, split between that of a blue-collar worker in the city and a successful entrepreneur and capitalist in the suburbs, mobilizes a fantasy of suburbanization as upward class mobility—of the move from a dependant, blue- or white-collar laborer to an independent owner-operator. But it does so at the same time as that possibility is foreclosed. Class mobility does not exist within the novel. No character successfully ascends. Instead of mobility, Galt offers the alternative of identification. In him, the subject position of the hardworking, blue-collar white worker fuses with that of the capitalist. What this scene ultimately reveals, then, is how a fantasy of white dispossession creates an ideological realignment in which the primarily male blue- and white-collar worker comes to distance himself from the social welfare state and to identify instead with capital.

Thus, while *Atlas Shrugged* undoubtedly mobilizes feelings of dispossession that Jurca rightly sees as underpinning white flight, the novel's perspective is ultimately not that of fleeing workers but that of capital itself. And this is why the novel cannot end in the enclave of Atlantis. While suburbanization, as David Harvey and others have shown, was crucial to solving the profitability crisis that marked the end of World War II, so too were the processes of creative destruction that played out in urban cores across the United States.[7] "Capital," Harvey writes, "cannot abide limits. When it encounters limits, it works assiduously to convert them into barriers that can be transcended or bypassed" (2011, 90). Following the war boom, that limit was the suburbs and, as William Whyte notes, the great postwar expansion of suburbia in the forties and fifties drew on the "romantic veneration of the frontier tradition" (1968, 1). But by the beginning of the 1960s, the frontier, as Charles Abrams noted in his 1965 book, had shifted to the city. Abrams was not alone in this observation. Just a year earlier, Lyndon Johnson had declared the city "the frontier of imagination and innovation." Indeed, as Christopher Klemek suggests, the very project of urban renewal was "conceived and executed as a kind of frontier assault, drawing red battle lines around entire districts and neighborhoods, advancing against blighted slums, imposing rational new form on cities" (2).[8]

Writing in the 1950s, Rand could not have known the specific shape that urban revalorization would take in the 1970s and 1980s once "the new urban frontier," in Neil Smith's apt lexicon, became "the frontier of profitability" (1996, 22). But what Rand was able to clearly see from early on was the continued importance of urban space to capital, even at the moment when urban space appeared to have been abandoned by capital or taken over by the state. Smith argues that with capital's return to the city, the imaginary of the urban similarly transformed from a "wilderness," a chaotic environment of decay and decline, to a "frontier" (16), a space of "economic progress and historical destiny, rugged individualism and the romance of danger, national optimism, [and] race and class superiority" (186). This is the transformation that both Dagny and the reader undergo as they reorient their perspective of the city from that of Eddie, who experiences the city as a hopeless battle against blight, to that of Galt, who embraces blight-ridden New York with all of the excitement of a cowboy heading west. Where the slums originally evoke a sense of terror in Dagny—at one point she cries out uncontrollably, "But this is New York City!" (1001)—Galt sees the slums as a laboratory. Literally. Inside his crumbling apartment, nested within a slum, Galt has built "the most efficiently modern laboratory [Dagny] had ever seen" (1005). And where Dagny, like Eddie, initially experiences the slumification of New York as a blight—a traumatic shock that threatens to destroy the city she loves—the men of the mind see in these slums the seeds of a new civilization that will supplant the looter state.

This change in perspective articulates the gulf that separates the subject positions of an embattled middle class and capital. While the middle classes fleeing the city experience the phenomenon of urban decay and blight as a constitutional shock that threatens the values of their houses and their identity, capital views these same processes as creating new spaces of potential redevelopment. One way we can think about the problem that *Atlas Shrugged* ultimately tackles, then, is how to shift the readerly perspective and identification from the position of a shell-shocked working- or middle-class subject who flees to the suburbs to that of capital, which understands both the suburbs and the city as integral.

Shocked Naturalisms

The novel finds its solution by turning shock and blight into a problem of literary genre. In her aesthetic opus, *The Romantic Manifesto* (1969), Rand develops a theory of her own literary genre that she terms "romanticism," which recognizes the truth that "all human actions are goal-directed, consciously or subconsciously; purposelessness is contrary to man's nature: it is a state of neurosis" (1975, 83).[9] She explains that her genre draws equally on "Aristotelianism, which liberated man by validating the power of his mind—and capitalism, which gave man's mind the freedom to translate ideas into practice" and aims to reveal man's ability to master both history and his own mind (103). Romanticism emerges as an explicit response to what Rand identifies as naturalism: the dominant literary genre of her moment and, according to her view, an expression of looter-state ideology. Naturalism, Rand writes, treats "misery [. . .] failure, frustration, defeat [. . . and] suffering" (125) as human nature for the explicit purpose of convincing man that he is "a helpless creature [. . . whose] destiny was held to be *society*" (124). It is this looter statism, Rand argues, in concert with its aesthetic forms, that has created a generation of people who "began to regard prosperity as unreal and present only misery, poverty, the slums, the lower classes [. . . and who] began to regard greatness as unreal and to present only the mediocre" (118).

Part of the education that the reader must undergo, then, is to recognize the novel's initial urban catastrophism as nothing but a naturalist vision of the city. Gerald Houseman suggests that cities have special importance to Rand as they represent "the triumph of creative people over nature" (162). *Atlas Shrugged* aims to restore this triumph over nature by revealing the anxieties of blight as an expression of naturalist ideology. Consider, for instance, the following scene, in which New York is depicted as literally crumbling back into nature:

> The inhabitants of New York had never had to be aware of the weather. Storms had been only a nuisance that slowed the traffic and made puddles in the doorways of brightly lighted shops. Stepping against the winds dressed in raincoats, furs and evening slippers, people had felt that a storm was an intruder within the city. Now, facing the gusts of snow that came sweeping down the narrow streets, people felt in dim terror that they were the temporary intruders and that the wind had the right-of-way. (465)

This scene evinces what many critics have identified as the primary trope of the naturalist novel: namely, the lack of control of the presumably lower- and middle-class urban inhabitants whose lives are, in the words of one prominent scholar of naturalism, "conditioned and controlled by environment, heredity, instinct, or chance" (Pizer, 11). These kinds of scenes repeat throughout the novel, tracking how New York City and its inhabitants desperately try and fail to exert control over their lives, always stumbling back into the seemingly natural forces of blight, decay, and decline. However, whereas these scenes appear at first as objective descriptions of reality, once Dagny begins the transformative work of becoming a man of the mind, she (alongside the reader) realizes that this feeling of powerlessness is actually an internalization of the generic tropes of looter ideology and a reflection of Eddie's, Dagny's, and the reader's failure of perception. That is, the city only *appears* to them as a chaotic space governed by the uncontrollable forces of nature, because they have misidentified with the vision of human stuckness, repetition, and lack of control held by naturalism.

Jennifer Fleissner has argued that, within naturalism, it is the characters' very "excessive attempt to gain control over one's surroundings that reveals [their] actual lack of control and concomitant frozenness in place" (43). It is this excessive and failed attempt to exert control that *Atlas Shrugged*, and Rand's genre of romanticism, critiques. Rand articulates this critique by placing two naturalist novelists, Keith Worthing and Balph Eubank, within *Atlas Shrugged*. Both of these writers, she emphasizes, hold important positions within the looter state and make their careers out of naturalizing stuckness, decline, decay, and anomie within both the built environment and the human subject itself. For instance, when Worthing is interviewed on the radio talk-show of the aristocratic and populist politician Kip Chalmers, he scoffs, "Freedom? [. . .] Do let's stop talk about freedom. Freedom is impossible. Man can never be free of hunger, of cold, of disease, of physical accidents. He can never be free of the tyranny of nature" (542). Similarly, Eubank, a modernist novelist and political lobbyist, explains that he is trying to create a new literature that "expresses the real essence of life [. . .] defeat and suffering" (128).

I opened this chapter by discussing the shocks that pervade Eddie Willers's experience of the city. I now want to suggest that Eddie's experience of shock, his compulsive descriptions of his fear, his powerlessness, his sense that things are happening "in some horrible way that [he] can't quite grasp" (205), and his mysterious, one-sided conversations with the nameless track fixer in the cafeteria who we later find out is Galt, all work to align him within naturalism's symptomology of shock and the uncanny (11). We can recall that in Freud's schema, the subject is governed by a death drive that seeks return to an earlier, "inorganic" state (1955a, 37) and thus experiences the invasion of stimuli as a form of traumatic shock. Freud suggests that, because the death drive wants to keep external stimuli out, it compulsively repeats all new stimuli in an attempt to "master the stimulus retrospectively" (31). Thus, in his essay on the uncanny, Freud will suggest that the experience of the uncanny—the belief that one's life is being governed by secret patterns or that a supernatural force that is ruling our fates, for instance—is simply the projection of an internal compulsion to repeat onto an outside or "daemonic" presence (1955a, 35). Eddie's sense of being haunted by some external logic, then, and his own repetition compulsion, position him as trapped firmly within this symptomology of shock and the death drive.

At least initially, Dagny doesn't fare much better. From the repetitive disappearances of key industrialists at the moment she needs them, to the sudden disasters that strike both her railroad and the industries she relies on to keep it running, Dagny and her railroad, too, appear to be haunted by that "fateful and unescapable" thing that Freud locates at the center of the uncanny (1995b, 236). Thus, while Dagny begins the novel by challenging Chalmers's and Worthing's views on life by fighting the blight of her city, the novel warns us that she does so on their terms. Dagny, like Eddie, remains trapped in the symptomology of naturalism: struggling against what seems like the unstoppable forces of nature as they wreak havoc on the economy and the social life of New York City and on their own psyches. The point is that while the reader may abhor the looter state, so long as they identify with the sense of powerlessness and defeat felt by Eddie (and initially Dagny), they are still trapped within it.

However, the novel's daemonic force, which is given the title of the "destroyer," is both real and symptomatic. Eddie's and Dagny's sense of being haunted—the mysterious disappearances; the recurring ghostly symphony of Dagny's favorite composer, Richard Halley, that has never been written; the cigarettes of a nonexistent brand with the "sign of the dollar [. . .] stamped in gold" (310)—are not quite external displacements of an internal compulsion to repeat. Everything they experience is the actual work of the men of the mind who *are* deliberately sabotaging them. But because they are unable to see clearly, because their attachment to the neurotic looter state has blinded them, they experience this reality as a traumatic form of repetition-compulsion. Dagny's attempts to save the railroad exemplify this thoroughly neurotic and "excessive attempt to gain control" that "reveals one's actual lack, instead of control" (Fleissner, 43). One of the first things that happens to those who cross over from the looters to the men of the mind is that they lose this compulsive attempt to gain control. They are able to escape from the naturalist novel. The coal baron Ken Dannager decides he would like to "take one of those excursion boat trips around the island of Manhattan" (413), the copper baron Francisco becomes a playboy, and John Galt takes on a menial job to which he is wholly unattached. "Only the man who does not need it, is fit to inherit wealth" (384), Francisco explains, and the principle extends to control. The desperate attempt to gain control reveals its ultimate lack: so long as Dagny is attached to the wildly neurotic and out-of-control looter city, she will compulsively continue to grapple at a power she can't possess, and the actions of the men of the mind will appear to her as traumatic shocks that further prove her lack of control.

Restoring Sight

The novel therefore suggests that what needs to change is not reality but simply Dagny's perception of it. Dagny must learn that what she initially perceived as a traumatic breakdown of the social order that renders her powerless and bewildered is actually the carefully planned and well-executed work of a striking capitalist elite whose goal is not the destruction of the city but instead the creation of a new, modern, and superior metropolis. And like the many modernist writers on whom Rand draws and from whom she breaks away, at the center of this problem of perception is the question of shock. As we've seen, throughout the late nineteenth and early twentieth centuries, artists and writers drew a connection between urban modernity, industrialization, traumatic shock, and the callousing of human consciousness. However, for Rand, unlike the modernists from whom she ultimately breaks away, shock is not constitutive to capitalist modernity or an expression of capitalism's internal contradictions. Shock is instead the self-regulating response of a fully rational capitalist system when faced with the unnatural and contradictory interventions of the state. Thus, the industrial accidents that recur throughout *Atlas Shrugged* are rational events caused by the growing bureaucratization of society that also does the necessary work of separating out the fit from the unfit, often literally "clearing the ground" for the new economic developments envisioned by the men of the mind. When a train crashes into the Colorado mountains as a result of a series of breakdowns along the chain of production, the narrator comments, "It is said that catastrophes are a matter of pure chance, and there were those who would have said that the passengers of the Comet were not guilty or responsible for the thing that happened to them" (560). The narrator challenges this by systematically going through the passengers of the sixteen cars, all of whom are teachers, professors, journalists, union men, and financiers who belong to the nanny-state apparatus of the looters. The chapter concludes, "These passengers were awake; there was not a man aboard the train who did not share one or more of their [the looters'] ideas" (562). There is no chance or chaos here. The accident is a result of a series of bureaucratic laws that hampered the railway industry from running in a safe and efficient manner while all of the people on the train were part of, and responsible for, this destructive process.

Throughout *Atlas Shrugged*, Rand suggests that it is not shock but the looter state's attempts to cushion the blows of shock—largely through anticompetition, foreign aid, social welfare, and arts funding programs—that is destroying society and blinding it to the state's destructive forces. Galt makes this point when the men of the mind take over a television station, and he delivers his famous laissez faire manifesto. His speech, with surprising precision, aligns the looter state with the death drive itself, which Freud identifies as an incessant urge to "lead organic life back into the inanimate state" (1955a, 40).[10] Galt accuses the state and looter society of being so intent on "avoiding death" (941) that, paradoxically, they have made the price of "life [. . .] the surrender of all the virtues required by life—and death by a process of gradual destruction is all that [such a] system will achieve" (945). In short, he concludes, the looters have created a religion of the "ideal zero, which is death" (945). This point is driven home in the myriad fates of the heads of the looter state, all of whom are either driven mad or literally killed by their own psychic contradictions, which the novel suggests are themselves reflections of the contradictions of their own policies. Both Orren Boyle, the head of the steel company of the looters, and James Taggart, the president of Taggart Transcontinental, suffer mental breakdowns, while James's wife, Cheryl, is so haunted by her husband's contradictions that she throws herself into the harbor, committing suicide.

In contrast, the men of the mind are unshockable. Or rather, because they have passed through the frontier of the death drive, they have come to identify with those shocks. The looter state discovers this once they kidnap Galt and subject him to a literal shock therapy machine, the Ferris Persuader, in a desperate attempt to convince him to change sides from the men of the mind to the looters. Not only does the machine fail to persuade him, but Galt ultimately breaks the machine for reasons that are remarkably psychoanalytic. The narrator explains that the machine is unable to work on Galt because he tries neither to "fight" the machine nor to "negate" it (1050). Rather, he defeats the machine by "surrendering" to its shocks (1050). For Freud, "negation" is the mechanism through which "the content of a repressed image or idea can make its way into consciousness" (667). It is a condition of the divided mind—and, as such, it is also the condition of Dagny, who maintains a hysterical attachment to the society she knows must be destroyed. Galt, in contrast, has already moved through his attachments to the past and society and no longer requires others to fulfill his drives; he has moved through the death drive and become, in the words of Dagny, a "single whole" (650).

Whereas Galt can inflict the most dramatic and devastating shocks to the looter state—destabilizing its cities, roads, railways, industries, international trade, and individual psyches—the looter state can't shock Galt because he—and, by extension, the men of the mind—is on the side of shock. While this scene is carried out in entirely psychological terms, the parallelism with the shocks and destructions visited upon New York City are exact. Just as the shocks of the Ferris Persuader work only on the looter state, only the looters or unconverted experience the shocks of urban decay, decline, and blight as traumatic. To those who have crossed over and come to identify with capital, these shocks are actually therapeutic, serving to rid the city of the decaying infrastructure of the older and contradictory state in order to make way for a new, rational, and prosperous city remade in the natural image of the market.

And here we finally arrive at the kernel of Rand's most dramatic intervention into midcentury politics and aesthetics: the forging of the neolib-

eral fantasy of shock therapy. She does so most dramatically by transforming the meaning of shock. Shock in *Atlas Shrugged* ceases to be—as it was
for Benjamin, Theodor Adorno, and numerous other modernists across
the political spectrum—something inherent within, and a result of, capitalist modernity (capitalism as Prometheus). Instead, the novel refigures
capitalist modernity as a strong, stable, and natural force (capitalism as
Atlas). According to this revision, shock and the death drive are refigured
as effects of the natural, self-regulating mechanism of a market that is attempting to purge itself of the impurities and sicknesses caused by state intervention. Second, the novel transforms the subject's experience of shock,
turning their anxious encounter with a world wracked by the struggle between the market and the looter state into a therapeutic force. Shock, the
novel promises, may be painful, but it will heal the subject, returning him
or her to a natural state of volition, force, and freedom. In carrying out this
transformation, the novel refigures the creative destruction of capitalist
modernity into a process of personal salvation: one that, if submitted to,
would lead to a stronger, more flexible human subject and, as we will see
shortly, a more modern, profitable, and healthy city.

Shock in *Atlas Shrugged* is at once reparative, ridding the system and
the self of unnatural aberrations, and evaluative, separating out the fit from
the unfit. Thus, the typically naturalist scenes of destruction, decline, and
shock faced by all of the characters become a test for the novel's readers.
Will they be dupes of the looter state and take on the anxiety of the characters? Or are they potentially men of the mind, who see these passages as
a rational and natural response to an irrational society and a salutary cleaning of blighted ground? The ultimate test is the explosion of Project X,
a thinly veiled representation of the atomic bomb. Project X is a sound
weapon created by the head scientist of the looters, Robert Stadler, which
explodes when one of the scientists accidentally pulls its lever (1040). The
explosion is described as destroying everything "within the circle of a ra-
dius of a hundred miles, enclosing parts of four states. [. . .] Telegraph poles
fell like matchsticks, farmhouses collapsed into chips, city buildings went
down as if slashed and minced by a single second's blow" (1041). I'd like
to take the short leap from Rand's vision of telegraph poles falling "like
matchsticks" to Benjamin's famous striking of the match. In "On Some
Motifs in Baudelaire," Benjamin argues that the striking of the match sym-
bolizes the many nineteenth-century inventions whereby "a single abrupt
movement of the hand triggers a process of many steps" (1999, 328). For
Benjamin, this process is central to understanding the almost supernatural
power man now possesses in modernity and, as with Shelley's *Frankenstein*

and Marx's sorcerer, the uncontrollable nature of the creations this power can conjure. The eruption of Project X is also caused by a single "abrupt movement of the hand" (328)—in this case, a looter's accidental "yank[ing of] a lever of the xylophone" (1041). Yet, significantly, only the looters experience this disaster as an uncontrollable and traumatic disaster akin to Freud's railway disasters or World War I. From the perspective of the men of the mind, Project X is a rational outcome of the looters' laws and a final rational shock that clears the ground for the emergence of a new laissez-faire system.

It is Project X—and the myriad other destructive policies of the looters—that allows *Atlas Shrugged*'s ultimate victory: the retaking of a now cleared-out New York. The novel ends with the banker Midas Mulligan sitting at his desk, "listing the assets of his bank and working on a plan of projected investments. He was noting down the locations he was choosing: 'New York—Cleveland—Chicago . . . New York—Philadelphia . . . New York . . . New York . . . New York . . .'" (1072). Meanwhile Judge Narragansett sits in his farm drafting new laws that forbid the "abridging of production and trade" (1073), and finally, Galt stands at the road (presumably back to New York) and announces: "The road is clear. [. . .] We are going back to the world," at which point he traces the sign of the dollar "over the desolate earth" (1074). Reading these final few pages, it is difficult not to be struck by the uncanny prescience of this scene, which was realized following the near-bankruptcy of New York in the 1970s and the structural adjustment programs of privatization, deregulation, financialization, and gentrification that followed in its wake (Tabb). And like the frontier narratives of gentrification that would follow, Rand too is able to turn the destruction of New York City's urban core into a bildungsroman narrative for the embattled, white-flight reader who comes to identify capital's victory over the welfare state with their own personal success and salvation.

Conclusion

When read against the historical trajectory of New York City, what appears in *Atlas Shrugged* as the zero point or death drive of the subject is really the frontier of the welfare state and its attendant political and legal structures, aesthetic forms, and subjectivities. Dagny is purged of the vestiges of collective responsibility, the novel is purged of its sympathetic identification with the disenfranchised and dispossessed, and New York is purged of its social safety net and market controls. What remains is an empty space of which the financiers, judges, and industrialists can take control. However, while Dagny passes through the death drive, and the city passes from welfare state to laissez-faire, the novel remains haunted by the conditions of its own success.

Most telling here is the novel's need to purge the two middle-class characters most closely associated with the novel's own presumed readership: Cheryl Taggart and Eddie. The novel begins with Eddie and Cheryl in the city and the men of the mind out of the city—Dagny on a train, Hank in Philadelphia, Francisco gallivanting and philandering across the world, Galt underground—and ends with the displacement of Eddie and Cheryl and the return of the men of the mind to the metropolis. Why? Most obviously, Eddie and Cheryl are prototypical naturalist figures, the shopgirl and the white-collar worker, who embody what Fredric Jameson identifies as the bourgeoisie's "desperate fear [. . .] of déclassement, of slipping down the painfully climbed slope of class position and business or monetary success, of falling back [. . .] into working class misery itself" (2015, 149). Cheryl is a *Sister Carrie* figure, a salesgirl whom James Taggart meets at a dimestore in "what had once been a busy neighborhood" (241), and who immediately recognizes him from his picture in the newspaper. Taggart, taken with her admiration of him, invites her to his house for drinks where she tells him the story of her life: her "stinking poor" family who refused to do anything to help themselves (244), and her move from Buffalo to New York in search of a better life.

Cheryl should be a proto-man of the mind. She is a woman of action, a woman who "saw pictures of New York and [. . .] thought, somebody built those buildings—he didn't just sit and whine that the kitchen was filthy and the roof leaking and the plumbing clogged" (249), a woman who saw opportunity and took it. Cheryl is one of the few other characters, and the only other woman, to undergo a transformation from looter to man of the mind, to see the truth that what appeared as "greatness" was really "its enemy" (817), and who realizes the truth of the principle, "my life is the highest of values, too high to give up without the fight" (820). By the end of the novel, not only has Cheryl converted, explaining that she has no "sympathy for that welfare philosophy" (800), but she even resembles Dagny in both style and appearance, gaining what the novel describes as a "smooth efficiency" and "poise" (799). Even James comments that "she was no longer an incongruous little freak, dwarfed by the luxury of the residence which a famous artist had designed; she matched it. [. . .] She wore a tailored housecoat of russet-colored brocade that blended with the bronze of her hair, the severe simplicity of its lines serving as her only ornament" (799). And yet, the novel cannot let Cheryl rise to the status, and class

position, of the men of the mind. The best fate the novel can give her is a
noble suicide in which she throws herself into the harbor, becoming, as Stacey Olster points out, a "spokesperson for the underlying sense of anomie"
that animates the novel (289). But why can she rise only to suicide? And
similarly, why does the novel strand Eddie, who appears to be very much
on the side of the men of the mind, on an abandoned railway somewhere
in the Arizona desert, "sobbing at the foot of the engine, with the beam of
a motionless headlight above him going off into a limitless night" (1072)?
Why can he not undergo a similar transformation to that of Dagny?

While there is a veritable cottage industry in Rand studies justifying
this narrative decision, I want to suggest that their excision from the plot
has more profound implications for the novel.[11] Eddie and Cheryl represent the fissure between changing one's perspective and changing one's
class position that the novel aims to efface. And here we arrive at the most
important difference between Jurca's white diaspora novels, which remain
trapped in a "fantasy of victimization" (9), and *Atlas Shrugged*. While the
latter animates this sense of victimization—Dagny spends most of the novel
feeling victimized by some mysterious force she cannot control—it does
so only to demand that the reader overcome their victimization, which is
revealed to be either misidentification or, worse, a symptom of not being
on the right side of history. While no characters actually transcend their
class position within the novel, the failure to transcend is always coded as
a personal failing, and so the reader must identify with capital if they are
to identify with the novel's developmental arc. The reader must identify
with Dagny and Galt while they remain trapped in the positions of Eddie
and Cheryl.

And it is ultimately here—in this space between the fate that awaits
the working- and middle-class characters in the novel and the presumed
middle-class reader's identification within the novel—that *Atlas Shrugged*
offers a remarkably canny and prescient model of shock therapy as a form
of reidentification. In the most naked and clear-eyed manner, the novel
lays out the cynical ways that a small group of economic elites can systematically hollow out and destroy urban infrastructure in order to take it over
for capital. And it also lays out the devastating effect that their policies
can have on the white middle-class subjects whose disaffection the novel
animates. That the novel's ending is considered a happy one can occur only
because the reader no longer identifies with the victimized middle class
but rather with the forces of capital. This is Ayn Rand's shock therapy. It
is the transformation of shock from a traumatizing, but potentially revolutionary, force that could lead to collective uplift and transformation, into

an individualizing force that leads not to a change in status or position but rather to a change in individual identification. Shock therapy creates entrepreneurial subjects whose lives appear to them—to return to Matthew Huber's observations—as a "coherent space of privatized freedom [. . .] entirely produced by and reducible to one's own life choices and entrepreneurial efforts" (xv). The result of this reconceptualization is as follows. If the subject's life is entirely of their own making, they have two choices when economic or personal disaster occurs: they can either identify with the winners, those who profit from the shocks, or they can identify with the losers, those who succumb to them. As the novel's conclusion, and more recently history shows, the choice, at least for white Americans, is clear.

CHAPTER 5

Fallen Corpses and Rising Cities:
The Bell Jar and the Making
of the New Woman

At the center of Sylvia Plath's *The Bell Jar* are two transformations: New York's transformation from the nineteenth-century industrial city of slums, tenements, and factories to a shiny new metropolis, and the transformation of Esther, who begins the novel as an anxious, sick, and needy tenderfoot but ends the novel as a seemingly independent, liberated, and autonomous subject. Throughout this book, I've been arguing that the correlation between urban transformations and the transformation of the subject is not incidental. Rather, key processes of transformation playing out in urban and suburban space effectively helped to shape the emergence of a new kind of subjectivity. In this chapter, I argue that *The Bell Jar* offers one of the first fully developed critiques of the racial violence underpinning the formation of this new entrepreneurial subject. Moreover, I suggest that it confronts the limit of this model of entrepreneurial freedom on its own terms.

Published in 1963, *The Bell Jar* is set in 1952 — a date the novel marks by two events that emblematize the overlapping and intersecting dynamics of Cold War history and the transformations taking place in New York City:

the construction of the United Nations Building, which was completed by the end of that year, and the execution of Julius and Ethel Rosenberg on June 19, 1953. Esther arrives into this scene having won a fashion magazine contest that lands her a coveted internship at a women's magazine in New York "for a month, expenses paid, and piles and piles of free bonuses, like ballet tickets and passes to fashion shows and hair stylings at a famous expensive salon and chances to meet successful people in the field of our desire" (3). Through Esther's wide-eyed arrival into Manhattan, Plath provides one of the first comprehensive literary representations of New York in the age of urban renewal. This was a New York composed of the "slick marble and plate-glass fronts along Madison avenue" (2) that housed a booming, postindustrial creative economy marked by an endless parade of commodities and an all-encompassing phantasmagoria of mass cultural forms, from ladies' magazines and commercial radio to movie theaters.

These urban and geopolitical markers have historically been underplayed in *The Bell Jar* criticism, which has largely forefronted how the double bind of consumer mass-culture and patriarchal 1950s values traps and confines women. Within this frame, *The Feminine Mystique* (1963)—that 1950s bible of suburban feminist liberation—is read as the novel's paratext (Dowbnia; Leach), with Esther's mental breakdown becoming both a symptom and a condemnation of frustrated female desire and ambition that reveals the fate of "talented yet powerless women" (Wagner-Martin, 61), or the bodily effects of a "gender-segregated knowledge economy" that doesn't support "Esther's hope of becoming a writer" (Jernigan, 4). Within such a reading, the novel's ending—her escape from New York, her assertion of (a rather circumscribed) sexual agency, and her becoming the author of the memoir we now hold in our hands—serves as evidence of an at least partial triumph in which Esther escapes from the vapidity of women's magazines such as *Ladies' Day*, on the one hand, and the misogynist psychiatric system represented by Dr. Gordon, who tries to shock her into submission, on the other.

The points made by these critics are not wrong. But while these readings often appear to us as feminist, progressive, or even anticapitalist critiques of the liquefying power of the culture industry or the repressive nature of Cold War politics, they are themselves frequently imbricated within racialized processes of urban respatialization and can be seen to aid in the consolidation of new and individualized subjects. In this case, Esther's transformation from the leaky and symptomatic female subject associated with naturalist heroines in the work of Theodor Dreiser, Edith Wharton, or Kate Chopin, to the rugged individualist subject of the Western, enacts the female West Cure we saw emerge in *The Price of Salt* and thus depicts this process of entrepreneurial subject formation.

Esther's personal transformation occurs alongside a recoding of the meaning of shock: from a tool of critical disruption (her use of the Rosenberg execution as an aesthetic and social shock), to a tool of social control and the commodification and domestication of the female body (as with Dr. Gordon's suburban psychiatric hospital), and finally to a tool of healing and liberation in the hands of Dr. Nolan. Shock's transformation from a traumatic to a redemptive force aligns with its recoding into a tool for the consolidation of the body of the white middle-class woman, whose newfound solidity and contentment, in turn, metonymically shores up and protects the United States from the overlapping threats of the Red Scare, fears of urban unrest, and the cultural anomie of suburbia.

All of this, however, turns out not to undermine but to strengthen the importance of considering *The Feminine Mystique* as the novel's paratext. Friedan's forceful critique of the confining limits that patriarchal systems of commodity capitalism place on women through domestication was itself built on an effacement of both the labor of black and poor women, as well as the uneven processes of urbanization and suburbanization that created very different kinds of oppression for different women. As bell hooks put it in her equally canonical critique of *The Feminine Mystique*, Freidan

> did not discuss who would be called in to take care of the children
> and maintain the home if more women like herself were freed from
> their house labor and given equal access with white men to the profes-
> sions. She did not speak of the needs of women without men, without
> children, without homes. She ignored the existence of all non-white
> women and poor white women. She did not tell readers whether it was
> more fulfilling to be a maid, a babysitter, a factory worker, a clerk, or a
> prostitute than to be a leisure class housewife. (1)

While Friedan may have shied away from these questions, however, Plath does not. *The Bell Jar* effectively highlights the often violent erasures of the racialized and ethnic working-class women whose labor helped create this limited vision of white middle-class female liberation.

This process of erasure is forefronted in the novel's depictions of both Esther's psychological vision and also her narrative journey. As Marie Ashe points out, Esther's own identity is often that of an ethnic, poor, and queer woman. Throughout the novel, she compares herself to a Chinese woman (18) and an Indian (118) while her name suggests a Jewish ethnicity; she is working-class, financially precarious and dependent on the wealthy donor Philomena Guinea; and her own sexuality is leaky and fluid as she finds herself tempted by what Marie Ashe describes as the "other-then-heterosexual possibility that recurs throughout *The Bell Jar*," particularly in her relationship to Doreen (223). In this sense, as in *The Price of Salt*, *The Bell Jar*'s narrative of redemption both aligns with, and is about the alignment of, Esther's salvation with the shedding of her working-class position and the shoring up of her whiteness and heterosexuality. But the novel makes explicit the connections between the consolidation of Esther's subjectivity and the physical violence visited on those foreign, poor, or queer bodies that Esther must reject in this process of individual salvation—most notably, through the corpses of the Rosenbergs and then Joan, who become the collateral damage in shaping this new model of white, middle-class, and maternal subjectivity. Moreover, even what on first blush appears to be liberation within the novel turns out to be far more ambivalent. After all, the form of salvation that Esther receives is exactly what she initially wanted to avoid: a domestic life defined by motherhood. Thus, I want to suggest that the novel is at least as much about the formation of the white, middle-class, suburban mother that we assume to be trapped as it is about the entrapment of that middle-class suburban mother. In its dual critique, *The Bell Jar* places the questions of femininity and feminism at the center of the process of neoliberal subject formation. It offers a trenchant critique of both the material violence visited upon foreign and queer bodies that underpinned the construction of this new feminine subjectivity, as well as the limited model of freedom available to her.

Native Agents and Foreign Bodies

The Bell Jar is one of the first novels both set in, and explicitly about, a renewed Manhattan and its psychic sensorium. The novel centers this vision on two emblematic architectural sites: the newly built United Nations (UN) headquarters on Manhattan's East Side, which Esther's window at the Amazon overlooks, and the concrete-and-glass, curtain-walled office buildings lining Manhattan's main drags in which Esther works. Plath's choice of buildings could not be more pertinent. As Samuel Zipp argues:

> The United Nations was the most apt crystallization of the ideals behind New York's ambitious ethic of city rebuilding precisely because it supported Manhattan's claim to world capital status. [. . .] Not only would the city-rebuilding ethic clear slums, rehouse the poor,

and attract new uses to the city center, but it would also remake the
cityscape in the image of the United Nations, implanting in the island's
schist a new urban form that would give all of Manhattan a profile
equal to its title as capital of the world. (37)

The building of the UN headquarters was at once a catalyst for urban
renewal—it was, in fact, a Title 1 project, constituting, as essayist E. B.
White observed, "the greatest housing project of them all" (710)—as well
as an architectural and ideological symbol of a renewed New York. While
the story of New York's bid for the UN has been well-rehearsed, it is worth
briefly repeating here, in order to grasp the significance of the UN headquarters within the novel.[1] Following World War II, city officials began
lobbying with the goal of New York becoming the chosen site for the new
UN headquarters. In early 1946, then New York mayor William O'Dwyer
formed a committee of prominent citizens whose job was to locate and
pitch a location to the UN. They decided on a site near Flushing Mead-
ows in Queens, but the UN site committee refused, citing both technical
problems and the area's relative isolation. It began to appear that New York
would lose its bid. Soon thereafter, however, John D. Rockefeller stepped in
with an $8.5 million offer to purchase several blocks of land in Turtle Bay on
Manhattan's East Side—an area that Robert Moses termed "a malodorous
slaughterhouse district" (Moses 4)—that were owned by real-estate magnate William Zeckendorf. The agreement was that the city would acquire
and give the UN the remaining land in exchange for the UN's agreement
to "construct its permanent headquarters at this location" (2).[2]

For Moses, this arrangement was a double gift. Not only did securing
the UN headquarters bring New York a step closer to his vision of it as a
global capital, but its construction became a prototype for his expansive
vision of renewal.[3] Politically, the UN exemplified the 1949 Housing Act's
vision of public-private partnerships wherein the state would clear away
blighted and "malodorous" districts while private interests would construct new buildings that would both serve a public good and catalyze the
revalorization of entire neighborhoods. Architecturally, the UN helped to
realize Moses's vision for a city in which the dirty and crowded walk-ups
of the old industrial landscape would be replaced by the new glass-skinned
and curtain-walled skyscrapers.[4] In short, the UN brought together Cold
War visions of the United States' safe-and-secure global hegemony alongside more local imaginaries of a new kind of safe-and-secure urbanism: a
prosperous city free from what Le Corbusier, drawing on these entangled

Cold War and renewal metaphors, called "the 'invading and hostile confusion' of unchecked urban development and decay" (qtd. in Zipp 2012, 59).

The Bell Jar is set within this shimmering new city. Esther works in these glass-skinned buildings, her hotel windows overlook the UN, and she has escaped her working-class roots to become what Allison Isenberg has identified as the "quality" consumer that redevelopers sought to lure back downtown (188). And yet, the novel opens with a symbol of both the slums and the war that the UN was meant to efface: the execution of the Rosenbergs. "I knew something was wrong with me that summer," the novel famously opens, "because all I could think about was the Rosenbergs and how stupid I'd been to buy all those uncomfortable, expensive clothes, hanging limp as fish in my closet, and how all the little successes I'd totted up so happily at college fizzled to nothing outside the slick marble and plate-glass fronts along Madison Avenue" (2). Isenberg argues that throughout the 1950s, redevelopers and downtown investors "pinned their future survival on a disappearing white, middle-class customer base" (175). The problem, Isenberg explains, was that since urban centers were becoming increasingly plagued by parking issues, run-down buildings, and a "'ring' of blight" (188)—itself code for mixed and older neighborhoods— they risked losing the white, suburban consumer base they needed to survive. This "urban redevelopment drama" (175) is replayed in *The Bell Jar* as the image of the Rosenbergs disrupts both the acts and spaces of redeveloped middle-class consumption.

Plath's choice of the Rosenbergs is as significant as her choice of the UN. On June 21, 1953, three days after the Rosenbergs' execution, the *New York Times* published a joint obituary that opened, "The Depression brought Julius and Ethel Rosenberg to communism" (E6), and then explained, "Born on Manhattan's poverty-ridden East Side, [the Rosenbergs] embraced the Communist movement in their teens while millions of Americans were out of work and Franklin D. Roosevelt was struggling to put a splintered economy back into one piece" (E6). This obituary wasn't unique. It reflected an oft-repeated connection between the Rosenbergs' early life in the slums and their identity as Russian spies.[5] The slums, as we have seen, were regularly envisioned as being like Third World countries: foreign spaces whose lack of development and modernization made them susceptible to left-wing and seditious influences that could, if uncontained, spread and infect all of American society. The Rosenbergs gave form to such fears.

The Bell Jar plays on this connection between slums and Cold War fears of a foreign threat by transforming the Rosenbergs into a foreign body that invades and infects Esther, alienating her from the shiny promises of postwar prosperity. Their execution, Esther explains, haunted her "like the first time I saw a cadaver. For weeks afterward, the cadaver's head—or what was left of it—floated up behind my eggs and bacon at breakfast" (2). One of Esther's defining features is her hunger, a hunger for experience, particularly sexual ones, for material objects, and especially for food. Unlike the other girls who watch their weight, Esther declares that her "favorite dishes are full of butter and cheese" and that she always picks "the richest, most expensive dishes" at the free luncheons (25). Plath links this hunger to the broader cultural desire for commodities following the deprivations of the Great Depression.[6] But her hunger is also, as Renée Dowbnia points out, "symbolic of the expression and tempering of her larger desires: the freedom not to know what she wants to be (or to balance more than one role) as an adult, sexual freedom and control over her reproduction, and access to the luxuries and privileges of an upper-class lifestyle" (568–69). For Esther, New York has become metonymic of these desires, and she arrives in New York famished for all of it: for experience, upward mobility, and new forms of sexual and economic freedom. And so Esther consumes, voraciously and often to excess. Just as she luxuriates in the mountains of gifts she receives, and just as she seeks out new experiences, so she "paves" her plate with chicken slices, "covers" those chicken slices "thickly" with caviar (28), and "tackles" avocado and crabmeat salad (29).[7]

But this excess is literally poisonous. Shortly after one free lunch, Esther becomes violently ill because, as she is later told, the crabmeat "was chock-full of ptomaine" (50). Ptomaine literally translates as fallen body or corpse and is one of a series of corpse images that connect the world of *Ladies' Day* to that of the Rosenbergs. Importantly, this fallen-corpse lunch occurs immediately after the women receive a tour of the "glossy kitchens" in which the magazine shoots its "lush double-page spreads of technicolor meals" (26). As Kate Baldwin notes, *The Bell Jar* was written in the wake of, and deeply informed by, the so-called "kitchen debate" between Soviet premier Nikita Khrushchev and US vice president Richard Nixon, in which American suburbanism became a key weapon in the Cold War as the achievement of the suburban lifestyle—individual home and car ownership, strict division of male labor and female domesticity, and plentiful and efficient consumer goods—became the measure of American capitalism's superiority over Soviet-style communism (Tyler May, 21). In linking the fallen corpses of the Rosenbergs with the fallen corpses in her avocado and crabmeat, Plath suggests that this most domestic and most contained space, or at least the commodified version put forward by *Ladies'*

Day, is haunted by the Cold War specter of the Rosenbergs and the slums they represent.

It is, I suspect, this insight that underpins the numerous readings of *The Bell Jar* as a critique of the commodified and reified mass-cultural space of postwar urban America and particularly American femininity. In this reading, the Rosenbergs act as something of a reality check or a return of the real: an eddy in the flows of capital that commodity culture hasn't yet penetrated. Here, they provide Esther with a vision of the violence and tumultuous forces lurking beneath the shiny surfaces of consumer culture, and potentially even awaken within her a desire for something different. In this reading, as "foreign bodies," the Rosenbergs function as an archetypal modernist shock capable of shattering the reified façade of daily life.

And yet, the novel rejects this narrative of critical awakening. Esther does not, ultimately, become a critic of this commodified version of New York, or at least not in the way we might hope. Rather, Esther's objections to the vapid commodity culture of this new glass-sheeted world are rooted in her critique of the increasing foreignization of New York: in which both the Rosenbergs and the renewed metropolis become symptoms of a city becoming altogether too foreign. Throughout the novel's opening sections, Esther connects this foreignness with the UN Building, which she describes as hanging in her window like a "weird, green, Martian honeycomb" (19–20). For her, the UN Building is literally responsible for the influx of foreigners to whom she is exposed, while she also worries that this imbrication of new mass culture and foreign bodies is making the city itself foreign. In turn, Esther is concerned that this foreignness is infecting white women, degrading their values and social mores, and turning them into foreign bodies.

Esther is not unique in making this connection. Eric Avila argues that, within the imaginary of white-flight popular culture, white men and women's transgressions of "socially prescribed boundaries"—particularly dominant gender or sexual codes—were implicitly linked with the rise of what he calls "the promiscuous world of the black city" (2004, 81). We see this most clearly in the figure of Doreen: one of the other contest winners, and a southern belle to whom Esther is immediately drawn. Shortly after the novel begins, Esther and Doreen decide to skip a magazine party at the behest of a disc jockey named Lenny Shepherd, a "man in the blue lumber shirt and black chinos and tooled leather cowboy boots" (8), who approaches their taxi and invites them to join him and a friend for a drink before taking them back to his apartment, which is a cross between a frontiersman's cabin and the glass-skinned buildings of Madison Avenue.

In true modern style, Lenny has had "a few partitions knocked down to make the place broaden out" (15), but Esther emphasizes that the place feels like a "ranch, only in the middle of a New York apartment house" (15). Lenny's place is even furnished like a cabin: "Great white bearskins lay about underfoot, and the only furniture was a lot of low beds covered with Indian rugs. Instead of pictures hung up on the walls, he had antlers and buffalo horns and a stuffed rabbit head" (15). In Lenny's home, the modernist frontier cabins of *Atlas Shrugged*'s Atlantis are transported to the city—and with this move, the racial undertones implicit in *Atlas Shrugged* are brought to the surface. In this new and implicitly racialized space of the urban frontier, the line between whiteness and blackness begins to blur as their sexual mores begin to loosen.

Throughout the novel's opening pages, Doreen is an object of fascination and fetishization for Esther as an emblem of whiteness. So much so that when she puts on a white dress, Esther comments that it makes her appear "so white she looked silver" (10). However, as Doreen moves deeper into the promiscuous world of New York, her skin begins to change until she becomes "dusky as a bleached blonde negress" (12). When Lenny puts on music and they begin to dance, the intermingled racialization and sexualization of Doreen's body intensifies until her breasts literally spill out of her dress, "swing[ing] out slightly like full brown melons" (18), and she begins to bite Lenny in a lascivious and wild frenzy. Strangely, though, Esther relates to this scene not as a foreigner in an American city, or even as a suburbanite in an urban center, but instead as a US businessman in the decolonizing Third World. Watching Lenny and Doreen dance, she tries "to look devout and impassive like some businessmen I once saw watching an Algerian belly-dancer" (17), but is unable to and ultimately runs of the apartment. Once outside, Esther fares no better because New York itself has become a foreign country: she is accosted by the "*tropical*, stale heat the sidewalks had been sucking up all day" which "hit [her] in the face like a last insult" (18, emphasis mine). Later, she will comment that the rain in New York isn't "the nice kind of rain that rinses you clean, but the sort of rain I imagine they must have in Brazil" (42). This peculiar transmutation in which a white southerner and a northern disc jockey transform into a Third World belly dancer/negress and a frontiersman emblematizes the bizarre overlapping of urban renewal discourses that link together the frontier, the decolonizing Third World, and Avila's promiscuous black city.

The sympathy we feel for Esther's antipathy toward the vapid commodity culture of *Ladies' Day* rubs up uncomfortably against her racial aversion to the city. There are moments, Kate Baldwin suggests, when *The Bell Jar* shifts from "desire and identification" with Esther to "distance and perhaps even dislike" (22). Her construction of the city as foreign is, or at least should be, one of these moments. That is, while the novel is sympathetic to her critique of the commodified culture of New York, it is less sympathetic to how that critique of commodification transforms into a critique of the city's foreignness, and also to how Esther's solidarity with the Rosenbergs is replaced by a hysteria about the city's foreignness as a material and existential threat to her being.

The Bell Jar highlights the critical distance we are meant to feel by emphasizing the exact nature of this perceived danger or threat. The new international and cosmopolitan nature of New York forces Esther to confront her own failings: her lack of worldly knowledge, and the limits of her significance and import. This becomes clear when her boss, Jay Cee, calls her into the office for her seeming disinterest with her work. Esther tries to list her aspirations—"getting some big scholarship to graduate school or a grant to study all over Europe, and then I thought I'd be a professor and write books of poems" (33)—but all of these visions of herself disintegrate as Jay Cee tells her what she needs to succeed: namely, more foreign languages. After all, she explains, "Hundreds of girls flood into New York every June thinking they'll be editors. You need to offer something more than the run-of-the-mill person" (35). With this warning, Esther's dreams unravel, as she realizes that both her assumed value, and her assumed trajectory of upward mobility, might not be as secure as she previously thought.

Esther's marked lack of value, her lack of "specialness," becomes more explicitly apparent when she visits the UN as the guest of Constantin, the simultaneous interpreter with whom her boyfriend's mother puts her in touch. When she first hears of Constantin, she expects that he will love her "passionately the minute he [meets her]" (54). She expects to play the role of the desired white woman, but that is not what happens. When Constantin takes her to the UN, she begins to confront her own limitations: "I couldn't speak German or read Hebrew or write Chinese. I didn't even know where most of the odd out-of-the-way countries the UN men in front of me represented fitted on the map" (79). And this realization about her lack of knowledge—of other languages and of the world at large— triggers an additional series of painful apprehensions: "For the first time in my life, sitting there in the sound-proof heart of the UN building between Constantin who could play tennis as well as simultaneously interpret and the Russian girl who knew so many idioms, I felt dreadfully inadequate. The trouble was, I had been inadequate all along, I simply hadn't thought about it" (80). And it is here that the real nature of Esther's anxiety and aversion to New York reveals itself: she can't compete. "I felt," she explains, "like a racehorse in a world without race-tracks or a champion college footballer suddenly confronted by Wall Street and a business suit" (80). What this suggests is that her anxiety about the foreignness of the city is not, as we might expect, about the decaying of the city—the loss of its quality, character, or value—but rather a confrontation with her *own* quality and character, with the loss of her *own* value.

This context is central to the novel's critique of what initially appears as a rehashing of white-flight beliefs that cast the city as a space of decline, danger, and anomie. Indeed, in *The Bell Jar*, the primary threat that foreign men seem to pose to Esther is that they *don't* want her. Even when the novel most explicitly traffics in the trope of dangerous and lascivious foreign men, namely the scene where Esther is almost raped by Marco, a man from Peru—a place where, as Esther tells us, "they're squat" and "ugly as Aztecs" (108)—it is nevertheless marked by the foreign man not really desiring her but instead his cousin. Meanwhile, Constantin won't even seduce her when she crawls into his bed. The novel emphasizes the imbrication of race and rejection by aligning this moment of failed seduction with both Constantin's "tanned skin" darkening such that it appears to be "almost black" (86), and Esther's descent into a deep insecurity. Lying beside him, she thinks, "if only I had a keen, shapely bone-structure to my face or could discuss politics shrewdly or was a famous writer Constantin might find me interesting enough to sleep with" (86). Reversing the noir codes, these scenes suggest that the real threat to Esther is not the promiscuous black city, which doesn't really want her anyway. Rather, it is that the foreign and racializing city forces middle-class white womanhood to confront its own inadequacies and limitations, and to confront the waning value of whiteness itself. *The Bell Jar* thus suggests the ways in which white-flight fantasies that cast white flight as an escape from a morally degraded city to a better, more prosperous and superior city might also be understood as a flight away from, and a fear of, one's own inadequacy.

The Rest Cure

However, if the city is a source of trauma, the cure—her flight from the city and to the safety, security, and homogeneity of the suburbs—fares no better. In fact, the suburbs come to appear like a vision of Silas Weir Mitchell's "rest cure," a prescription for all female nervous disorders that called for the removal of all stimulus and particularly that of intellectual and physical work.[8] Its most famous critique, Charlotte Perkins Gilman's 1892 novel *The Yellow Wallpaper*, aimed to show that stripping women of intellectual labor and artistic expression also stripped them of their subjectivity and exacerbated the very nervous diseases the rest cure meant to treat. *The Bell Jar* depicts Esther's return to the suburbs within the ambit of such a cure, both by comparing the suburbs to a prison and by aligning the suburbs with the opposite of writing and creative endeavors. Not only does Esther compare her mother's car to "a prison van" (120), and the "white, shining, identical clapboard houses with their interstices of well-groomed green [. . . to] one bar after another in a large but escape-proof cage" (120), but upon entering the car/prison carriage, her mother informs her that she "didn't make that writing course" (120), and thus instead of going to Cambridge, Esther will be stuck in the suburbs with the possibility of writing taken away from her.

But the clearest twinning occurs when Esther is taken to undergo shock therapy at the private hospital of Dr. Gordon in Waltham. The hospital is notably marked by "yellow clapboard walls" (148) with a "green dome of the lawn" on which no one walks (148): details that echo both the wallpaper and garden of Perkins Gilman's story. The shock that Dr. Gordon inflicts on Esther brings out her worst fears about the execution of the Rosenbergs. At the novel's beginning, she worries that being shocked would feel like being "burned alive all along your nerves" (1). Dr. Gordon's shocks bear this out. She describes her experience of being shocked thusly: "Then something went down and took hold of me and shook me like the end of the world. Whee-ee-ee-ee-ee, it shrilled, through an air crackling with blue light, and with each flash a great jolt drubbed me till I thought my bones would break and the sap fly out of me like a split plant" (151). Moreover, when Esther wakes up and finds herself sitting on the porch with the other women in the clinic, she seems to have become a cadaver. Or at least not quite alive. She explains that she feels as if she were "sitting in the window of an enormous department store," only "the figures around me weren't people, but shop dummies, painted to resemble people and propped up in attitude counterfeiting life" (149–50).

By now, we have seen a few other dummies: namely, the lynched mannequins in *Invisible Man*, and the dolls Therese sells in *The Price of Salt*, both of which express what Hal Foster identifies as the "uncanny changes wrought upon bodies and objects in the high capitalist epoch [. . . particularly the] remaking of the body (especially the female body) as commodity" (126). Mannequins, Foster contends, evoke the "uncanny confusion between life and death" (126) that lies at the heart of a Taylorist regime of

mass production, consumption, and commodification. Foster's interpretation of the mannequin's uncanniness draws on a remarkably Benjaminian
account of industrialization and the processes through which the automation of labor and urbanization effectively discipline and commodify the
body—and particularly, as we saw in *The Price of Salt*, the female body.

Foster's account of the commodification of the female body, however,
differs greatly from the accounts of commodification that underpin most
critiques of the novel. Whereas for Foster, the process of commodification is tied up with the subsumption of bodies into capital—and specifically how industrial and Taylorist work both disciplines and mechanizes
the body—for critics of *The Bell Jar*, commodification becomes entirely
tied to consumption.[9] This difference can partially be explained by the
theoretical inclinations of Plath critics who have tended to eschew Marx-
ist frameworks for more culturalist or consumerist accounts of modernity
and the novel. But more profoundly, what these critics are reflecting is an
important material shift occurring *within* capitalism, a shift of which *The
Bell Jar* is acutely aware: namely, the retrenchment of traditional gender
roles and the retethering of femininity to domesticity that occurred as suburbanization and the so-called postwar deal brought a certain stratum of
largely white women workers back into the home.[10] With this change, the
locus of the uncanny moves from labor to consumption. Thus, unlike in
the earlier naturalist novels (and in novels like *The Price of Salt* that are still
at least partially linked to the naturalist novels) where it is the shopgirl figure who is associated with mannequins and automation, in *The Bell Jar*, Esther becomes the mannequin only once she has left the workforce and the
industrialized space of northern cities (and particularly the shop windows
within them). Her commodification, in other words, traces the white-flight
path of the female worker-turned-shopper from the glass-skinned office
towers and department stores downtown back to suburban domesticity.

The shifting of the locus of feminine commodification from the city to
the suburbs occurs alongside the novel's recasting of the suburban hospital
as part of the very nineteenth-century industrial spaces that renewal sought
to clear: with its "table on wheels with a machine on it" (151), "smelly
grease" used to prepare her skin, and the "two metal plates" placed on her
head and the wire she needs to bite (151).[11] Like the paint factory in *Invisible Man*, the space of shock in the novel is an outmoded industrial space.
In *The Bell Jar*, however, Plath places this space in the suburbs: that is, the
very safe-and-secure enclave of white middle-class domestic femininity.
It is neither work nor racialized urban mass-culture but rather suburban
femininity that ultimately transforms her into a corpse or automaton.

Indeed, following her shock therapy, Esther seems to be completely transformed into a lifeless state that is tellingly defined by her lack of productive work—in terms of both paid labor as well as socially useful activity. She spends her days "circling" the public garden, feeding the pigeons "dead"-tasting peanuts, sitting on benches staring blankly at beaches and sandbars, and listlessly "pushing round magazines and candy and flowers" at a hospital ward (171). For Esther, while the shocks of New York were traumatic, the suburban rest cure is tantamount to death. The only thing that seems to prevent Esther from killing herself is the fact that she is too tired to perform, or incapable of carrying out, the labor necessary to do so. She thinks about jumping off a building but concludes that "if you didn't pick the right number of storeys, you might still be alive when you hit bottom" (144); she considers cutting herself in a bathtub but realizes that her "dallying had used up the better part of the morning and that my mother would probably come home and find me before I was done" (157); she tries swimming out "until I was too tired to swim back" but somehow returns unscathed; she tries to hang herself, but is too "poor at knots and had no idea how to make a proper one" (167). Stripped of all purpose, Esther is left to linger within the realm of the undead. When Esther finally does figure out how to kill herself, it is in the most passive way possible: she crawls into in the breezeway of her mother's basement—a site that evokes both the haunted spaces of domesticity, and the damp, decayed spaces of the prerenewal city—surrounds herself in darkness, lugs "heavy-dust-covered logs across the hole mouth," takes at "least fifty pills," and lets them rush her "to sleep" (179).

The Urban West Cure

Of course, Esther's near-death in the crawlspace—like the Invisible Man's move to the underground and Dagny's arrival in Atlantis—is not an actual death but a symbolic one: a key moment in the construction of a new kind of subjectivity. While the first half of the novel tracks the movement from city to suburb, and symbolically into death, the second part repeats this movement, but with a difference. Instead of tracking a journey toward death, Esther's movement from the city to the suburbs becomes a journey of rebirth and transformation. Why? I suggest that in this repetition, the novel comes to allegorize a new pact between suburbanization and a limited and specifically white, middle-class form of female liberation.

In order to effect this transformation, however, the meaning of the city must change. In the first part of the novel, the city is a frontier: clean, new, postindustrial, and modern, while the suburbs are associated with the outdated machines of an industrial past. In the second part of the novel, this reverses. The suburbs become the healthy, modern, and natural space envisioned by modernist architects and planners while the city becomes an outmoded space of cultural poverty and backwardness. This recoding of the city within a developmentalist logic of backwardness is crucial to Esther's psychological "healing." She must abandon her earlier positions of affinity (most notably with the Rosenbergs) and inferiority (in relation to the UN workers) and come to see the city and its inhabitants as backwards. This transformation occurs through a shift in scene from New York to Boston, and more specifically, to the *public* mental hospital in Boston. When Esther wakes up from her suicide attempt, she finds herself in the psychiatric ward in the city hospital, which is marked by the "negro orderly" who brings the patients their food (191). Esther is immediately repulsed and enraged by him. She describes, in painstaking detail, how he "bang[s] down the tureens and then the dinted silver and the thick, white china plates" and how "he gawp[s] at us with big, rolling eyes" (191), and she is convinced that he is there to test her when he brings a "wodge of macaroni, stone-cold and stuck together in a gluey paste" and "two kinds of beans" (192), commenting that "he was just trying to see how much we would take" (192).

Reading this interaction in the context of the Cold War, Baldwin argues that it serves to "link the discontent of white middle-class women to racial emancipation and the demystification of the Soviet other" (36). She further suggests that the encounter between Esther and the "negro" is an image of "the black worker peering into Esther's prison [. . . while] peering out from his. What we learn from this passage is that her imprisonment relies in part on his and vice versa" (35). While their respective imprisonments may very well be linked, this is certainly not how Esther experiences the encounter. Moreover, such a reading ignores the ways in which the entire hospital in Boston is coded as both a public and racialized space: a space beneath Esther, and a space from which she must escape. After all, it's not just the orderlies who are black. It is also the doctor who, notably, "looked very like Doctor Gordon, except that he had black skin where Doctor Gordon's skin was white" (189–90). The point of the Boston hospital scene is not one of solidarity. Quite the opposite. It serves to rewrite the far more vexed space of New York as both too cosmopolitan and too good for her, into the far more familiar codes of the city as a decaying, racialized, and substandard space not fit for white femininity: a space from which she must be rescued.

This recoding occurs alongside Plath's reinterpretation of the suburbs. If they previously served as an appropriate backdrop for a Silas Weir
Mitchell–style rest cure, they now became a frontier setting for his "camp,"
or West Cure. This is why it is so important that, while the private hospital looks "like a country club" (196), it is connected to Native American
history—such that when she arrives, a "handsome white-haired doctor"
explains to her "about the Pilgrims and Indians and who had the land after
them, and what rivers ran nearby" (198). What distinguishes Dr. Nolan's
clinic from that of Dr. Gordon, the novel suggests, is the shift from the
manicured garden associated with the rest cure to the untrammeled "outdoors" epitomized by the West Cure. This new hospital is able to bring together the frontier cultures of both the rugged wilderness and New York,
while placing them within a suburban setting. But unlike *Atlas Shrugged*,
what is at stake in *The Bell Jar* is not the strengthening and remasculiniz-
ing of the urban businessman but instead the (re)formation of the modern
suburban woman. What this suggests is Plath's own sense that perhaps the
new figure of US global dominance was not the cowboy businessman that
it was at the turn of the century (Kuenz; Will) but rather the modern suburban woman.

What makes this conclusion so peculiar is that this West Cure occurs
via the very process the novel has thus far rejected: namely, through *shock*.
Timothy Melley argues that we should conceive of *The Bell Jar* as part of
the broader tendency of postwar literature to deploy "the image of elec-
troconvulsive therapy" as a metaphor for brainwashing: and particularly
with the kind of brainwashing associated with "the construction of Cold
War femininity" (161). Melley here aligns with the dominant readings I've
tracked thus far in which the novel's politics, and above all its feminist
politics, lie in its assertion of the importance of the individual against an
increasingly powerful, domineering, and patriarchal Cold War state. But
these readings are unable to account for the novel's concluding gesture.
How can we simultaneously read this novel as a critique, and particularly a
feminist critique, of the manipulation and brainwashing of women by the
Cold War state when the novel ends with Esther's cure being carried out
through shock therapy and specifically through a form of shock therapy
carried out by a woman in a private clinic? And not just any woman but,
as Linda Wagner-Martin points out, the central "mother figure" in the
novel (60)?

When Dr. Nolan tricks Esther into undergoing yet another round of
shock therapy, Esther is pleased to discover that—unlike the shocks she

experiences from the memory of the Rosenbergs, or the shocks she under-goes at Dr. Gordon's hospital—these shocks are stripped of their relation-ship to the uncanny or to brainwashing. Instead, her experience of shock therapy apes the promises offered by its proponents such as Ewen Cam-eron, who believed that shock could "break up old pathological patterns" by "depatterning the subject" and returning "the mind to a state [. . . of] tabula rasa" (Klein, 36). It is precisely this language that Esther uses when she describes her experience being shocked as being "wiped out like chalk on a blackboard" (226). Here, shock moves from away from its previous iterations as a destabilizing force connected to the city and its dangerous and leaky urban scene, or a controlling and deadening force, connected to the suburbanization and entrapment of women, and becomes instead a safe and controllable force that resets the subject: clearing them of their confu-sion, their symptomatic body, and their irrational desires.

At first, Esther's experience of shock under the watchful eye of Dr. Nolan does appear to be a genuinely liberatory and feminist form of shock therapy, one which allows her to achieve what she has been looking for all along: notably, the loss of her virginity. And this is why, although Dr. Nolan's hospital might initially echo that of Dr. Gordon, they are clearly distin-guished. Whereas Dr. Gordon's Waltham hospital, as the wallpaper makes clear, shocks women into mannequins and creates submissive and beaten-down feminine subjects, this new hospital is staffed by female doctors and promotes women's emancipation. Furthermore, Dr. Nolan herself is the also the chief exemplar of this new model of womanhood: elite, profes-sional, independent, and sexually liberated. Dr. Nolan is a psychiatrist, she smokes, and she dresses stylishly, wearing "a white blouse and a full skirt gathered at the waist by a wide leather belt, and stylish, crescent-shaped spectacles" (197). Moreover, while the entire clinic's approach to mental health is effectively that of a finishing school—replete with "white linen table-cloths and glasses and paper napkins" (198) and populated with "fashionably dressed and carefully made up" women who play music on the grand piano or play bridge and chat and even go "shopping downtown" (217–18)—unlike boarding schools, it is a space where sex and sexuality are permitted and even encouraged. Dr. Nolan, for instance, goes so far as to get Esther an appointment to acquire a still-illegal diaphragm. How-ever, while Dr. Nolan is not exactly antisex, what she prescribes for Esther and what Esther experiences is less about sexual experience or the libidinal than it is about a negotiation of white middle-class female sexuality in a safe, contained, and controlled way.

Sex and sexuality are associated with danger in *The Bell Jar*. Whether it is the attempted rape of Esther, the queer desire of Joan, or the violent sexual encounter between Doreen and Lenny, sex is a dangerous and uncontrollable force that transgresses boundaries. It is Dr. Nolan's job to help the women she treats control and contain those forces, and it is ultimately this containment that is achieved in this New England version of the West Cure. Esther's devirgination crucially plays two key roles here. First, it rewrites the Constantin scene. Esther's sense of inadequacy brought on by the female Russian interpreter is replaced through Olga, "A large, bosomy Slavic lady in a bulky sweater of natural sheep's wool, purple slacks, high-heeled black overshoes with Persian lamb cuffs and a matching toque" (239), whom Irwin rejects for Esther, thus restoring Esther's whiteness as a marker of desirability. Second, it creates the controlled danger necessary for Esther's West Cure. However, like Mitchell's West Cure, such a danger was only ever a patina; the West Cure was never meant to be actually dangerous. In his descriptions of these forays west, he discusses the importance of good guides and plenty of food. It was, as Will reminds us, "far less 'confrontational'" and dangerous than his writings suggested it might be (301). What was accomplished by a move to the great outdoors in the traditional Western novels of Wister et al. is here accomplished through sex. Thus, while Esther's loss of virginity is dangerous—Esther is literally wounded by it and ends up hemorrhaging—her wound is fully healable, and she can be bolstered and recontained. As her doctor puts it, "I can fix it all right" (235).

The Bell Jar ends with the assertion, "I am, I am, I am" (256), a statement not unlike Ellison's protagonist who proclaims, "I yam what I yam what I yam," but stripped of its irony. At the end of the novel, Esther calls Irwin and presents him with a bill for twenty dollars. When he asks when she'll see him again, she replies "never," hangs up the phone, and—realizing that his voice "had meant nothing to her"—comments, "I was perfectly free" (255). She is what she is. But what is the meaning of this perfect freedom and, relatedly, what is this new subject position that Esther achieves? Her sense of freedom and identity are intricately linked to the erasure of the numerous doublings that haunt her throughout the book. Ashe suggests that we read *The Bell Jar*'s ending "as a figurative 'killing' of Ethel Rosenberg [. . .] the distancing, displacement, and banishment—through the construction of Esther Greenwood—of a troubling model of 1950s woman, a model of disturbingly unsuccessful marriage and motherhood culminating in destruction" (222). By the end of the novel, the Rosenbergs and their corpses do seem to have finally been laid to rest. And yet, their corpse returns in a different form, this time in the body of Joan, a friend of Esther who commits suicide. Like the Rosenbergs, Joan is another double of Esther, and like the Rosenbergs, she is a double that Esther must disavow. The nature of the threat that Joan poses to Esther is not racialized, but sexualized. Unlike Esther, Joan is entirely unafraid of her desire. She just states it. "I like you," she tells Esther. "That's tough," Esther replies, "You make me puke" (232). Shortly thereafter, Joan fulfills her role as the tragic lesbian figure Patricia Highsmith radically broke with: helping Esther when she begins to hemorrhage after her sexual encounter with Irwin before vanishing from the novel by hanging herself.

Joan's corpse brings us back to the ptomaine, the fallen corpse, and again to the Rosenbergs, a doubling the novel emphasizes when Esther compares Joan to a "martian" (231) and thus implicitly to the UN, where the novel began. But again with a difference. When Joan dies, Dr. Nolan assures Esther that she doesn't need to attend the funeral, but Esther goes anyway and throughout wonders "what I thought I was burying" (242). The answer comes through Esther's description of the funeral:

> At the altar the coffin loomed in its snow pallor of flowers—the black shadow of something that wasn't there. [. . .] Behind the coffin and the flowers and the face of the minister and the faces of the mourners, I saw the rolling lawns of our town cemetery, knee-deep in snow now, with the tombstones rising out of it like smokeless chimneys. There would be a black, six-foot-deep gap hacked in the hard ground. That shadow would marry this shadow, and the peculiar, yellowish soil of our locality seal the wound in the whiteness, and yet another snowfall erases the traces of newness in Joan's grave. (242)

This remarkable passage outlines very clearly what Esther is burying: her old self, the parts of her that need to be sloughed off to embody her new subject position. Specifically, through the burial of her queerness via Joan, Esther also buries her association with the Holocaust and Jewishness through the "smokeless chimneys," and her association with the ethnically and racially mixed city through the "black [. . .] gap" and "yellowish soil," all of which is healed and "sealed" with the "whiteness" of snow. This language of "sealing" is also an echo of the sealing she must undergo to staunch the wound of her lost virginity, and it is this final sealing—at once sexual, racial, and ethnic—that leads to her declaration of identity formation, "I am, I am, I am" (256).

By the end of the novel, Esther is free. She has purged herself of the Rosenbergs, of Joan, and of her own racial and sexual indeterminacies. And we finally arrive at the real form that shock takes on in *The Bell Jar*: not Cold War brainwashing but instead a crucial tool in the production of a new kind of female subject, one predicated on a new political pact that transforms suburbia from a space of domestic incarceration to one of sexual liberation. If Highsmith shows us the how the city becomes rebuilt in the suburbs, Plath shows us how the suburbs takes on the veneer of the city. In both cases, however, we conclude in spaces that take on the excitement of the city, but stripped of its foreign, racialized, and working-class elements.

Unlike Highsmith, Plath is far more ambivalent about the kind of freedom Esther achieves. Like *Invisible Man*, *The Bell Jar* begins at its end—it is framed as a personal reflection of a character who is trying to explain how they became who (and where) they are. In this case, though, what we learn about Esther is limited: simply that she has kept the "the make up kit" she received (4) and that she is now a mother. "I use the lipsticks now and then," Esther explains, "and last week I cut the plastic starfish off the sun-glasses case for the baby to play with" (4). That is all. We don't know if she is a writer. In fact, we don't know anything else about her. All we know is that she is a mother, a highly ambivalent ending for a novel that began by comparing suburban domesticity to death. Thus, while Melley is right that the novel offers a critique of electroshock therapy as a metaphor for the larger social transformations occurring in the postwar period, its primary site of critique is not the brainwashing Cold War state, or even the mass culture industry of feminization, but rather the privatization, individualization, and lactification of women's liberation.

What makes *The Bell Jar* such a remarkable novel, however, is that it doesn't take middle-class white women's misery as the ultimate horizon of politics. *The Bell Jar* is not *The Feminine Mystique*, and it is not just that Esther's solution is unsatisfactory. Rather, the novel links Esther's psychic misery with the far more material violence visited on those racialized, poor, and queer subjectivities that Esther rejects: most notably through the corpses of the Rosenbergs and then Joan, who all become refigured as the collateral damage in shaping this new model of white, middle-class, and maternal subjectivity. *The Bell Jar* limns both the process through which white middle-class women's horizons for freedom are foreclosed, and that process's relationship to urban underdevelopment and suburban over-development; the alienation and vilification of queerness and foreignness;

and the very material violences visited upon racialized and queered bodies alongside the reimprisonment of the middle-class white woman. What we receive at the end, then, is a picture of the very uneven processes through which a new suburban white feminism is forged, and ultimately a model of what neoliberal freedom looks like: a model of freedom that turns out to be not so free at all.

Conclusion: *The Siege of Harlem* and Its Commune

In a book about shock and the 1950s, it is tempting to look ahead toward postmodernism and make a claim for the 1950s' import in the shaping and unleashing both the rebellious energies of the 1960s and, through that, the stylistic and theoretical experimentalism and energies of postmodernism. I resist this temptation by turning not to the real future but to a counterfactual one, a future in which Harlem declares independence from New York and the United States and becomes a great black capital: a center of a new vision of global modernity in which shock is notably absent. To do so, however, I shift from one temptation to another: to end my account of urban renewal with the compulsively repeated, if often factually wrong, tale of the seemingly improbable and triumphant fall of Robert Moses at the hands of Jane Jacobs.

The myth of how Jacobs and the Committee to Save the West Village successfully fought to save Greenwich Village from Moses's Lower Manhattan Expressway proposal is now something of a legend. Throughout the 1950s and 1960s, at the height of his career, Moses made three attempts to redevelop Greenwich Village and its surrounding areas. First, in the early 1950s, he attempted to build a road through Washington Square Park.

Second, in 1961, he attempted to designate the West Village for renewal, declaring it a "predominant non-residential area characterized by blight and suitable for clearance, replanning, reconstruction or rehabilitation" (qtd. in Klemek, 313), and putting forth a proposal that included plans to clear the mixed-use houses and warehouses near Jacobs's home to make room for a high-rise, low-income public housing project. Third, in 1962, he attempted to build an expressway across Broome Street that would have destroyed much of the neighborhood that became SoHo. In each of these battles, Jacobs and what Moses archly and offensively called her "bunch of mothers" (qtd. in Fishman, 125) defeated him, essentially marking an end to his reign and that of urban renewal more broadly.[1]

Jacobs's victory over Moses is often read as the victory of the "walkers" over the planners" (11) or of the "view from the ground" over the "view from the tower" (Zipp 2012, 11). It was the heroic and necessary symbolic defeat of what James C. Scott calls "authoritarian high modernism" (87), itself typified by Moses's slash-and-burn approach to urbanism: the cutting of freeways into the heart of ethnic working-class communities, and the bulldozing of entire neighborhoods for modernist housing projects, cultural centers, or hospitals, all in the interests of a ruthless administrative order. It is also a story of the rise of the local—of citizens' power and the importance valuing and preserving what Jacobs famously called the "intricate ballet of the city sidewalk" (61). Finally, it is a narrative that fits nicely into a genealogy that includes the barricades of Paris 68 and the Reclaim the Streets parties of the alter-Globalization movement at the turn of the millennium. And yet, it is an account that feels oddly out of step with—or better yet, segregated from—the largely black and Puerto Rican, and often Communist Party (CP)—supported, urban struggles and campaigns of the 1940s and 1950s that explicitly linked struggles over urban space to larger struggles against white supremacy, US imperialism, and capitalism.

More pointedly, the story of the West Village isn't just out of step with, or separate from that story. Rather, the victory of Jacobs's call for the withdrawal of the activist, modernist state and her vision of what Scott Larson terms "democratic individualism" (10) often ended up exacerbating the urban poverty, ghettoization, and segregation that these campaigns were struggling against. In the coming years, Jacobs's vision of the urban village itself was easily transformed into a marketing slogan to sell high-priced condos in often poor or low-income areas, thus driving out local residents and capitalizing on the rent gaps created by state neglect. In other words, if Moses's actions shaped the first round of "negro removal" and urban redevelopment, Jacobs's vision of the urban village underpinned the second: allowing a new generation of planners and developers to, in the words of one city official, "build like Moses with Jacobs in mind" (qtd. in Larson, 3).

Eric Avila has gone so far as to call Jacobs, in language that echoes Moses's own condemnation of Jacobs, the "mother of neoconservatism" (2014, 67). As he explains:

> She railed against the interventions of government and its audacious figureheads but she said nothing about the radical forces of capitalism that ravaged her neighborhood, pushing out factories, affordable housing, and struggling artists while enforcing broader disparities of race, wealth and poverty. Her color-blind polemic altogether ignored these patterns of rising inequality, even as they made a starker imprint on the landscape of the postwar American city. (67)

Sharon Zukin similarly argues that the problem with Jacobs's vision, and thus with our celebrating of Jacobs's legacy, is that she fundamentally misread the political situation and thus mistook the enemy. By 1960, when Jacobs had finished *The Death and Life of Great American Cities*, Zukin explains, the city clearly "lay in the grip of two malevolent forces, government and developers" (2009, 220). But instead of targeting either developers, or the state's increasingly close relationship with developers, Jacobs "directed her ire at architects and bureaucrats" (220), who were only secondary figures. And this misidentification, Zukin argues, made her unable to see that her own vision of the urban village would "even without concerted planning by the state" ultimately "grease the wheel of developers' high-stakes, large-scale projects" (227), projects that would ironically replace the very landscapes Jacobs was fighting to preserve with new landscapes of generic chain stores and uniform condominiums, creating an updated and even more pernicious and antipoor version of top-down, homogeneous modernism.

If Jacobs misidentified the sources of power, and thus of the problem, there were many postwar intellectuals and activist groups in the United States who did not. Building on its long history working with interracial tenant groups on the question of housing and ghettoization, the New York Communist Party (CP) in the postwar period argued that housing should be a strategic priority as it was a key site where "the interlocking oppression of white supremacy and American capitalism" occurred (Biondi, 127).[2] Thus, throughout the 1940s and 1950s, the CP worked in alliance with New York civil rights groups and tenant organizations, taking on segregated private housing developments like Metropolitan Life's Stuyvesant Town. For both the CP and the tenant and neighborhood groups, labor activists, political groups, and civil rights organizers with whom they worked, housing was part of a larger struggle to create an inclusive, international urbanism that served working-class communities instead of capital.[3] While the political and intellectual influence of this Communist-inflected Left waned in response to internal divisions, Nikita Khrushchev's "secret speech" that revealed the extent of the horrors of Stalinism, and the anticommunist crusade of Truman and the Red Scare, it did not vanish.

Instead, this resolutely internationalist and anticapitalist urban vision lived on, finding its way into the radical reading groups and student organizations, which formed at the expanding community college and state university systems in California and New York, and which contributed to the founding of groups like the Black Panther Party, Young Lords, and Black Workerist parties.[4] These groups, like many other 1960s organizations, came out of cities, organized in cities, thought seriously about cities, and offered trenchant theorizations of the role that cities played within the larger horizon of US imperialism and its increasingly global circuits of capital. Moreover, the forms of organizing these new groups carried out— in factories, apartment blocks, schools, churches, and in the streets—also did the work of creating a new strand of anti-imperialist urban internationalism, a resurgent form of Commune thinking. Why, then, aren't the numerous urban struggles carried out by these radical movements considered alongside, or evaluated against, those of Jacobs? Moreover, why aren't the intellectual architects of these movements such as Huey Newton, José Jiménez, or James Boggs considered foundational urban thinkers or theorists?

I want to conclude by taking up this counterurbanism and the threads of postwar Commune thinking developed therein, by considering how it was registered in a somewhat unlikely place: Warren Miller's 1964 *Siege of Harlem*, a vexing and strange novel written by a Jewish journalist that imagines a counterfactual history in which Harlem secedes from New York and the United States, thus "originat[ing] itself as one of the great black capitals of this earth" (7–8). I do so not because it is a particularly "good" or "radical" novel—it is neither—but rather because of the politics its historical, generic, and temporal strangeness allows us to recuperate. Carlo Rotella and others have suggested that *Siege*'s "ghetto insurrection anticipates a reading of the 1960s riots" (240). This is true, but it is a novel that is as much about the New York's residual two-decade-old, and often CP-led, civil rights movement as it is a novel about the emergent regime of black power and urban rebellion. Poised on the fulcrum between these two periods, *Siege* registers the longer thread of international urbanism connecting the two that propounded a very different kind of modernity: a vision that is both rooted in, and a challenge to, the contradictions of the new regime of segregation and expanded accumulation that emerged in the postwar period.

The Siege of Harlem begins seventy-five years after Harlem declares independence. Employing and subverting the form of the Uncle Remus stories and the plantation romance, *Siege* unfolds through the recollections of an elderly Harlemite as he recounts the story of Harlem's struggle to survive its first year against the ideological, military, diplomatic, and mass-cultural onslaught of the United States, or what it calls the "Privileged People," to his grandchildren—who all have names like Ngomo, Jomo, Mboya, Sekou, and Shabad. Like all the novels this book has examined, *Siege* is very much about the landscapes created by the violent processes of urban renewal, and it is also a novel whose very imaginative premise relies on urban renewal projects: in this case, what E. B. White terms the "greatest housing project of them all," the United Nations. It is the watchful eye of the UN, and particularly of the representatives of Third World member states who reside in New York as a result of its presence, that enables Harlem's secession to occur, and that prevents the United States from engaging in an outright military invasion. As Lance Huggins, the charismatic House of Commons member turned revolutionary leader, repeatedly emphasizes, it is only because of their "good friends in the international picture down at the UN. It was on account of outraging this opinion" that the United States didn't invade Harlem to reunite the country (15).

Unlike many of the other novels reviewed thus far, however (with the exception of *Atlas Shrugged*), *Siege* conforms to the genre of what Fredric Jameson, in "The Politics of Utopia," terms the "textual utopia" (2004, 36). Jameson argues that the textual utopia centers on a world in which the "root of all evil," however the author defines it, "has been eliminated" (36). For instance, he explains that in Thomas More, "what every reader famously takes away—as from Plato, too—is the abolition of private property" (36). In *Siege*, as well, private property (and thus class) is abolished. "That thing of class," comments Jomo, one of the children of the future, is "so archaic" (17). And indeed, Harlem's first acts of independence include the nationalization of the "Hudson River Day Line" and "every stick and stone of property in Harlem" via the "Harlem Land Reform" (21). They even go so far as to nationalize the numbers racket.

Siege, however, doesn't immediately present itself as utopic. Rotella, for instance, argues that while the novel reads the riots as "postcolonial uprising" (240), the novel doesn't "advocate postcolonial separation" (257). Rather, he contends, it critiques "the growing tendency across the spectrum of urban intellectuals and representations to regard the ghetto, inextricably intertwined with the rest of the metropolis, as a separate world: colony, enemy, alien land" (257). In this, Rotella suggests, the novel is not utopic but instead a satire of black nationalism and a defense of a more integrationist liberalism, coming down firmly on the side of the latter (257). There is much to support this reading. As in *Invisible Man*, there are numerous send-ups of black nationalism, most notably, the presence of "Tribal People"—karate-practicing, knife-wielding separatists—who, in revenge for US incursions into Harlem, begin murdering Harlem's white working-class residents, such as "an old fruit peddler with a family of six youngsters, and a former Hungarian refugee" (90). Furthermore, as Rotella aptly shows, liberal integrationism is at the heart of Miller's larger literary trajectory such as *The Cool World* (1957).

    And yet, the novel's politics turn out to be far less contained, far less liberal than it might appear. While Rotella is right that *Siege* offers a scathing rejection of racial separatism, it offers an equally scathing rejection of liberal integrationism, which turns out to be little more than the carrot masking the stick of invasions, sanctions, and violence. But the project of an independent Harlem succumbs to neither the Scylla of racial separatism nor the Charybdis of liberal integrationism. Instead, perhaps even against its author's own political commitments, *Siege* identifies a horizon of anticolonial and anticapitalist politics, one that often took the city as its starting position and the international as its endpoint and that heralded a resurgence of the Commune.[5]

A Great Black Capital of the World

In 1966, James and Grace Lee Boggs penned their remarkable essay "The City Is the Black Man's Land." It opens with two facts: first, that African Americans were expected to become the majority in fifty major cities by the 1970s; and second, that, according to both US democratic principles and historical precedent, this should mean that black Americans would take "over the leadership of municipal government" (162). But, the authors argue, racism is so deeply entrenched in the American psyche that "every conceivable strategy" is being used to prevent this ascension to power (162). They list three examples: "urban renewal or Negro removal; [the] reorganization of local government on a metropolitan area basis; [and] population (birth) control" (163). This stand-off between the facts of population trends and American democratic traditions on the one hand, and racist fear on the other, had brought US cities to a crossroads where they were faced with two choices: either the state enacts wholesale extermination and/or forced migration of black urban dwellers, or the city becomes governed by "the black majority organized behind leaders and organization of its own creation and prepare[s] to reorganize the structure of city government and city life from top to bottom" (163). For James and Grace Lee Boggs, there is no choice. The city will become the black man's land.

Within this framework, the Boggses turn to the riots they saw erupting across the nation and argue that these struggles represented nothing less than a "Civil War between black power and white power" (163). Their representation of riots as a "Civil War" is a nod to Marx, who challenged popular media accounts of the Paris Commune as either a riotous orgy of the urban rabble or a foreign invasion and instead described the Commune as a "Civil War in France" that presaged a revolutionary situation. For the Boggses, the urban unrest in the United States, too, presages such a revolutionary situation. "Revolution," they explain, "involves the conquest of state power by oppressed strata of the population," but it also requires "a fundamental problem involved that can be solved only by the political power of the oppressed" (163). For them, that problem was the large-scale deindustrialization of American cities. While this tendency is national, they argue that black urban workers are the vanguard because they are "the ones who have been made most expendable" under this regime of deindustrialization, and thus "the revolution must be a black revolution" (163), and an urban one.

James and Grace Lee Boggs were not alone. Over the following decade, many civil rights, black power, and antiwar organizations would turn not to the nation-state but to the city over the nation as the site of revolutionary struggle.[6] While black power's vision of the city was at times nationalist, black power also exceeded this framework. Huey P. Newton's famous open letter to the National Liberation Front of South Vietnam in 1970 is a key instance of this, as he delivered his forceful anti-imperialist critique of black nationalism. "We cannot be nationalists," he argued, "when our country is not a nation, but an empire. We have the historical obligation to take the concept of internationalism to its final conclusion—destruction of statehood itself" (197).

The destruction of statehood itself. This concept, too, dates back to the Commune, which Marx described as "the direct antithesis to the empire" (72) because of its commitment to the "destruction of [. . .] state power" (74). The resonances between the thought of James and Grace Lee Boggs,

Newton, and Marx are not incidental. The Boggses and Newton, like many revolutionary black leaders, were avid readers of Marx. They were committed to a rigorous rethinking of him alongside and in tension with Third World revolutionary thinkers like Che Guevara, Frantz Fanon, and Mao Zedong, and in relation to the specific struggles of the historical moment in which they found themselves. Moreover, the situation of American cities in the 1960s, as David Harvey repeatedly notes, bore resemblances to Paris in the lead-up to the Commune. Most notably, both had recently emerged from periods of urbanization characterized by massive, debt-backed projects whose bills were coming due. Also common to both scenarios was an upsurge in urban working-class movements, state repression, and violence (Harvey 2012).

One of the more striking aspects of *Siege* is the extent to which it deploys the idiom—and, as we shall see in a moment, the internationalist ethos—of the Commune: namely, the slogan and the barricade. In *The Emergence of Social Space*, Kristin Ross unpacks the legacy of this potent pair of political symbols, arguing that their significance is derived from the specific ways in which they seized onto and reappropriated both everyday objects and ways of life. By the 1860s, Ross explains, the meaning of sloganeering shifted from a "rallying cry" to "a brief, striking phrase used in advertising or commercial promotion" (1988, 151). By the time of the Commune, the slogan came to exist at the nexus between marketplace and revolutionary desire, continually negotiating and mobilizing the energies of the other. The Commune's use of slogans—most notably its battle cry, "Vive le Commune!"—served to reseize the slogan, to deploy the commercial phrase for revolutionary ends. Similarly, Ross reads barricades as objects of "*bricolage*" (131) in which the "previous 'whole' (social context, dominant organization of space, of bodies) must be sabotaged to allow for new functions, pieces put back together" (131). In both cases, the social structures and objects of everyday life—saturated as they were in the logics of commodification and mass culture—began to transform alongside and through the Commune's transformation of the quotidian.

Ross could just as easily have been discussing the role of the barricade and the slogan in *Siege*'s newly independent Harlem. Not only do the barricades take the dominant forms of organization—ghettoization, segregation, and policing—and invert them such that Harlem ceases to be a space of imprisonment and entrapment, and instead a space of freedom and liberation, but *Siege*'s barricades are also consciously entangled with the logic of the commodity. The barricades, we are told, are constructed out of "abandoned automobiles, mattresses, orange crates, and such" (11), and thus metaphorically work to transform the looted commodities that were so often a symbol of the 1960s riots into the raw materials of revolution. *Siege*'s Harlem also makes ready use of the slogan, appropriating the tools of advertisement to announce the revolutionary present. As the grandfather recalls, they would paint the barriers "with slogans of our own, famous sayings by our famous sons," such as, "The problem of the twentieth century is the problem of the color line" (33), as well as slogans made up for the occasion such as, "We shall be a living petition," and "Peace is the presence of justice" (33).

Beyond the idiom and the objects of the Commune, *Siege*'s Harlem also echoes the internationalism of the Commune. Whether pro- or anti-Commune, contemporary writers all pointed to its fierce internationalism.[7] Marx's description is especially notable here. He observed how the Commune "made a German working man its Minister of Labor" at a time when the French government was hunting down Germans in France (81); it "honoured the heroic sons of Poland by placing them at the head of the defenders of Paris" at a time when the French government was betraying Poland (81); and it "pulled down that colossal symbol of martial glory, the Vendôme Column," rejecting the entire history of French imperialism and military conquest (81).

The grandfather continually emphasizes the internationalism of Harlem. Its first finance minister is a "Puerto Rican gentleman [. . .] from East Harlem and had formerly been a certified public accountant" (21). The composition of Harlem is described as "multi-national [. . . comprised of] African, Puerto Rican, Chinese, and Gypsy too" (52). The children of Harlem have African names and speak French, while its grocery stores are part of the "Great African & Pan-Islamic cooperative grocery chain" (50). And finally, Harlem's survival depends on its internationalism: from the shipment of tea given by "our Chinese brothers," to the importance of solidarity from their friends in the UN who help them deal with the diplomatic maneuvering of Mister Eddie, the US ambassador (70–71).

What these resonances suggest is that while, as Rotella notes, *Siege* does read the 1960s riots as postcolonial—though "anticipatory," as we will see, might not be the correct word, as numerous activists and intellectuals understood black unrest as a postcolonial uprising immediately—the iteration of postcolonialism it evokes is not based on "postcolonial separation" (257) as he assumes. Instead, it draws on a specifically Fanonian or Césairian strand of postcolonial theory that frames postcolonialism as a fight against both the territorial imperialism that dominated British hegemony and what Kwame Nkrumah calls the "neo-colonialism" that would take flight under

US hegemony (1974). This strand of postcolonial thinking recognized that so-called national liberation was not the endpoint of colonialism but rather the precondition for the United States' new iteration of it. This was a postcolonialism that recognized that decolonization struggles would not ultimately take place between decolonizing nation-states and colonial nation-states but between what Newton termed "revolutionary intercommunalism" and "capital's reactionary intercommunalism" (qtd. in Hilliard and Cole 319). In Newton's revolutionary intercommunalism, therefore, we find an anticolonialism whose horizon of struggle was not the creation of separate, capitalist nation-states but rather the dismantling of the global capitalist-state system itself.

What makes it so difficult to see this form of communal internationalism within *Siege*, and what makes it so tempting to read *Siege* within the frame of a postcolonial nationalism, as Rotella does, is its focus on race, which makes it appear as if "*Siege* imagines being a black American as a separate state" (Rotella, 258). For Jameson, what made Marx a more developed utopian thinker than More is that where both wanted to "eliminate individual property relations" in order "to lead to a situation in which classes as such disappeared" (2004, 37), More's utopia was fixated on greed as an intrinsic part of human nature that had to be done away with. On the other hand, Jameson argues, Marx's vision did not "include a concept of human nature" (2004, 37), because for him, human nature is itself historically constructed, "the result of human praxis," as he puts it, and thus also variable at different historical moments (2004, 37). Similarly, *Siege* moves away from cultural or psychological explanations for the riots that were circulating at the time, which became doxic with the famous claim of the Moynihan Report (or its official name, *The Negro Family: The Case for National Action*) that the urban uprisings of the mid-1960s could be blamed on "the deterioration of the Negro family" (Moynihan 5) and thus the "Negro community" (5) and "character" (5). By contrast, in *Siege*, the urban unrest that forms the prehistory of the novel cannot be read as anything but protorevolutionary.

I also want to suggest that *Siege*'s Harlem, too, eschews innate concepts of race. That is, while Harlem takes the *appearance* of racial separatism, what the novel stages is not a race war between black and white America but a war of the proletariat[8] against a capitalist and imperialist state: a war that—because of what Chris Chen articulates as "the racialization of unwaged surplus or superfluous populations" (217)—can be played out only on racial terms. But what is ultimately at stake in *Siege*'s Harlem is two different visions of modernity. Shortly after the barricades come up, the "Privileged People" attempt to seduce Harlemites back to their side with promises of commodities. Specifically, they offer Harlemites a "free trip to Miami; a color teevee set; a complete set of forty copper-bottomed pots and pans; an electric swizzle stick; a lifetime subscription to *House & Garden* magazine" (16). This assortment of gadgets, print culture, and travel represents in a condensed form the promise of a suburban American modernity that much of this book has been tracing. Its vision is that of a privatized freedom that is identical with the nuclear family, home ownership, and the ability to participate in the economy of mass-produced goods.

It is from within this vision of modernity that Harlem gets cast in the terms of the Moynihan Report and of developmentalist discourses more broadly. It is the "Majority People," or "Privileged People," as they are alternately called, that view Harlem as a "jungle" in which crime is rampant and people can't get their needs met (88), a place that is desirous for, and simply needs the trappings of, this new capitalist, domestic modernity. But from the other side of the barricade, the situation appears quite different. In a fascinating presage of the encounters between the Students for a Democratic Society and the Students' Afro-American Society (SAS) as well as black power groups like SNCC, the Harlem Mau Maus, and United Black Front of Harlem that did take place at Columbia in 1968, in the novel white students from Columbia University encounter this newly liberated Harlem and are filled with "a longing" for their "freedom" (87).[9] If not trips to Miami, an electric swizzle stick, or a complete set of pots and pans, what is this vision of freedom that Harlem instills? It is a notion of freedom embedded in the destruction of the wage relation and private property, it is the freedom of unalienated labor, and freedom from the violence of the state.

It is this vision, this radically alternative notion of freedom and modernity, that makes Harlem so dangerous. It is why the Privileged People must wage information wars proclaiming that "HUGGINS [is] UNABLE TO PROTECT HIS PEOPLE [from] MUGGINGS AND MURDERS" (88), and it is why lurking beneath the PR battle being waged on the airwaves between Radio Free Harlem and WEBDuBois Radio (Harlem's radio station), and through the diplomatic channels of the UN, is the ever-present threat of military invasion. This threat comes not only from the official US state—which has eschewed a direct frontal assault in favor of a mix of economic and cultural warfare mixed with infiltration—but also from numerous paramilitary groups, all of which take up the imagery and symbolism of Confederacy: from "'Fabus' Own Fusiliers" and "Strom Thurmond's Light Horse" to "Bull Connor's Canines and Volunteer Armored Truck" (17).

In its allusions both to the Civil War and to the United States' primarily strategies of controlling rebellious Third World countries—namely, economic strangulation, cultural warfare, and only paramilitary intervention—*Siege* refigures black urban struggle, including the riots, as a form of civil war. Like the Commune, which I'm arguing functions as an analogue within the novel, it is a Civil War where what is at stake is not racial separatism but a revolt against private property, a class-based society, and alienated labor: a Civil War that, because of its historical circumstances, takes the form of a race war.

The Riot. The Occupation. The Commune

That this new form of Commune thinking should emerge in the 1960s United States is no accident. In *Riot. Strike. Riot: The New Era of Uprisings*, Joshua Clover calls for a rejection of moralizing or normative accounts of the riot, which see it as the violent counterpart to the strike, and instead argues that riots and strikes are expressions of two sides of capitalist accumulation: that while strikes are production struggles carried out by those within the wage relation, riots belong to the category of "circulation struggles" carried out in the sphere of reproduction, and which includes "the blockage, the occupation, and at the far horizon, the commune" (31). While, Clover argues, circulation struggles are always present, they tend to erupt, or become a "privileged tactic," overtaking the strike, at moments in which capitalism itself shifts from a production-dominant phase to one of circulation. And deindustrialization is, of course, the term used to describe the shift from production to circulation within the United States in the 1960s.

The riot and the Commune. Whatever the limits of *Siege*, however—and there are many—what the book is able to register is the resurgence of the Commune and Commune thinking within the riots erupting across the United States. And it registers the ways in which the eruption of Commune thought and praxis was able to grasp midcentury urbanization—and particularly the urban renewal projects that became the precursor to gentrification—as a frontier of imperialist struggle.

Reading urban renewal as a precursor of gentrification suggests we rethink postwar urban conflicts not only as struggles against the racist violence implicit in the state interventions that marked the era of Keynesianism and culminated in Lyndon Johnson's Great Society but also as vanguard struggles against the onslaught of a process that would come to be understood as neoliberalism: that is, as struggles against the transformation of the largely racialized city into the new frontiers of finance capital (of which real estate is always front and central) that emerged once the productive processes that marked the postwar boom began to decline. It also proposes that we consider the wide-ranging urban social movements—from the labor movement, to the Indian, Puerto Rican, and black liberation movements, to the gay and feminist liberation movements—that erupted across the 1960s and 1970s as both objects to be alternatively destroyed or appropriated by neoliberalism's recuperation of their demands for freedom, and as vanguard struggles against the urban colonization that has become a central part of neoliberal globalization.

The riots at the end of *Invisible Man*. The fire that swallows New York and clears the ground for Rand's men of the mind. The law-and-order state that Lee finds at the end of *Naked Lunch*. The effacement of the working-class city in *The Price of Salt*. The death of Rufus in *Another Country*. These are the landscapes of Civil War, the prehistories to our present. And they also help show the ways in which we should understand contemporary forms of urban redevelopment—including gentrification—as a battle in a Civil War that is still ongoing. Shortly after the Watts riots, Vice President Hubert Humphrey declared that "the biggest battle we're fighting today is not in South Vietnam; the toughest battle is in our cities" (qtd. in Boggs and Boggs, 193). We should take seriously the truth of this claim. Humphrey understood that the city was the other space in which the United States was fighting in its imperial wars. As with its incursions into socialist countries abroad, its incursions into urban spaces—whether by way of developers, planners, or the police—were battles over the future of US empire and a US-led global capitalist system. These were the battles that produced the geographies, politics, and landscapes of struggle that mark our current moment, and thus they are battles to which we need to return, to reevaluate and redeem.

My grandfather was born in the Bronx to Russian-Jewish refugees and was able to attend university only because both tuition and textbooks were free at the City University of New York at that time. He received an engineering degree there and went on to become a very successful chemical engineer. His life is composed of the contradictions this book explores. He made his money working on Marshall Plan–era large-scale economic development projects rooted entirely in the new regime of petro-capitalism; he participated in a kind of white flight, moving from New York City to Great Neck on Long Island, where my dad grew up; and yet he was also—alongside my grandmother—a member of the Communist Party until 1956; and he remained a lifelong social justice and antiwar activist (even joining Facebook to organize against the Iraq War) until he died at the age of ninety-four. Not only did he pay for my undergraduate education, and not only was he an intellectual mentor, but in many ways the contradictions of his life form the story underwriting this book.

More expansively, this book is primarily a product of two institutions: Simon Fraser University and the University of Warwick. At Simon Fraser University, I was taught how to think like a geographer and literary theorist. I owe this to Carolyn Lesjak, Jon Smith, Geoff Mann, and Mathias Nilges, as well as to Jeff Derksen, Jerry Zaslove, and Mike Everton. Thank you also to Emily Fedoruk, Dave Gaertner, Peter McDonald, Matt Risling, Naava Smolash, Jason Starnes, and to Christa Grundringer and the rest of the office staff for their tireless work and patience. In Vancouver, the Lacan Salon was both an intellectual and social center. Huge thanks to Clint Burnham, Hilda Fernandez, Jesse Proudfoot, and especially to Andrew Shmueley. Andrew introduced me to the work of Marshall Berman; my conversations with him about cities influenced and shaped this book in ways I couldn't at the time even begin to imagine; and it was his careful reading and comments that brought the book to its completion. Last but not least, I was lucky enough to belong to the political community that surrounded the Teaching Support Staff Union. Thanks to Marika Albert,

Usamah Ansari, Sam Bradd, Caelie Frampton, David Huxtable, Krisztina Kun, Veronica Miralles Sanchez, and Jason Tockman. Most of what I know about neoliberalism I know from struggling against it with them.

At Warwick, I was not only lucky enough to have fabulous colleagues, but also to have found the intellectual and political home that brought the book to its conclusion: Ajay Chandra, Craig Gent, Jane Hudson, Daniel Katz, Nick Lawrence, Tina Lupton, Emma Mason, Michael Meeuwis, Mike Niblett, Stephen Ross, Laura Schwartz, Leon Sealey-Huggins, Rochelle Sibley, Jonathan Skinner, Mark Storey, Arianna Tassinari, Kat Zeltner, and the Warwick Research Collective more broadly. Heather Pilbin, Alison Lough, and the office saved me more times than I can count. Most of all, however, thank you to Stephen Shapiro, who over the past four years has provided his guidance, mentorship, support, and even (at great personal cost) his office. Thanks to my comrades at the UCU and the Student Staff Solidarity Group for being my political home and compass.

Bridging my time within these institutions was a year in Boston. Which was hell. And yet, I am forever grateful for getting to work with Jack Matthews, whose mentorship, careful and brilliant readings, advice, and support were and continue to be invaluable, and for Nicole Aschoff, Molly Geidel, Patricia Stuelke, and Lucas Freeman, who are the reasons this is a book. Thank you to the Social Sciences and Humanities Research Council, whose Ph.D. and postdoctoral funding supported this project.

Thank you to my families, who have provided the emotional labor on which this was built: Zelda Abramson, Eric Tucker, Zachary Tucker-Abramson, Lisa Brand, and John Lynch; Jennifer Scott, Valerie Zink, Lian Beveridge, John Diamond-Gibson, Lucas Fitch, Mike Toews, Jessica Liebster, Daniel Gladstone, and Mabel Liebster-Gladstone, Mark Willson, Meghan Jezewski, Carleton Gholz, Caitlin Erskine Smith and Owen Coggins, Elyssa Livergant, Xanthe Whittaker, Vix Thompson, and Nora Parr. And thank you to everyone at Fordham University Press, but especially John Garza and Richard Morrison, who made this process nearly effortless thanks to their kindness, attentiveness, the exceptional readers to whom they sent it, and the care they've shown throughout.

It seems to have become standard to conclude one's acknowledgments by reprivatizing and thanking one's spouse or primary romantic partner with increasing fervor. It's as if 1970s queer and feminist politics and theory never happened. So, for Sylvia Federici, for creating the ground on which so many of us walk, and to Jessa Crispin, for being brave enough in 2017 to demand nothing short of the abolition of marriage. For Caitlin and Jessica, for refusing to marry, and for Jen, who, though married, has the most capacious and queer sense of family of anyone I've ever met. My final thanks are to them.

Sections of Chapter 1 appeared in an earlier version as "Blueprints: *Invisible Man* and the Housing Act of 1949," *American Studies* 54, no. 3 (2015): 9–20. Sections of Chapter 4 appeared in an earlier version as *"Atlas Shrugged*'s Shock Therapy," *Modern Fiction Studies* 63, no. 1 (2017): 73–94.

INTRODUCTION

1. For more on the Haussmannization of Paris, see Harvey 2003b; and Berman.

2. As soon as the act passed, Robert Moses submitted a report to Mayor O'Dwyer calling for the clearance of 1,320 acres of "five notorious slum districts"—Lower Manhattan, Harlem, Bedford-Stuyvesant, Brownsville, and South Central Bronx—by 1955 (New York City Committee on Slum Clearance 1949, 2). This initial report was quickly followed up by the *Second Report to Mayor William O'Dwyer from the Mayor's Committee on Slum Clearance by Private Capital* (January 23, 1950), which became the blueprint for many of the Title 1 projects that would be carried out over the following decade.

3. I am riffing here on Samuel Zipp's 2013 article "The Roots and Routes of Urban Renewal."

4. There is a vast literature on the decline of the American city (see, for instance, Beauregard; Teaford; Mollenkopf; and Gelfand).

5. The name comes from Catherine Bauer's book *Modern Housing*, published in 1934.

6. The creation of long-term and low-cost mortgages, which were the basis of the FHA and US housing policy, were based on ranking systems of insurability and risk. In both policy and practice, these ranking systems prioritized white suburban communities while they undervalued and effectively redlined urban neighbourhoods that were older, racially mixed, and densely populated (Jackson). For more on the relationship between postwar federal policies and race, see Kenneth Jackson's pathbreaking *Crabgrass Frontier*; Sugrue; Hirsch 2009 and 2000; and Self.

7. See Harcourt.

8. The Housing Act offered billions of dollars in federal loans and grants though the Housing and Home Finance Agency (HHFA) to local governments for the "acquisition and clearance of slum areas" (HHFA 2). Title I, the section dealing with slum clearance, drastically extended the powers of eminent domain to municipalities, allowing the government to condemn

any land deemed a slum in order to hand it over, as Robert Caro explains, to "individuals for them to build [. . .] projects agreeable to government" (1974, 777) and remake the geography of the city. As historian Jon Teaford puts it, urban renewal tried to "beat suburbia at its own game" (7). Urban renewal policies sought to deal with the economic devaluation of downtown by solving what was perceived to be the main causes: a postwar housing shortage caused by over a decade of lost development, and the increasingly racialized character of downtown business districts, which were spilling over into other at-risk areas.

9. There were two reasons that the 1949 Housing Act ended up solidifying these patterns of segregation. First, where previous housing bills had linked slum clearance to the building of public housing, one of the Housing Act's innovations was to delink the two and to focus instead on private investment. Second, this bill did not contain within it an antidiscrimination clause, which effectively meant that federal funds and powers consolidated the structure of racial inequality rooted in the racially discriminatory housing policies such as redlining on a national scale (Jackson). As Edgar Brown, director of the National Negro Council, warned at the bill's hearings, when segregation "becomes good business, when it is capitalized in bonds and banks, when the American Government drives them back, then, [an African American's] last chance is gone" (n.p.). The delinking of slum clearance with public housing and the absence of antidiscrimination clauses meant that while slums were cleared, what often replaced those slums was not public housing but (often segregated) middle-class housing projects like those in Stuyvesant Town, or large-scale complexes such as the Lincoln Center and even the United Nations Building. In 1952, FHA administrator Albert Cole clearly spelled out the effects of this absence, stating that "it is not incumbent on the federal government to impose integration in federally insured and federally aided housing in violation of the attitude, customs and practices of the local community" (qtd. in Biondi, 121). The issue of Title 1 funds being used to fund segregated housing or not was an explosive one, hotly debated by community groups such as the Urban League, NAACP, and the Communist Party, in the pages of housing and architecture magazines, and in Congress. For more on the struggles over housing discrimination, see Biondi 2003; D. King; Massey and Denton; and Abrams.

10. The "rent gap" is a theory of gentrification developed by Neil Smith in his 1979 article "Toward a Theory of Gentrification," which challenged dominant narratives that explain gentrification through hypotheses based on the sovereignty of consumer choice. In contrast, Smith argues that gentrification is not the unexpected result of discrete choices but an expected process that occurs when the rent gap—what he defines as "the disparity between the

potential ground rent and the actual ground rent capitalized under the represent land use" (1979, 545)—is wide enough that "developers can purchase structures cheaply, can pay the builder's costs and profit for rehabilitation, can pay interest on mortgage and construction loans, and can then sell the end product for a sale price that leaves a satisfactory return to the developer" (545). Smith develops this term in "The Evolution of Gentrification" (2011); in *The New Urban Frontier: Gentrification and the Revanchist City* (1996); and in "Gentrification and the Rent Gap" (1987).

11. For more on the radicalization of New York in the postwar period, see Biondi; and Freeman. For more on the Soviet Union's criticism of poverty in US cities, see O'Donohue; Melamed 2011; and Von Eschen.

12. In *Satchmo Blows up the World*, Von Eschen draws out the state violence implicit within these modernization programs through her focus on the Jazz Ambassador program. She argues that as the "jazz tours moved through regions rich in those quintessential Cold War commodities oil and uranium" (146), they were also moving through the sites of some of the United States' most violent Cold War interventions: a year after Dizzy Gillespie's visit to Syria, CIA operatives supported a military coup against a pro-Communist government (127); at the same time Louis Armstrong and his band were touring Africa, the CIA was plotting its assassination of the Belgian Congo's recently elected prime minister, Patrice Lumumba; and Duke Ellington was brought to Iraq shortly after the CIA supported a 1963 coup led by General Ahmad Hassan al-Bakr as part of its broader attempt to "reduce Iraqi dependence on the Soviet Union" (132–33).

13. For more on New York City's 1975 bankruptcy as a key originary moment of neoliberalism, see Harvey 2005 and 2007; Hackworth; Moody; O'Connor; Peck; and Tabb. For more on Proposition 13, see M. Davis 1992; Self; and McGirr.

14. For more on the university, see Nick Mitchell's "The Fantasy and Fate of Ethnic Studies in an Age of Uprisings" (2016), which traces the "birth of the adjunct" to San Francisco State University's accommodation of the Third World Liberation Front and Black Student Union demands for a college of ethnic studies. There is an immense body of work tracking neoliberalism's absorption and accommodation of radical demands of 1960s and 1970s social movements (see, for instance, Puar; McRobbie; Melamed 2011; Reddy; Fraser; Stuelke; and Spade 2015).

15. See, for instance, Freund; Matthew Lassiter, *Silent Majority: Suburban Politics in the Sunbelt South* (Princeton, N.J.: Princeton University Press, 2006); Kruse and Sugrue; McGirr; Kruse; and M. Davis 1992.

16. See, for instance, "Genres of Neoliberalism," ed. Jane Elliott and Gillian Harkins, special issue, *Social Text* 31, no. 2 (2013); "Neoliberalism

and the Novel," ed. Emily Johansen and Alissa G. Karl, special issue, *Textual Practice* 29, no. 2 (2015); and *Neoliberalism and Contemporary Literary Culture*, ed. Mitchum Huehls and Rachel Greenwald Smith (Baltimore: Johns Hopkins University Press, 2017).

17. It has recently become commonplace to root accounts of neoliberalism in the forms of reason and economic platforms put forward by the so-called Mont Pelerin Society, which emerged at a conference organized by Frederich Hayek in 1947 (see, for instance, Steadman Jones; Peck; Mirowski and Plehwe; and Foucault).

18. I am particularly indebted to Leo Panitch and Sam Gindin's *Making of Global Capitalism: The Political Economy of American Empire* (2013), which shows that while Keynesianism and neoliberalism deployed radically different playbooks, they were more complementary than is often assumed, and functioned as two equally necessary components for what Panitch and Gindin have termed the United States' "making of global," and I would add racial "capitalism."

19. While the most famous iteration of this argument is Alan Nadel's *Containment Culture: American Narratives, Postmodernism, and the Atomic Age* (1995), which reads narratives of communist containment and conformity as defining the entire cultural field of the high Cold War period (from 1946 to 1964), much of our thinking about 1950s US writing has remained locked within a containment framework that reads the 1950s as a series of political declines: the decline of a vigorous left-wing politics of aesthetics, or of the importance of class. The foundational texts in this vein are Lawrence Schwartz, *Creating Faulkner's Reputation* (1988); Thomas Schaub, *American Fiction in the Cold War* (1991); Barbara Foley, *Radical Representations: Politics and Form in US Proletarian Fiction* (1993), and, more recently, Greg Barnhisel, *Cold War Modernism: Art, Literature, and American Cultural Diplomacy* (2015). Bruce McConachie makes a similar argument about the rise of containment culture with regards to theater in *American Theater in the Culture of the Cold War: Producing and Contesting Containment, 1947–1962* (2003).

20. In *Postmodernism or the Cultural Logic of Late Capitalism* (1991), Jameson argues that Benn Michaels's *The Gold Standard and the Logic of Naturalism* (1987) enacts what he argues is New Historicism's method, a "return to immanence and to a prolongation of the procedures of 'homology' which eschews homology's theory and abandons the concept of structure" (187).

21. New York was certainly the only site where such work can occur. In an earlier article (2017), I make a similar argument about Atlanta, and in Chapter 3, I show the relationships between the urban renewal projects carried out in New York and the modernization projects carried out in decolonizing spaces like that of Tangier. But New York is a particularly useful site

of inquiry due to both the proliferation of novels written about New York at this moment and also New York's import to the project of US hegemony. New York, in short, is not exceptional, but exemplary.

22. For more on the debate between Adorno and Benjamin and the development of Benjamin's positions on the role of shock and art through his writings, see Buck-Morss 1979.

23. In the 1950s, psychoanalysis and psychology ceased to be the purview of the upper middle class and became a fundamental part of American popular culture and discourse. As Ellen Herman argues, Cold War anxieties about loyalty gave rise to a neo-Freudian discourse of "national character" (1995b, 32). At the same time, psychology became a cornerstone of military strategy—including propaganda as well as more invasive forms of psychological testing from drugs to shock therapy (126)—and of social policy, which began to understand crime, social deviancy, and social unrest not as responses to social, structural, and political issues but as a psychological problem that could be solved through self-help books, therapy, education, and public health and propaganda campaigns. Across these diverse fields, psychology was both a site of anxiety as discourses of the decline or weakening of the national character spread and a new site of battle as military strategists, urban planners, and social psychologists all began to imagine the potential to manipulate and shape human subjectivity.

1. BLUEPRINTS: *INVISIBLE MAN* AND THE GREAT MIGRATION TO WHITE FLIGHT

1. Ellison joined the CCF in 1956 (Purcell, 917). The CCF was part of a larger anticommunist Cold War campaign that sought to turn black American cultural producers into ambassadors of American capitalism. In addition to the CCF, this campaign also led to the creation of the Goodwill Jazz Ambassadors, which sent black jazz musicians like Benny Goodman, Dizzy Gillespie, Dave Brubeck, and Duke Ellington to Europe, Latin America, and Africa. For more on the Jazz Ambassadors, see Von Eschen.

2. For more on the relationship between neoliberalism and criminality, see Harcourt; and Wacquant 2009b. For more on the relationship between race and mass incarceration, see Alexander; Gilmore; A. Davis; and Angela Davis, "Race, Gender, and Prison History: From the Convict Lease System to the Supermax Prison," in Prison Masculinities, ed. Donald Sabo, Terry A. Krupers, and Willie London (Philadelphia: Temple University Press, 2001).

3. See, for instance, Ellison, "Judge Lynch in New York," which tells the story of three southern migrants who encounter the same Jim Crow violence they thought they've escaped when they are beaten by a couple of white boys for crossing the invisible line of Amsterdam Avenue. The article

ends ominously by claiming that if these "incidents" continue, they "are sure to precipitate the sort of emotional reaction that made for the riots of 1935" (1939, 17).

4. I'm drawing here largely on Hal Foster's definition of surrealism as mirroring the actions and categories of Freud's uncanny, namely "an indistinction between the real and the imagined, [. . .] a confusion between the animate and the inanimate, [. . . and] a usurpation of the referent by the sign or of physical reality by psychic reality" (7). Dorothea Fischer-Hornung points out that Ellison "was acquainted with the famous 1936 exhibit 'Fantastic Art, Dada, Surrealism at the [MOMA]'" and suggests that New York's position as "the focal point of Surrealist activity [. . .] may account for the strong trend toward surrealistic effects in the story" (249).

5. According to Janet Abu-Lughod, "in the eight-month period that ended in June 1932, some 186,000 families had [. . .] been served with dispossession notices" in New York City (179). See also Lipsky 1970.

6. William Shack explains that the men chosen to fight in this unit were not working-class, but members of Du Bois's "talented tenth." In *Invisible Man*, too, the veterans are elite: "doctors, lawyers, teachers, Civil Service workers; there were several cooks, a preacher, a politician, and an artist. One very nutty one had been a psychiatrist" (74).

7. As writers and critics like Robin D. G. Kelley, Franklin Rosemont, Amanda Stansell, Michael Richardson, and Krzysztof Fijałkowski suggest, surrealism emerged on the fault lines of de/colonization. For instance, in 1926, the surrealists, inspired by the anticolonial Rif Rebellion in Morocco, joined the communists in supporting the rebels, and in 1931, they protested the Colonial Exhibition in Paris by hosting a counterexhibit called *The Truth about the Colonies* that featured "a black child with a begging bowl" as one of their "European fetishes" (Richardson and Fijałkowski 4). Recent work by the critics above has also begun to focus on the surrealisms created by students from the colonies who were living in France, most notably Etienne Léro, Jules-Marcel Monnerot, and Pierre Yoyotte. The lone issue of their journal *Légitime Defense* heralded the creation of a Caribbean surrealism, while joining it with an appreciation of Western philosophy, European surrealists, and African American writers like Langston Hughes and Claude McKay (see Kelley). Soon thereafter, another group led by Aimé Césaire, Leon Damas, and Léopold Sédar Senghor came together and founded their own journal, *L'etudiant Noir*. It was from here that Aimé Césaire and the negritude movement emerged, and it was the negritude movement that most clearly drew the "direct link between the logic of colonialism and the rise of fascism" (Aimé Césaire, *Discourse on Colonialism* [New York: Monthly Review Press, 2001], 12). When Césaire moved back to Martinique, he and his wife, Suzanne, and

René Ménil formed *Tropiques*, a journal of black consciousness, antifascism, and international surrealism.

8. In 1947, the city authorized the wiping out of "warehouses, carpet and cleaning stores, a printing plant, a few shops, about 1,400 jobs [. . . and] thirty-nine tenements" to make space for the NYU–Bellevue Medical Center on the East Side (J. Schwartz, 217).

9. For instance, the "Demonstration of Slum Conditions" section of *North Harlem. Slum Clearance Plan under Title 1 of the Housing Act of 1949* (New York City Committee on Slum Clearance 1951) argues that 73 percent of the buildings are "run-down" and that the buildings are "ancient, poorly lighted, badly laid out, inadequately ventilated, and generally occupied by more families than they were originally designed to accommodate" (36). The report further explains that currently there is a net density of "1,385 persons per net acre of residential use," and that the new development "will have a density of 417 persons per net residential acre" (42).

10. The path of Clifton's funeral takes the marchers past this sight before turning back to the park where the protagonist gives his final speech. The funeral, we are told, begins in a park, winds through the "poorer streets at first," and then "turned into Seventh Avenue and down and over to Lenox" (451) before returning back to the park where "a brother in the Park Department had opened the lookout tower, and [. . .] at our signal he struck the bell and I could feel my eardrums throbbing with the old, hollow, gut-vibrant Doom-Dong-Doom" (451). Based on the street names and directions Ellison gives us, we can assume that the parade heads north up Lenox Avenue to the 130s and 140s, before turning left down Seventh and heading back to the Mount Morris Park. Moses released his plans for the North Harlem Title I project—whose boundaries were Lenox Avenue, West 143rd Street, Harlem River Drive, Fifth Avenue and West 139th Street (see "Private Financing Sought to Replace 7 City Slum Areas," *New York Times*, January 22 1951)—in January 1951. This scene also contains a further nod to Moses. The park where they meet is Morris Park (now Marcus Garvey Park): a prominent park in central Harlem famous for the fire lookout tower that was built in 1857. In the 1930s, the Parks Commission under Moses's watch revitalized the park, adding playgrounds, a child sanitation station, and baseball diamonds and rebuilding the fire tower. During the funeral, the novel mentions a "brother in the park department" who opens the lookout tower (451). We can assume that the brother was one of the park workers helping to rebuild the tower during the 1930s.

11. Adrienne Brown, too, reads the novel's final descent underground as a descent into the suburbs, suggesting that the "protagonist's 'warm hole, full of light' probes to share some key similarities with the new middle-class developments popping up outside many major US cities" (179).

2. THE PRICE OF SALT IS THE CITY: PATRICIA HIGHSMITH
AND THE QUEER FRONTIERS OF NEOLIBERALISM

1. Legal theorist Dean Spade identifies a shift in LGBT organizing from the "anti-police activism of the 1960s and 70s," such as Stonewall and Compton's Cafeteria riots, to a new "law and order" activism that emerged in the wake of September 11 and the subsequent launching of the so-called War on Terror (2009, 353). For instance, in 2009, the Obama administration added the Matthew Shepard Law Enforcement Enhancement—which expanded the 1969 federal hate-crime law to include crimes that targeted a victim because of their gender, sexual orientation, gender identity, or disability—to the National Defense Authorization Act for 2010. This artful uniting of antihomophobic hate-crime legislation with a military budget, Spade points out, bolstered the prison industrial complex at home by providing an extra $10 million for "police and prosecutorial resources" (2009, 338) in the name of LGBT rights, while also securing liberal consent for a $680 billion Pentagon budgetary measure that funded a US military personnel surge in Afghanistan to the tune of almost one hundred thousand soldiers. For more on the appropriation of queer practices, theories, and politics into American neoliberalism, see Reddy 2011; Agathangelou, Bassichis, and Spira 2008; Puar 2007; Duggan; and Puar and Rai 2002.

2. The Lavender Scare adopted the structure of the Red Scare. As Robert Corber argues, it "recalled the hysteria produced by the McCarthy witch hunts, which reflected the fear that communists had infiltrated the nation's political and social institutions, and were secretly conspiring to overthrow them by recruiting naïve and unsuspecting Americans to their cause" (4). It also drew a line between the two, suggesting that gays and lesbians were themselves a security risk and that homosexuality was a "psychological maladjustment that led people toward communism" (D. Johnson, 16). For more on the Lavender Scare, see Canaday 2009; and Robert Corber, *In the Name of National Security: Hitchcock, Homophobia, and the Political Construction of Gender in Postwar America* (Durham, N.C.: Duke University Press, 1993).

3. This dichotomy is largely reflected in contemporary criticism. For instance, Heise; and Rotella focus on the urban literature of the period, while Hoberek; Beuka; and Jurca focus on suburban literature of the period. Rare works that are able to think about urban and suburban culture together are Avila 2004; and Hayden.

4. The term "neurasthenic strain" was developed by George Miller Beard, an early neurologist and physician in the 1880s, to explain a new condition he was seeing in his patients, marked by migraines, exhaustion, depression, and poor digestion. Beard argued that these symptoms were a result

of the capacities and energies of the nervous system being exhausted by the stresses of modern and particularly urban life (Murison, 158–62).

5. For more on the literature of the Left and the Popular Front, see Denning; Foley 1993; Wald 1994; Rabinowitz 1991; Daniel Aaron's *Writers on the Left* (New York: Columbia Univeristy Press, 1961); and Rideout.

6. For more on lesbian pulp novels in the 1950s and 1960s, see Keller; Katherine V. Forrest's *Introduction to Lesbian Pulp Fiction: The Sexually Intrepid World of Lesbian Paperback Novels, 1950–1965* (Minneapolis: Cleis, 2005); Stryker; Zimet; and Server. For an examination of lesbian pulp in film, see Corber.

7. Rabinowitz points out that their encounter, "the young woman fed and clothed by the older, experienced woman—begins much lesbian fiction of the early period" (195–96).

8. The ideational origins of the national highway system are generally traced back to the phenomenally popular *Futurama* exhibit, sponsored by General Motors at the 1939 World's Fair in New York. The *Futurama* exhibit conceptualized a system of freeways that would eliminate the crowding, chaos, and congestions of city streets and, by facilitating the movement of people and goods, would bring prosperity back to the nation's centers and thus the nation itself (Fotsch, 67). This vision was translated into policy through two major highway reports: the 1939 Bureau of Public Roads' *Toll Roads and Free Roads*, which drew the link between highway building and urban redevelopment by suggesting that freeway construction could facilitate slum clearance, and the 1944 National Interregional Highway Committee's *Interregional Highways*, which provided a blueprint for a 40,000-mile interregional highway network (Mohl, 677). These reports, alongside the lobbying efforts of state highway engineers, road builders, and a newly emerging highway lobby, pushed Congress to pass the Federal-Aid Highway Act of 1944, which approved the construction of the highways that would eventually be financed in the 1956 Federal Highway Act. For more on *Futurama*, see Fotsch; and Norman Bel Geddes, *Magic Motorways* (New York: Random House, 1940). For more on the history of freeway construction and urban redevelopment, see Mohl; Avila 2014; and Rose and Mohl.

9. Jane Kuenz argues that the new Anglo Saxon cowboy birthed in Wister's *The Virginian* positioned the white cowboy, and thus model of masculinity, as a force "against the twin terrors of modernization, both images of dangerous or degrading mixtures of races [. . .] or a mix of classes" (102). See also Bold.

10. Matthew Huber, for instance, argues that suburbanization was enabled by newfound access to fossil fuels but also that suburbanization became a

model through which the American-run fossil-fuel industry was exported globally: expanding and consolidating US international dominance and helping "power what others have called 'the real subsumption of life under capital,' where subjectivity itself mirrors the entrepreneurial logics of capital" (xv). See also Jason Moore, *Capitalism in the Web of Life* (New York: Verso, 2015); Stephanie LeMenager, *Living Oil: Petroleum Culture in the American Century* (London: Oxford University Press, 2013); and Frederick Buell, "A Short History of Oil Cultures: Or, the Marriage of Catastrophe and Exuberance," *Journal of American Studies* 46, no. 2 (2012): 273–93.

3. *NAKED LUNCH*, OR, THE LAST SNAPSHOT OF THE SURREALISTS

1. Unless otherwise noted, all citations to *The Naked Lunch* in this chapter refer to the 2001 Grove Press edition edited by James Grauerholz.

2. For more on the earlier history of the battle over Washington Square Park, see Shannon; Abrams; and Jacobs.

3. For more on the anticolonial struggles in Morocco, see Walonen; Zisenwine; Finlayson; and Vaidon.

4. The history of Morocco's independence is often seen to begin with the arrival of US troops in the region alongside Roosevelt's subsequent meetings with Morocco's sultan, Muhammed Ben Youssef, wherein Roosevelt assured the sultan that he would support the Moroccans in their struggle to gain independence from France. (Bernard, 3).

5. See also Aboul-Ela, which both offers an excellent account of the transformation from "old world colonialism, with their heavy administrative policing elements overlaying colonial ideology" to this new American coloniality, which "reinforce[d] privileged US access without ever bothering with official colonization of any of the region's countries" (10–11).

6. Along these lines, Fiona Ngô has similarly traced a long trajectory of elisions between the western frontier and the East. Turning to a 1923 pamphlet called *Our Araby: Palm Springs and the Garden of the Sun*, which aimed to promote East Coast travelers to California, Ngô observes the ways in which the tract—often drawing on the Orientalist imagery of Hollywood—fuses together West and East: "Because Hollywood imagery reduces 'Araby' to the desert, and the desert is 'presented as the essential unchanging décor of the history of the Orient,' an Arabic desert is essentially interchangeable with one in California. This US desert provides additional scenery as the untamed site of the wild West and is thus 'associated with productive, creative pioneering, a masculine redeemer of the wilderness.' Here the romantic and religious lure of the desert is mobilized to entice settlers to uncivilized regions of the US imperial expansion" (182–83).

7. For more on the irreal, see Löwy and the Warwick Research Collective.

8. The 1966 trial, or "Boston trial," as it came to be known, centered on the question of whether Burroughs's inflammatory writing was destructive and antisocial or whether its excesses could be construed as art that served a larger moral and social purpose. Professor Thomas H. Jackson was asked whether he felt that there were "details and points in this book that you feel you may not be able to explain because, in effect, they have no meaning and are intended only for shock value?" The manuscript continues: "A. 'Actually, no.' / Q. 'Everything in this book has meaning then?' / A. 'As a literary man I have to assume it does, yes.'" (*Attorney General v. A Book Named Naked Lunch*). This was not the first time *Naked Lunch* had been put on trial. In 1960, the University of Chicago literary magazine, *Big Table*, which included Burroughs's "Ten Scenes from *Naked Lunch*," was taken to court on obscenity charges that arose largely as a result of Burroughs's contribution. In that case, the trial judge, Julius Hoffman, found that "Ten Scenes" was not obscene. Citing the 1957 Roth decision that set the legal definition of obscenity as "material which deals with sex in a manner appealing to prurient interest" (*Big Table, Inc. v. Schroeder*, 259), Hoffman argued that as long as literature appeals to "some other interest than the prurient" (261), it is not obscene and thus concluded that Burroughs's use of drugs was not obscene because it was part of a larger strategy of "shocking contemporary society, in order perhaps to point out its flaws and weaknesses." Noting *Naked Lunch*'s similarity to Burroughs's 1952 novel *Junky* in both theme and content, Whiting argues that what made the former obscene over the latter was *Naked Lunch*'s lack of "a unified consciousness and the standard continuities of time and space that characterize conventional novels," remarking further that "there was little that could serve as a reference point, much less a center of gravity for moral concerns" (158). He concludes by observing how, in *Junky*, "the single voice of addiction was delegitimated by the moral universe of the genre"—presumably naturalism—while in *Naked Lunch*, Burroughs inhabited the subject position of both "addiction and its condemnation" (159). In other words, for both Whiting and Ronell, what made *Naked Lunch* obscene was its Romanticist refusal to reject intoxication, and even its seeming elision of literature and intoxication.

9. "Deposition" is an addendum that appears at the beginning of the 1960 Grove edition and the end of the restored text edition (see Appendix 1).

10. In *Forces of Habit: Drugs and the Making of the Modern World*, historian David Courtwright offers a model for thinking about the relationship between the emergence of drug types and regimes and periods of global hegemony. Between 1500 and 1789, Courtwright explains, the world witnessed a "psychoactive revolution," a term he uses to describe the popularization and globalization of increasingly powerful drugs that provided people "more, and

more potent, means of altering their ordinary waking consciousness" (2001, 3). Courtwright contends that this revolution, which had its "roots in the transoceanic commerce and empire building of the early modern period" (2), brought into being the global drug trade through caffeine, nicotine, and alcohol. Extrapolating from Courtwright, we can identify two other psychoactive revolutions that align with the global hegemonies of Britain and the United States. First was the "isolation and commercial production of psychoactive alkaloids such as morphine and cocaine" (76), alongside the development of hypodermic drugs, and the discovery and manufacture of synthetic drugs and "semisynthetic derivatives." Second was the development of new synthetic and chemical drugs that occurred in the wake of World War II—such as amphetamines, barbiturates, hallucinogens, and steroids—which offered more precise manipulations of the nervous system, and which became a cornerstone of US foreign and geopolitical policy.

    11. See, for instance, Fang 2003; M. Davis 2000; and Courtwright 2001.

    12. Drawing on this cocaine craze, the French chemist Vin Mariani created a wine-cocaine cocktail called Vin Mariani that was marketed as a tincture for "brain workers" by giving it a couth form of ingestion, upping its effects via alcohol, and making it a salve for white-collar, upper-class workers (Gootenberg, 26).

    13. What Burroughs is bringing up here is also the long relationship between drugs and the management of racial anxieties. In *The American Disease: Origins of Narcotic Control* (1973), for instance, Musto discusses how, in the nineteenth century, the rise of cocaine use in the United States brought about entirely new kinds of racial fears in the South: "The fear of the cocainized black coincided with the peak of lynchings, legal segregation, and voting laws all designed to remove political and social power from him" (7). The myths that circulated such as "cocaine ma[king] blacks almost unaffected by mere .32 caliber bullets" (7) gave voice to white fears and provided fodder for the maintenance and promotion of repressive race laws.

    14. In the postwar era, the kinds of psychoactive drugs Burroughs places in Benway's lab were increasingly used as part of what Ellen Herman calls the "military-psychology combination" (58), which was developed in response to fears of Chinese and Soviet Communists brainwashing American POWs (58). Herman goes so far as to argue that the "Cold War was, above all, a psychological phenomenon, just as total world war had been. While the Cold War presented the U.S. military with new challenges [. . .] nothing could have offered clearer evidence for the World War II maxim that war was fundamentally a battle for hearts and minds" (63).

    15. Hygiene was also an important aspect of urban renewal. See, for instance, Shannon's article "Claes Oldenburg's 'The Street' and Urban Renewal

in Greenwich Village 1960" (2004). Focusing on "The Big Sweep," an annual street-cleaning campaign that began in 1956, Shannon argues that hygiene campaigns "formed one front in the battle for a more ordered city" (138).

16. For a remarkable evocation of the connections between hygiene, modernization, and US coloniality, see William Faulkner's 1955 short story "Hog Pawn," in which a southern family's drive to build an indoor bathroom collides with an oil company's desire to build a filling station on a strip of their land.

17. The "cut up" method comes from the famous story that, upon receiving its proofs, Burroughs decided "not to reread the chapters that he had selected in order to determine an appropriate sequence in which they might appear on publication, but instead to submit the chapters in the entirely arbitrary sequence in which they had been put to the side when the selection process had taken place" (Sheehan, n.p). Whether this is true is difficult to say. Burroughs also claimed that parts of *Naked Lunch* "were written as a tract against Capital Punishment in the manner of Jonathan Swift's *Modest Proposal*" (205), and that the cut-up method came from a book called *Theory of Games and Economic Behaviour* (Burroughs and Gysin, 32). Both claims seem spurious at best, especially given Burroughs's own proclamation that he was a "huckster" (Loranger, 1999). But neither is exactly true. While the Interzone section itself may be out of time and chaotic, and while there are substantial shifts between the editions released by Big Table, Olympia Press, and the two versions put out by Grove Press, the overall structure—that is its movement into and out of the Interzone—is remarkably consistent across the drafts (see Appendix 1).

18. Burroughs, like the rest of the Beats, was also an ardent admirer of the surrealists and met them in Paris. Jean-Jacques Lebel tells the story of the Beats and the surrealists meeting up at an international poetry fest: "Burroughs was stoned and mute as always. Corso got drunk and cut off Duchamp's tie with a pair of scissors, emulating what he thought was a typical Dadaist action. Allen, too, was drunk, he went down on his knees in front of Duchamp and kissed the bottom of his trousers" (87).

19. On Wordsworth, see Sudan 2013; and Kitson; on Charles Lamb and Samuel Coleridge, see Fang. See also Zieger; Fulford and Kitson; and Leask.

20. Burroughs emphasizes the importance of curare by having his protagonist recount its history: "An explorer in sun helmet has brought down a citizen with blow gun and curare dart. He administers artificial respiration with one foot. (Curare kills by paralyzing the lungs. It has no other toxic effect, is not, strictly speaking, a poison)" (34). In *Poison Arrows* (2005), Stanley Feldman fleshes out this story: curare was a toxin used for centuries by indigenous populations in South America as a poison on their arrows that could kill game or their enemies. Feldman explains that curare works by preventing

the message carried in nerves from translating into muscular activity. This effect could both kill and be mobilized to give the medical establishment greater control over, and access to, the nervous system, and thus become a key part in the development of anesthetics and electroshock treatment (see also Shepherd and Watt 752).

21. See, for instance, Mullins's argument that the Interzone is a utopic counterspace to the West. In this space, he writes, "encounters between people from different nations, cultures, and religions were transacted, in part, through sexual activity and drug use [. . .] served to break down other social and psychic barriers" (5).

22. "Latahs" is the term for a person who suffers from "Latah," a "culture-specific startle-syndrome" in Malaysia and Indonesia that is often associated with erratic and skittish behaviour and also with "forced obedience" (Bakker et al., 371).

23. Interestingly, however, if the queered, nationalist Arab is one site of invasion in the development imaginary, the other site is that of the racist, southern whites who also weirdly seem to populate the Interzone. Crucial here are Clem and Jody, who are described as "two old-time vaudeville hoofers, cop out as Russian agents whose sole function is to present the US in an unpopular light" (132). They tell the story of being "arrested for Sodomy in Indonesia" and defending themselves by proclaiming to the magistrate, "It ain't as if it was being queer. After all they's only Gooks" (133), before exclaiming in a seeming non sequitur, "So I shoot that old nigger" (133). In addition to the Clem and Jody scene, Burroughs references the "nigger-killing sheriffs" in the south of Texas (14), the area known as "Dead Coon County, Arkansas ['Blackest Dirt, Whitest People in the U.S.A.—Nigger, Don't Let The Sun Set On You Here']" (36, square brackets in original). Jennifer Rae Greeson has pointed to the ways in which the South has come to embody the disavowed coloniality of the United States: "simultaneously colonial and colonized, it diverges from the nation writ large on the basis of its exploitativeness as the location of the internal colonization of Africans and African Americans in the United States—and on the basis of its exploitation—as the location of systemic underdevelopment, military defeat, and occupation" (3). Clem and Jody, the ostensible Russian spies, are everything that both the Jazz Ambassadors and urban renewal was trying to defend against: the figure of the backwards southern racist and the Yankee imperialist.

24. For more on the racial, sexual, and gendered underpinnings of the hard-boiled genre, see Pepper; Orr; Breu; Abbott; E. Smith; Pfeil; M. Davis 1992; and Avila 2004.

25. Important here is the history of drug criminalisation. Noted drug

historian David Musto notes that, beginning in 1951, "the Federal statute was dramatically strengthened [. . .] by making first convictions carry a mandatory minimum penalty of two years and by omitting provision for either suspension of sentences or probation on second and subsequent convictions" (230). Similarly, Gerald M. Oppenheimer argues that the "draconian" Boggs Act of 1951 and the Narcotics Control Act of 1956 "significantly hiked minimum sentences and almost completely eliminated parole for those found guilty of selling or possessing narcotics" (498). For further discussions of the criminalization of addicts and addictions that occurred during the midcentury, see R. King; and Lindesmith. In part, this turn toward criminalization is precisely what *Naked Lunch* argues against in its concluding coda, "Deposition: Testimony Concerning a Sickness," where Burroughs, like many of the drug reformers of the time, argues for a return to medical conceptions of drug use and addiction. Notably, "Deposition," which is the clearest and most linear section of the book, is also the most reformist—that is, it is the section that most explicitly addresses the state and interacts with state policy.

26. I am grateful to Dan Grausam for this insight.

4. SHOCK THERAPY: *ATLAS SHRUGGED*, URBAN RENEWAL, AND THE MAKING OF THE ENTREPRENEURIAL SUBJECT

1. There is a vast literature on the decline of the American city. See, for instance, Isenberg; Beauregard; Teaford; Mollenkopf; and Gelfand.

2. For more on the emergence of the term blight, see Fogelson; Weiss; and Wood.

3. The two most notable books that solidified the use of the term blight were Mabel Walker's *Urban Blight and Slums: Economic and Legal Factors in their Origin, Reclamation, and Prevention* (1938); and Edith Elmer Wood's *Slums and Blighted Areas in the United States* (1939).

4. In "The 'Public Menace' of Blight: Urban Renewal and the Private Uses of Eminent Domain" (2003), Wendell Pritchett highlights the relationship between the term "blight" and shifts in racial policy. He explains that the most important court case on the topic of urban renewal, *Berman v. Parker*, was argued four months after the monumental *Brown v. Board of Education*. At issue in *Berman v. Parker* was the question as to whether clearing a blighted area in and of itself constituted "public use," even if the cleared land would be given over to private developers. The case concluded that such condemnations were constitutional (1). Thus, Pritchett argues, both the *Berman* and the *Brown* case "were intimately related" because "the urban renewal program that the Court approved allowed cities to redistribute their populations, increasing residential segregation" (44). Urban renewal, in other words, became a policy of segregation by other means.

5. Kenneth Jackson explains this process in his pathbreaking *Crabgrass Frontier: The Suburbanization of the United States* (1987). The Home Owners Loan Corporation (HOLC) refinanced and restabilized millions of mortgages across the country and revolutionized how mortgages worked, creating the twenty-five-year loan and laying the groundwork to transform the United States into a nation of homeowners. HOLC also carried out the first large-scale appraisals of urban space. They divided cities into neighborhoods, developed elaborate questionnaires, and then created standardized measures of the value of all urban neighborhoods in the United States. Their system, however, "undervalued neighborhoods that were dense, mixed, or aging," characterizing them negatively as fourth grade or "red." This system came to effectively underwrite federal housing policy from that point forward. For instance, in 1934, Franklin Delano Roosevelt created the Federal Housing Administration (FHA) to ensure and guarantee mortgages, thus bringing down interest rates and making home ownership available on a wide scale. The FHA used HOLC's rating system and refused to ensure mortgages that fell within the "red" line. These processes, Jackson argues, guaranteed the underdevelopment and ghettoization of urban, racialized populations, and the overdevelopment of suburban, white populations (97–210).

6. Thomas Sugrue, Kevin Kruse, and Robert Self have all made similar arguments.

7. See, for instance, Harvey 2008; Florida and Jonas; and D. Walker.

8. It is worth noting here that politically Rand would in no way have been an ally of urban renewal. Her disciple Martin Anderson, whose book *The Federal Bulldozer: A Critical Analysis of Urban Renewal, 1949–1962* (1964) became a textbook of conservative urban policy, attacked urban renewal for failing to solve the housing problem and indeed making it worse before concluding that the only thing that can save us from the quagmire of urban development is, unsurprisingly, "free enterprise" (230). The point of reading *Atlas Shrugged* in the context of urban renewal, in other words, is not to align laissez-faire or protoneoliberal urban policy with urban renewal but rather to show the ways in which these neoliberal policies were able to at once profit from the infrastructures created by renewal while ideologically resignifying the meaning and lessons of the failure of renewal.

9. Rand clearly distinguished her iteration of "romanticism" from the "Romanticism" of writers like Shelley, Keats, and Wordsworth, explaining that her literary definition is hers alone and "not a generally known or accepted one" (1975, 102–3).

10. In "The Actuality of Ayn Rand" (2002), Slavoj Žižek transcodes the looter state and its "ideal zero" or "zero point" into Lacanian terms as "subjective destitution" (222), the point the subject must pass through to become

wholly actualized. But such a transcoding removes our ability to situate Rand in her properly modernist context amid a diverse range of other novelists and writers who, as we have seen throughout this book, were engaged in the problem of shock. By keeping our language within the terms of Freud's death drive, we are better able to historicize and understand the critiques that Rand is leveling at the psychological and economic tenets of modernism and the welfare state.

11. This is a common topic on Rand forums, and Rand herself partially answered this in one of her letters where she explains that "Eddie Willers is not necessarily destined to die; in a free society, he will live happily and productively; in a collectivist society, he will be the first to perish. He does not have the ability to create a new society of his own, but he is much too able and too honest ever to adjust himself to collectivism" (1997, 564).

5. FALLEN CORPSES AND RISING CITIES: *THE BELL JAR* AND THE MAKING OF THE NEW WOMAN

1. For a more in-depth discussion of New York's bid for the UN headquarters and its subsequent construction, see "Clearing the Slum Called War," in Zipp 2012; and Mumford 1956b.

2. As the report explains, "the City acquired by condemnation, at its own expense, the balance of the privately-owned land in the block bounded by East 47th Street, First Avenue, East 48th Street and Franklin D. Roosevelt Drive, and deeded all of it, except for a narrow strip required for the widening of East 48th Street, to the United Nations. East 43rd, 44th, 45th, 46th and 47th Streets were closed between First Avenue and the Drive and also transferred" (Moses, 2).

3. In Moses's report to O'Dwyer's successor, Mayor Vincent R. Impellitteri, he wrote: "The story of the United Nations would not be complete without describing the changes in the surrounding neighborhood. The site was originally a malodorous slaughterhouse district and the source of many complaints by its residential neighbors to the north and west. Properties were offered at ridiculously low prices and there were no takers. Today the same parcels have doubled and tripled in value, and are being held for as much as $65 per square foot. The Carnegie Foundation has purchased a plot at the northwest corner of First Avenue and East 46th Street and started constructing a new building. A prominent savings bank intends to construct a new bank and office across the street from the site. [. . .] The great activity in real estate points to the rehabilitation of this area by private investment which has been attracted by the United Nations. A large part of this area is old and substandard and it would have required aid from the City through public housing or slum clearance through the use of Title I of the National Housing

Act of 1949 with a write-down of values sufficiently to attract the private capital that is now quite apparently entering the area. This alone will eventually save the City more than the amount it has expended in aiding the United Nations" (4).

4. The UN also had its detractors. Lewis Mumford didn't just hate the design of the UN Building, which he called "a fragile aesthetic achievement, whose main lines conform to the ideals of a boom period of shaky finance and large-scale speculation" (1956b, 43–44), but he also warned that its reliance on Rockefeller created a shaky foundation on its own. "It was," he wrote, "bad symbolism to let Mr. Rockefeller get mixed up with the United Nations headquarters. [. . .] [T]o some of our more difficult brothers overseas, Mr. Rockefeller is Monopoly Capitalism, and the fact that it was he, and not the City of New York or the federal government, who gave this site to the United Nations, will not, unfortunately, lessen their suspicions" (1956b, 25). For Mumford and others, in other words, the UN was not a symbol of clearing "this slum called war" (White, 710) but rather a symbol of the rapacious reconsolidation of capitalism under US hegemony.

5. For more on the relationship between the Rosenbergs as spies and New York's urban landscape, see Moore; and A. Ross.

6. Esther compares the excess of New York to a memory of her grandmother, who "cooked economy joints and economy meat-loafs and had the habit of saying, the minute you lifted the first forkful to your mouth, 'I hope you enjoy that, it cost forty-one cents a pound,' which always made me feel I was somehow eating pennies instead of Sunday roast" (27).

7. As Christina Britzolakis argues, throughout *The Bell Jar*, "food and spectacle become interchangeable" (36).

8. Weir Mitchell famously treated Perkins Gilman and issued her the following orders: "Live as domestic a life as possible. Have your child with you all the time . . . Have but two hours' intellectual life a day. And never touch a pen, brush or pencil as long as you live" (Perkins Gilman 1972, 96).

9. Garry Leonard, for instance, has astutely observed that the image of the bell jar and Esther's repeated sense that she is being encased in glass acts as a metaphor for the "the plate-glass windows of department stores, where 'women' (mannequins) strike a 'feminine' pose with such perfection that only a dead woman could hope to rival it" (62). Renée Dowbnia makes a similar point, arguing that Esther's "conspicuous consumption [. . .] attests to Horkheimer and Adorno's claim that culture is simultaneously commodified and used to control the masses, who become commodities themselves under capitalism" (571).

10. There is an important body of feminist scholarship that has tied the gendered division of labor, and particularly women's entrapment within the

prison of domesticity, to larger processes of capitalist expansion and colonialism. Sylvia Federici and Mariarosa Dalla Costa and Selma James have all argued that the division of labor and women's oppression are not leftovers from feudalism but are instead at the core of capitalist accumulation. Similarly, in *Patriarchy and Accumulation on a World Scale: Women in the International Division of Labour* (1999), Maria Mies argues that the process of what she terms "housewifization" and colonialism have always been interlinked. As she puts it, "The conquest and exploitation of the colonies from the 16th century onwards was the basis for capital accumulation in Europe. But equally important was the destruction of the autonomy of women over their bodies and life during the witch pogroms" (5). Hazel Carby applies a similar analytic with respect to race and gender ideologies in the antebellum South, arguing that the two "opposing definitions of motherhood and womanhood for white and black women which coalesce in the figures of the slave and the mistress" (20) emerged alongside, and in response to, the passing of laws that made it illegal to import more slaves. She contends that because "the slave followed the condition of his or her mother [it] necessitated the raising of protective barriers, ideological and institutional, around the form of the white mother, whose progeny were heirs to the economic, social, and political interest in the maintenance of the slave system" (20). My analysis here of the changing role of women in the changing conditions of capital is deeply indebted to these accounts.

11. We can compare this to the very clinical and modern experience of shock she has at Dr. Nolan's as she is wheeled through the hallways of "bright, white lavatory tile" and the pipes threading through the "glittering walls" that appear like "an intricate nervous system" (225). Similarly, when she undergoes the experience of shock, she describes a nurse "smoothing" a "salve on [her] temples and fitting small electric buttons on either side" of her head (226).

CONCLUSION: *THE SIEGE OF HARLEM* AND ITS COMMUNE

1. Numerous articles and books have been written on this set of struggles. For books that largely repeat this myth, see Lang and Wunsch; Hirt and Zahm; Flint; Gratz; and Jennifer Hock, "Jane Jacobs and the West Village: The Neighborhood against Urban Renewal," *Journal of the Society of Architectural Historians* 66, no. 1 (2007): 16–19. For a more critical evaluation of Jane Jacobs's legacy, see Alfred; Larson; Zukin 2009 and 2006; J. Schwartz 1993, "Full Exposure" chapter; and Berman. For work that challenges the myth of Jacobs and Moses and offers a more nuanced and historically accurate account of the political and economic forces that led to Moses's fall, see Ballon and Jackson; and Caro, esp. chaps. 45–49.

2. For more on the interrelationship between the Communist Party and urban organizing in Harlem, and often the Caribbean roots of both, see Naison; Maxwell; James; and Stevens.

3. For more on the history of radical housing activism in New York City, see Biondi. See also Freeman; and Roberta Gold, *When Tenants Claimed the City: The Struggle for Citizenship in New York City Housing* (Champaign: University of Illinois Press, 2014).

4. Donna Jean Murch's *Living for the City: Migration, Education, and the Rise of the Black Panther Party in Oakland, California* makes the compelling case that the roots of the Black Panther Party lie in the "litany of Black nationalist and radical groups" that "spring up on the urban campuses of the East Bay's public colleges and universities" (5). As well, Assata Shakur discusses the key role that reading groups at CUNY campuses played in her radicalization.

5. In *Philosophy and Revolution: From Hegel to Sartre and Marx to Mao* (1982), Raya Dunayevskaya, too, draws a connection between black urban unrest and the Paris Commune.

6. The National Organization for Black Power, for example, formed in Detroit. They were the inspiration for much of the Boggses work—declaring, in their founding statement, that "We must struggle to control, to govern cities, as workers struggled to control and govern the factories of the 1930s" (167). Shortly before his assassination, Malcolm X also turned to the city, proclaiming that "Harlem is ours!" (qtd. in Boggs and Boggs, 165).

7. Kristin Ross's chapter "Beyond the 'Cellular Regime of Nationality'" in *Communal Luxury: The Political Imagination of the Paris Commune* (2016), makes this point particularly well. Matthew Beaumont's survey of the explosion of "cacotopic" or anti-Commune dystopias in England also drives home the importance of the Commune's internationalist dimension, revealing the extent to which the British upper class saw it as the product of the "seething imaginations of foreign conspirators" (Lord Salisbury qtd. in Beaumont, 467). See also John Merrman, *Massacre: The Life and Death of the Paris Commune of 1871* (New York: Basic, 2014); and Bargain-Villéger.

8. Nick Dyer-Witherford distinguishes between the "working class," which "includes all labourers," and the "proletariat," which "opens to the explicit inclusion of the unemployed and paupers" (13).

9. For more on the SDS and SAS occupation of Columbia, which called for an end to both Columbia incursions into Harlem via a proposed gym and its "affiliations with the Institute for Defense Analyses," see Bradley, 72.

Abbott, Megan E. 2002. *The Street Was Mine: White Masculinity in Hardboiled Fiction and Film Noir*. London: Palgrave.

Aboul-Ela, Hosam. 2007. *Other South: Faulkner, Coloniality, and the Máriategui Tradition*. Pittsburgh: University of Pittsburgh Press.

Abrams, Charles. 1965. *The City Is the Frontier*. New York: Harper and Row.

Abu-Lughod, Janet L. 1999. *New York, Chicago, Los Angeles: America's Global Cities*. Minneapolis: University of Minnesota Press.

Adorno, Theodor W. 1991. *Notes to Literature, Volume 1*. New York: Columbia University Press.

———. 1997. *Aesthetic Theory*. Translated by Robert Hullot-Kentor. Minneapolis: University of Minnesota Press.

Agathangelou, Anna M., Daniel Bassichis, and Tamara L. Spira. 2008. "Intimate Investments: Homonormativity, Global Lockdown, and the Seductions of Empire." *Radical History Review* 100:120–43.

Alexander, Michelle. *The New Jim Crow: Mass Incarceration in the Age of Colorblindness*. 2010. New York: New Press.

Alfred, Johan. 2015. "'Wilding' in the West Village: Queer Space, Racism, and Jane Jacobs Hagiography." *International Journal of Urban Regional Research* 39 (2): 265–83.

Anderson, Martin. 1964. *The Federal Bulldozer: A Critical Analysis of Urban Renewal, 1949–1962*. Cambridge: MIT Press.

Arrighi, Giovanni. 1994. *The Long Twentieth Century: Money, Power, and the Origins of Our Times*. New York: Verso.

Ashe, Marie. 1995. "*The Bell Jar* and the Ghost of Ethel Rosenberg." In *Secret Agents: The Rosenberg Case, McCarthyism, and Fifties America*. New York: Routledge.

Attorney General v. A Book Named Naked Lunch. 1966. 351 Mass. 298, Suffolk County, 1966.

Avila, Eric. 2004. *Popular Culture in the Age of White Flight: Fear and Fantasy in Suburban Los Angeles*. Berkeley: University of California Press.

———. 2014. *The Folklore of the Freeway: Race and Revolt in the Modernist City*. Minneapolis: University of Minnesota Press.

Baker, Houston A., Jr., and Dana D. Nelson. 2001. "Preface: Violence, the Body and "the South." *American Literature* 73, no. 2 (June): 231–44.

Bakker, Mirte, J., et al. 2013. "Latah: An Indonesian Startle Syndrome." *Movement Disorders* 28, no. 3 (March): 370–79.

Baldwin, James. 1962. *Another Country*. New York: Vintage.

Baldwin, Kate A. 2004. "The Radical Imaginary of *The Bell Jar*." *Novel: A Forum on Fiction* 38 (1): 21–40.

Ballon, Hilary, and Kenneth T. Jackson. 2007. *Robert Moses and the Modern City: The Transformation of New York*. New York: Norton.

Banks, Ann, and Aaron Siskind. 1981. *Harlem Document: Photographs, 1932–1940*, Providence, R.I.: Matrix.

Bargain-Villéger, Alban. 2014. "The Scarecrow on the Other Side of the Pond: The Paris Commune of 1871 in the Canadian Press." *Labor/Le Travail* 74, (1): 179–98.

Bauer, Catherine. 1934. *Modern Housing*. New York: Houghton Mifflin.

Beaumont, Matthew. 2006. "Cacotopianism, the Paris Commune, and England's Anti-Communist Imaginary, 1870–1900." *ELH* 73 (2): 465–87.

Beauregard, Robert A. 1993. *Voices of Decline: The Postwar Fate of US Cities* Cambridge: Blackwell.

Benjamin, Walter. 1999. "On Some Motifs in Baudelaire." In *Walter Benjamin: Selected Writings, 1939–1940*, edited by Howard Eiland and Michael W. Jennings; translated by Harry Zohn, 4:313–35. Cambridge: Harvard University Press.

———. 2005. "Surrealism: The Last Snapshot of the European Intelligentsia." In *Walter Benjamin: Selected Writings, 1927–1930*, edited by Howard Eiland, Michael W. Jennings, and Gary Smith; translated by Edmund Jephcott, 2.1:207–21. Cambridge: Harvard University Press.

Berman, Marshall. 1982. *All That Is Solid Melts into Air*. New York: Verso.

Bernard, Stéphane. 1968. *The Franco-Moroccan Conflict, 1943–56*. New Haven: Yale University Press.

Beuka, Robert. 2004. *SuburbiaNation: Reading Suburban Landscape in Twentieth-Century American Fiction and Film*. London: Palgrave Macmillan.

Bewes, Timothy. 2002. *Reification, Or, the Anxiety of Late Capitalism*. New York: Verso.

Bialasiewicz, Luiza, and Lauren Wagner. 2015. "Extra-Ordinary Tangier: Domesticating Practices in a Border Zone." *GeoHumanities* 1 (1): 131–56.

Big Table, Inc. v. Schroeder. 1960. 186 F. Supp. 254 (U.S. Dist., 1960).

Biles, Roger, Raymond A. Mohl, and Mark H. Rose. 2014. "Revisiting the Urban Interstates Politics, Policy, and Culture since World War II." *Journal of Urban History* 40 (5): 827–30.

Biondi, Martha. 2009. *To Stand and Fight: The Struggle for Civil Rights in Postwar New York City*. Cambridge: Harvard University Press.

Boggs, James, and Grace L. Boggs. 1966. "The City Is the Black Man's Land." In *Pages from a Black Radical's Notebook: A James Boggs Reader*, edited by Stephen M. Ward, 162–70. Detroit: Wayne State University Press.

Bold, Christine. 2013. *The Frontier Club: Popular Westerns and Cultural Power, 1880–1924*. New York: Oxford University Press.

Bourgois, Philippe. 2003. *In Search of Respect: Selling Crack in El Barrio*. Cambridge: Cambridge University Press.

Bradley, Stefan. 2009. *Harlem vs Columbia University: Black Student Power in the Late 1960s*. Champaign: University of Illinois Press.

Breines, Wini. 2001. *Young, White, and Miserable: Growing up Female in the Fifties*. Chicago: University of Chicago Press.

Brenner, Robert. 2006. *The Economics of Global Turbulence: The Advanced Capitalist Economies from Long Boom to Long Downturn, 1945–2005*. London: Verso.

Breton, André. 1969a. *Manifestos of Surrealism*. Translated by Richard Seaver and Helen Lane. Ann Arbor: University of Michigan Press.

———. 1969b. "Political Position of Today's Art." In *Manifestos of Surrealism*, translated by Richard Seaver and Helen Lane. Ann Arbor: University of Michigan Press.

Breu, Christopher. 2005. *Hard-Boiled Masculinities*. Minneapolis: University of Minnesota Press.

Britzolakis, Christina. 1999. *Sylvia Plath and the Theatre of Mourning*. New York: Oxford University Press.

Brown, Adrienne. 2016. "'My Hole Is Warm and Full of Light': The Sub-Urban Real Estate of *Invisible Man*." In *Race and Real Estate*, edited by Brown and Valerie Smith. New York: Oxford University Press.

Brown, Edgar G. 1949. *Hearings before the Committee on Banking and Currency House of Representatives*. Eighty-First Cong.

Brown, Elaine. 2015. *A Taste of Power: A Black Woman's Story*. New York: Anchor.

Brown, Wendy. 2015. *Undoing the Demos: Neoliberalism's Stealth Revolution*. Cambridge: MIT Press.

Buck-Morss, Susan. 1979. *Origin of Negative Dialectics: Theodor W. Adorno, Walter Benjamin, and the Frankfurt Institute*. New York: Simon and Schuster.

———. 1986. "The Flaneur, the Sandwichman and the Whore: The Politics of Loitering." *New German Critique*, no. 39, 99–140.

———. 1991. *The Dialectics of Seeing: Walter Benjamin and the Arcades Project*. Cambridge: MIT Press.

———. 1992. "Aesthetics and Anaesthetics: Walter Benjamin's Artwork Essay Reconsidered." *October* 62, no. 1 (October): 3–41.

Burroughs, William S. 1959a. *The Naked Lunch*. Paris: Olympia.

———. 1959b. "Ten Episodes from Naked Lunch." *Big Table* 1:79–137.

———. 1962. *Naked Lunch*. New York: Grove.

———. 2001. *Naked Lunch*. Edited by James Grauerholz, and Barry Miles. New York: Grove.

———. 2008. *Junky: The Definitive Text of "Junk."* New York: Penguin.

Burroughs, William S., and Brion Gysin. 1978. *The Third Mind*. New York: Viking.

Canaday, Margot. 2009. *The Straight State: Sexuality and Citizenship in Twentieth-Century America*. Princeton, N.J.: Princeton University Press.

Carby, Hazel. 1990. *Reconstructing Womanhood: The Emergence of Afro-American Woman Novelist*. Oxford: Oxford University Press.

Caro, Robert A. 1974. *The Power Broker: Robert Moses and the Fall of New York*. New York: Knopf.

Carpentier, Alejo. 2001. *The Lost Steps*. Minneapolis: University of Minnesota Press.

Cassuto, Leonard. 2009. *Hard-Boiled Sentimentality: The Secret History of American Crime Stories*. New York: Columbia University Press.

Castronovo, David. 2004. *Beyond the Gray Flannel Suit: Books from the 1950s That Made American Culture*. New York: Bloomsbury.

Césaire, Aimé. 2000. *Discourse on Colonialism*. Edited by Robin D. G. Kelley. Translated by Joan Pinkham. New York: Monthly Review Press.

Chen, Chris. 2013. "The Limit Point of Capitalist Equality: Notes toward an Abolitionist Antiracism." *Endnotes* 3:202–23.

Clover, Joshua. 2016. *Riot. Strike. Riot: The New Era of Uprisings*. London: Verso.

Corber, Robert J. 2011. *Cold War Femme: Lesbianism, National Identity, and Hollywood Cinema*. Durham, N.C.: Duke University Press.

Courtwright, David T. 1982. *Dark Paradise: Opiate Addiction in America before 1940*. Cambridge: Harvard University Press.

———. 2001. *Forces of Habit: Drugs and the Making of the Modern World*. Cambridge: Cambridge University Press.

Cowan, Deb, and Nemoy Lewis. 2016. "Anti-Blackness and Urban Geopolitical Economy: Reflections on Ferguson and the Suburbanization of the 'Internal Colony.'" *Society & Space*. August 2, 2016. http://societyand space.org/2016/08/02/anti-blackness-and-urban-geopolitical-economy -deborah-cowen-and-nemoy-lewis/.

Dalla Costa, Mariarosa, and Selma James. 1972. *The Power of Women and Subversion of the Community*. Bristol: Falling Wall.

Davis, Angela. 2003. *Are Prisons Obsolete?* New York: Seven Stories.

Davis, Mike. 1992. *City of Quartz: Excavating the Future in Los Angeles*. New York: Vintage.

———. 2000. *Late Victorian Holocausts: El Niño Famines and the Making of the Third World*. London: Verso.

———. 2007. *Planet of Slums*. New York: Verso.

Deleuze, Gilles. 1992. "Postscript on the Societies of Control." *October* 59:3–7.

Denning, Michael. 1998. *The Cultural Front: The Laboring of American Culture in the Twentieth Century*. New York: Verso.

Dickstein, Morris. 2002. *Leopards in the Temple: The Transformation of American Fiction, 1945–1970*. Cambridge: Harvard University Press.

Dowbnia, Renée. 2014. "Consuming Appetites: Food, Sex, and Freedom in Sylvia Plath's *The Bell Jar*." *Women's Studies* 43 (5): 567–88.

Duggan, Lisa. 2003. *The Twilight of Equality: Neoliberalism, Cultural Politics, and the Attack on Democracy*. Boston: Beacon.

Dunayevskaya, Raya. 2003. *Philosophy and Revolution: From Hegel to Sartre, and from Marx to Mao*. Lanham, Md.: Lexington.

Dyer-Witherford, Nick. 2015. *Cyber-Proletariat: Global Labour in the Digital Vortex*. Chicago: University of Chicago Press.

Eburne, Jonathan P. 1997. "Trafficking in the Void: Burroughs, Kerouac, and the Consumption of Otherness." *Modern Fiction Studies* 43 (1): 53–92.

Edelman, Lee. 2004. *No Future: Queer Theory and the Death Drive*. Durham, N.C.: Duke University Press.

Edwards, Brian. 2005. *Morocco Bound: Disorienting America's Maghreb, from Casablanca to the Marrakech Express*. Durham, N.C.: Duke University Press.

Ehrenreich, Barbara, and Deirdre English. 1978. *For Her Own Good: Two Centuries of the Experts' Advice to Women*. New York: Random House.

Ellison, Ralph. 1939. "Judge Lynch in New York." *New Masses*, 15–17.

———. 1964. "Harlem Is Nowhere." In *Shadow and Act*. New York: Random House.

———. 1978. "The Little Man at Chehaw Station: The American Artist and His Audience." *American Scholar* 47 (1): 25–48.

———. *Invisible Man*. 1992. New York: Modern Library.

———. 1995a. "The Art of Fiction: An Interview." In *Shadow and Act*. New York: Vintage.

———. 1995b. "Change the Joke and Slip the Yoke." In *Shadow and Act*. New York: Vintage.

Elmwood, Victoria A. 2008. "The White Nomad and the New Masculine Family in Jack Kerouac's *On the Road*." *Western American Literature* 42 (4): 335–61.

Escobar, Arturo. 2011. *Encountering Development: The Making and Unmaking of the Third World*. Princeton, N.J.: Princeton University Press.

Esteve, Mary. 2012. "Queer Consumerism, Straight Happiness: Highsmith's 'Right Economy.'" *Post45: Peer Review.*

Eversley, Shelley. 2001. "The Lunatic's Fancy and the Work of Art." *American Literary History* 13 (3): 445–68.

Fang, Karen. 2003. "Empire, Coleridge, and Charles Lamb's Consumer Imagination." *Studies in English Literature, 1500–1900* 43 (4): 815–43.

Farland, Maria. 2000. "Sylvia Plath's Anti-Psychiatry." *Minnesota Review,* no. 55–57, 245–56.

Faulkner, William. 2005. *The Uncollected Stories of William Faulkner.* New York: Vintage.

Federici, Sylvia. 2014. *Caliban and the Witch: Women, the Body and Primitive Accumulation.* Brooklyn: Autonomedia.

Feldman, Stanley. 2005. *Poison Arrows.* Toronto: Hushion House.

Felski, Rita. 1995. *The Gender of Modernity.* Cambridge: Harvard University Press.

Fiedler, Leslie A. 1960. *Love and Death in the American Novel.* New York: Criterion.

———. 1964. *Waiting for the End.* New York: Dell.

———. 1971. "The New Mutants." In *The Collected Essays of Leslie Fiedler Volume 2.* New York: Stein and Day.

Finlayson, Iain. 1993. *Tangier: City of the Dream.* London: Flamingo.

Fischer-Hornung, Dorothea. 1979. *Folklore and Myth in Ralph Ellison's Early Works.* Stuttgart: Hochschulverlag.

Fisher, Louis. 2006. *In the Name of National Security: Unchecked Presidential Power and the Reynolds Case.* Lawrence: University Press of Kansas.

Fishman, Robert. 2007. "Revolt of the Urbs: Robert Moses and his Critics." In *Robert Moses and the Modern City: The Transformation of New York.* New York: Norton.

Fleissner, Jennifer L. 2004. *Women, Compulsion, Modernity: The Moment of American Naturalism.* Chicago: University of Chicago Press.

Flint, Anthony. 2011. *Wrestling with Moses: How Jane Jacobs Took on New York's Master Builder and Transformed the American City.* New York: Random House.

Florida, Richard, and Andrew Jonas. 1991. "U.S. Urban Policy: The Postwar State and Capitalist Regulation." *Antipode* 23 (4): 349–84.

Fogelson, Robert M. 2003. *Downtown: Its Rise and Fall, 1880–1950.* New Haven: Yale University Press.

Foley, Barbara. 1993. *Radical Representations: Politics and Form in US Proletarian Fiction, 1929-1941.* Durham, N.C.: Duke University Press.

———. 2003. "From Communism to Brotherhood: The Drafts of Invisible Man." In *Left of the Color Line: Race, Radicalism, and Twentieth-Century*

Literature of the United States, 163–82. Chapel Hill: University of North Carolina Press.

———. 2010. *Wrestling with the Left: The Making of Ralph Ellison's "Invisible Man."* Durham, N.C.: Duke University Press.

Foster, Hal. 1993. *Compulsive Beauty*. Cambridge: MIT Press.

Fotsch, Paul M. 2001. "The Building of a Superhighway Future at the New York World's Fair." *Cultural Critique* 48 (1): 65–97.

Foucault, Michael. 2008. *Birth of Biopolitics: Lectures at the Collège De France, 1978-79*. Edited by Michel Senellart; translated by Graham Burchell. New York: Palgrave Macmillan.

Francis, White E. 2001. *Dark Continent of Our Bodies: Black Feminism and the Politics of Respectability*. Philadelphia: Temple University Press.

Fraser, Nancy. 2013. *Fortunes of Feminism: From State-Managed Capitalism to Neoliberal Crisis*. London: Verso.

Freeman, Joshua. 2000. *Working-Class New York: Life and Labor since World War II*. New York: New Press.

Freud, Sigmund. 1955a. "Beyond the Pleasure Principle." In *The Standard Edition of the Complete Psychological Works of Sigmund Freud*, translated by James Strachey, vol. 18 (*1920–1922*), 1–64. London: Hogarth Press and the Institute of Psychoanalysis, London.

———. 1955b. "The Uncanny." In *The Standard Edition of the Complete Psychological Works of Sigmund Freud*, edited and translated by James Strachey, vol. 17 (*1917–1919*), 219–52. London: Hogarth Press and the Institute of Psychoanalysis.

———. 1974. *Cocaine Papers*. Edited by Robert Byck. New York: Farrar, Straus and Giroux.

———. 1989. "Negation." 1989. In *The Freud Reader*, edited by Peter Gay, 666–69. New York: Norton.

———. 1994. *The Interpretation of Dreams*. Translated by A. A. Brill. 3rd ed. New York: Barnes and Noble.

Freund, David. 2010. *Colored Property: State Policy and White Racial Politics in Suburban America*. Chicago: University of Chicago Press.

Fulford, Timothy, and Peter J. Kitson. 2005. *Romanticism and Colonialism: Writing and Empire, 1780–1830*. Cambridge: Cambridge University Press.

Geidel, Molly. 2015. *Peace Corps Fantasies: How Development Shaped the Global Sixties*. Minneapolis: University of Minnesota Press.

Gelfand, Mark I. 1975. *A Nation of Cities: The Federal Government and Urban America, 1933–1965*. New York: Oxford University Press.

Gilmore, Ruth W. 2007. *Golden Gulag: Prisons, Surplus, Crisis, and Opposition in Globalizing California*. Berkeley: University of California Press.

Goonewardena, Kanishka. 2005. "The Urban Sensorium: Space, Ideology and the Aestheticization of Politics." *Antipode* 37 (1): 46–71.

Gootenberg, Paul. 2008. *Andean Cocaine: The Making of a Global Drug.* Chapel Hill: University of North Carolina Press.

Gordon, Leah N. 2015. *From Power to Prejudice: The Rise of Racial Individualism in Midcentury America.* Chicago: University of Chicago Press.

Gratz, Roberta B. 2011. *The Battle for Gotham: New York in the Shadow of Robert Moses and Jane Jacobs.* New York: Nation.

Greeson, Jennifer R. 2010. *Our South: Geographic Fantasy and the Rise of National Literature.* Cambridge: Harvard University Press.

Hackworth, Jason. 2007. *The Neoliberal City: Governance, Ideology, and Development in American Urbanism.* Ithaca, N.Y.: Cornell University Press.

Harcourt, Bernard E. 2011. *The Illusion of Free Markets: Punishment and the Myth of Natural Order.* Cambridge: Harvard University Press.

Harris, Oliver. 2003. *William Burroughs and the Secret of Fascination.* Carbondale: Southern Illinois University Press.

Harris, Oliver, and Ian MacFayden, eds. 2009. *Naked Lunch@50: Anniversary Essays.* Carbondale: Southern Illinois University Press.

Harvey, David. 2003a. *New Imperialism.* Oxford: Oxford University Press.

———. 2003b. *Paris, Capital of Modernity.* New York: Routledge.

———. 2005. *A Brief History of Neoliberalism.* Oxford: Oxford University Press.

———. 2007. "Neoliberalism and the City." *Studies in Social Justice* 1 (1): 1–13.

———. 2008. "The Right to the City." *New Left Review* 42:23–40.

———. 2011. *The Enigma of Capital: And the Crises of Capitalism.* London: Profile.

———. 2012. *Rebel Cities: From the Right to the City to the Urban Revolution.* London: Verso.

Haut, Woody. 1995. *Pulp Culture: Hardboiled Fiction and the Cold War.* London: Serpent's Tail.

Hayden, Dolores. 2003. *Building Suburbia: Green Fields and Urban Growth, 1820–2000.* New York: Pantheon.

Heise, Thomas. 2011. *Urban Underworlds: A Geography of Twentieth-Century American Literature and Culture.* New Brunswick, N.J.: Rutgers University Press.

Hemmer, Kurt. 2009. "'The Natives Are Getting Uppity': Tangier and Naked Lunch." In *Naked Lunch@50: Anniversary Essays,* edited by Oliver Harris and Ian MacFadyen, 65–71. Carbondale: Southern Illinois University Press.

Herman, Ellen. 1995a. "The Career of Cold War Psychology." *Radical History Review* 1995 (63): 53–85.

———. 1995b. *The Romance of American Psychology: Political Culture in the Age of Experts.* Berkeley: University of California Press.

Hesford, Victoria. 2003. "Love Flung out of Space: Lesbians in the City in Patricia Highsmith's *Carol.*" *Paradoxa* 18:118–35.

———. 2005. "Patriotic Perversions: Patricia Highsmith's Queer Vision of Cold War America in *The Price of Salt, The Blunderer* and *Deep Water.*" *Women's Studies Quarterly* 33 (3/4): 215–33.

Hibbard, Allen. 2009. "Tangier and the Making of Naked Lunch." In *Naked Lunch@50: Anniversary Essays*, edited by Oliver Harris and Ian MacFadyen, 56–63. Carbondale: Southern Illinois University Press.

Highsmith, Patricia. 2004. *The Price of Salt.* New York: Norton.

Hilliard, David, and Lewis Cole. 2002. *This Side of Glory: The Autobiography of David Hilliard and the Story of the Black Panther Party.* Chicago: Chicago Review Press.

Hirsch, Arnold R. 2000. "Searching for a 'Sound Negro Policy': A Racial Agenda for the Housing Acts of 1949 and 1954." *Housing Policy Debate* 11 (2): 393–441.

———. 2009. *Making the Second Ghetto: Race and Housing in Chicago 1940– 1960.* Chicago: University of Chicago Press.

Hirt, Sonia, and Diane L. Zahm. 2012. *The Urban Wisdom of Jane Jacobs.* New York: Routledge.

Hoberek, Andrew. 2002. "Cold War Culture to Fifties Culture." *Minnesota Review* 55–57:146.

———. 2005. *The Twilight of the Middle Class: Post–World War II American Fiction and White-Collar Work.* Princeton, N.J.: University Press.

hooks, bell. 1984. *Feminist Theory: From Margin to Center.* Boston: South End Press.

Houseman, Gerald L. 1982. *City of the Right: Urban Applications of American Conservative Thought.* Westport, Conn.: Greenwood.

Housing Act of 1949, 81st Cong., 1st sess., July 15, 1949.

Housing and Home Finance Agency (HHFA). 1950. *A Handbook of Information on Provisions of the Housing Act of 1949 and Operations under the Various Programs.* Washington, D.C.: Office of the Administrator.

Huber, Matthew T. 2013. *Lifeblood: Oil, Freedom, and the Forces of Capital.* Minneapolis: University of Minnesota Press.

Hussey, Andrew. 2009. "'Paris Is about the Last Place . . .': William Burroughs in and Out of Paris and Tangier, 1958–60." In *Naked Lunch@50: Anniversary Essays*, edited by Oliver Harris and Ian MacFadyen. Carbondale: Southern Illinois University Press.

Isenberg, Allison. 2004. *Downtown America: A History of the Place and the People Who Made It.* Chicago: University of Chicago Press.

Jackson, Kenneth T. 1987. *Crabgrass Frontier: The Suburbanization of the United States*. New York: Oxford University Press.

Jacobs, Jane. 1961. *The Death and Life of Great American Cities*. New York: Vintage.

Jacques, Geoffrey. 2009. *A Change in the Weather: Modernist Imagination, African American Imaginary*. Boston: University of Massachusetts Press.

James, Winston. 1998. *Holding aloft the Spirit of Ethiopia: Caribbean Radicalism in Early Twentieth-Century America*. New York: Verso.

Jameson, Fredric.1981. *The Political Unconscious: Narrative as a Socially Symbolic Act*. Ithaca, N.Y.: Cornell University Press.

———. 1991. *Postmodernism, or, The Cultural Logic of Late Capitalism*. Durham, N.C.: Duke University Press.

———. 2004. "The Politics of Utopia." *New Left Review* 25:35–54.

———. 2015. *The Antinomies of Realism*. New York: Verso.

Jernigan, Adam T. 2014. "Paraliterary Labors in Sylvia Plath's *The Bell Jar*: Typists, Teachers, and the Pink-Collar Subtext." *Modern Fiction Studies* 60 (1):1–27.

Johnson, David K. 2009. *The Lavender Scare: The Cold War Persecution of Gays and Lesbians in the Federal Government*. Chicago: University of Chicago Press.

Johnson, Lyndon. 1964. "University of Michigan Commencement Address." May 22, 1964. http://www.lbjlib.utexas.edu/johnson/archives.hom/speeches.hom/640522.asp.

Johnson, Rob. 2009. "William S. Burroughs as 'Good Ol' Boy': Naked Lunch in East Texas." In *Naked Lunch@50: Anniversary Essays*, edited by Oliver Harris and Ian MacFadyen. Carbondale: Southern Illinois University Press.

Jurca, Catherine. 2001. *White Diaspora: The Suburb and the Twentieth-Century American Novel*. Princeton, N.J.: Princeton University Press.

Keller, Yvonne. 2005. "'Was It Right to Love Her Brother's Wife So Passionately?': Lesbian Pulp Novels and US Lesbian Identity, 1950–1965." *American Quarterly* 57 (2): 385–410.

Kelley, Robin D. G. 1999. "A Poetics of Anticolonialism." *Monthly Review* 51 (6): 1–21.

Kerouac, Jack. 1976. *On the Road*. New York: Penguin.

Kinder, Douglas C., and William O. W., III. 1986. "Stable Force in a Storm: Harry J. Anslinger and United States Narcotic Foreign Policy, 1930–1962." *Journal of American History* 72 (4): 908–27.

King, Desmond S. 1995. *Separate and Unequal: Black Americans and the US Federal Government*. New York: Oxford University Press.

King, Rufus. 1972. *The Drug Hang-Up: America's Fifty-Year Folly*. New York: Norton.

Kitson, Peter J. 2012. "The Wordsworths, Opium, and China." *Wordsworth Circle* 43 (1): 2–12.

Klein, Naomi. 2008. *Shock Doctrine: The Rise of Disaster Capitalism*. Toronto: Random House.

Klemek, Christopher. 2011. *The Transatlantic Collapse of Urban Renewal: Postwar Urbanism from New York to Berlin*. Chicago: University of Chicago Press.

Kotz, David M. 2015. *The Birth of Neoliberal Capitalism*. Cambridge: Harvard University Press.

Kruse, Kevin M. 2005. *White Flight: Atlanta and the Making of Modern Conservatism*. Princeton, N.J.: Princeton University Press.

Kruse, Kevin M., and Thomas Sugrue. 2006. *The New Suburban History*. Chicago: University of Chicago Press.

Kuenz, Jane. 2001. "The Cowboy Businessman and 'The Course of Empire': Owen Wister's *"The Virginian."* *Cultural Critique* 48 (1): 98–128.

Lang, Glenna, and Marjory Wunsch. 2012. *Genius of Common Sense: Jane Jacobs and the Story of "The Death and Life of Great American Cities."* Boston: David R. Godine.

Larson, Scott. 2013. *"Building Like Moses with Jacobs in Mind": Contemporary Planning in New York City*. Philadelphia: Temple University Press.

Le Corbusier. 1973. *The Athens Charter*. New York: Grossman.

———. 2007. *Toward an Architecture*. Translated by John Goodman. London: Francis Lincoln.

Leach, Laurie F. 1963. "Sylvia Plath's *The Bell Jar*: Trapped by *the Feminine Mystique* (1963)." In *Women in Literature: Reading through the Lens of Gender*, edited by Jerilyn Fisher and Ellen S. Silber. Westport, Conn.: Greenwood.

Leask, Nigel. 2004. *British Romantic Writers and the East: Anxieties of Empire*. Cambridge: Cambridge University Press.

Lebel, Jean-Jacques. 2009. "Burroughs: The Beat Hotel Years." In *Naked Lunch@50: Anniversary Essays*, edited by Oliver Harris and Ian MacFadyen. Carbondale: Southern Illinois University Press.

Leonard, Garry M. 1992. "'The Woman Is Perfected. Her Dead Body Wears the Smile of Accomplishment': Sylvia Plath and *Mademoiselle* Magazine." *College Literature* 19 (2): 60–82.

Levenson, Jacob. 2004. *The Secret Epidemic: The Story of AIDS and Black America*. New York: Pantheon.

Levin, Joanna. 2009. *Bohemia in America, 1858–1920*. Stanford: Stanford University Press.

Lindesmith, Alfred R. 1965. *The Addict and the Law*. Bloomington: Indiana University Press.

Lipsky, Michael. 1970. *Protest in City Politics*. Chicago: Rand McNally.

Loewinsohn, Ron. 1998. "'Gentle Reader, I Fain Would Spare You This, but My Pen Hath Its Will Like the Ancient Mariner': Narrator(s) and Audience in William S. Burroughs's *Naked Lunch*." *Contemporary Literature* 39 (4): 560–85.

Loranger, Carol. 1999. "'This Book Spill off the Page in All Directions': What Is the Text of *Naked Lunch*?" *Postmodern Culture: An Electronic Journal of Interdisciplinary Criticism* 10 (1): n.p.

Löwy, Michael. 2010. "The Current of Critical Irrealism: 'A Moonlit Enchanted Night." In *A Concise Companion to Realism*, edited by Matthew Beaumont, 211–24. Chichester: Wiley-Blackwell.

Lyndenberg, Robin. 1987. *Word Cultures: Radical Theory and Practice in William S. Burroughs' Fiction*. Urbana: University of Illinois Press.

Marglin, Stephen A., and Juliet B. Schor. 1992. *The Golden Age of Capitalism: Reinterpreting the Postwar Experience*. Oxford: Oxford University Press.

Marx, Karl. 1966. *The Civil War in France*. Translated by Friedrich Engels. Peking: Foreign Languages Press.

———. 1977a. *Capital, Volume I*. Translated by Ben Fowkes. Toronto: Vintage.

———. 1977b. "The Communist Manifesto." In *Selected Writings*, edited by David McLellan. Oxford: Oxford University Press.

———. 1988. *Economic and Philosophic Manuscripts of 1844*. Translated by Martin Milligan. New York: Prometheus.

Massey, Douglas S., and Nancy A. Denton. 1993. *American Apartheid: Segregation and the Making of the Underclass*. Cambridge: Harvard University Press.

Matthews, Tracye. 1998. "'No One Ever Asks, What a Man's Place in the Revolution Is': Gender and the Politics of the Black Panther Party, 1966–1971." In *The Black Panther Party Reconsidered*. Baltimore: Black Classic Press.

Maxwell, William J. 1999. *New Negro, Old Left: African-American Writing and Communism between the Wars*. New York: Columbia University Press.

McCann, Sean. 2000. *Gumshoe America: Hard-Boiled Crime Fiction and the Rise and Fall of New Deal Liberalism*. Durham, N.C.: Duke University Press.

McConachie, Bruce. 2003. *American Theater in the Culture of the Cold War: Producing and Contesting Containment*. Iowa City: University of Iowa Press.

McGirr, Lisa. 2001. *Suburban Warriors: The Origins of the New American Right*. Princeton, N.J.: Princeton University Press.

McRobbie, Angela. 2009. *The Aftermath of Feminism: Gender, Culture, and Social Change*. London: Sage.

Medovoi, Leerom. 2005. *Rebels: Youth and the Cold War Origins of Identity.* Durham, N.C.: Duke University Press.

Melamed, Jodi. 2006. "The Spirit of Neoliberalism: From Racial Liberalism to Neoliberal Multiculturalism." *Social Text* 24 (4): 1–24.

———. 2011. *Represent and Destroy: Rationalizing Violence in the New Racial Capitalism.* Minneapolis: University of Minnesota Press.

Melley, Timothy. 2000. *Empire of Conspiracy: The Culture of Paranoia in Postwar America.* Ithaca, N.Y.: Cornell University Press.

———. 2008. "Brainwashed! Conspiracy Theory and Ideology in the Postwar United States." *New German Critique* 35 (1): 145–64.

Mendes, Gabriel N. 2015. *Under the Strain of Colour: Harlem's Lafargue Clinic and the Promise of an Antiracist Psychiatry.* Ithaca, N.Y.: Cornell University Press.

Mies, Maria. 1999. *Patriarchy and Accumulation on a World Scale: Women in the International Division of Labour.* 2nd ed. London: Zed.

Miller, Warren. 1964. *The Siege of Harlem.* New York: McGraw-Hill.

Mirowski, Phil, and Dieter Plehwe. 2009. *The Road to Mont Pèlerin: The Making of the Neoliberal Thought Collective.* Cambridge: Harvard University Press.

Mitchell, Nick. 2016. "The Fantasy and Fate of Ethnic Studies in an Age of Uprisings." https://undercommoning.org/nick-mitchell-interview/

Mitchell, Silas W. (1871) 2004. *Wear and Tear: Or Hints for the Overworked.* Vol. 4. Edited by Michael S. Kimmel. Altamira, Md.: Rowman.

———. 1877. *Nurse and Patient and Camp Cure.* Philadelphia: Lippincott.

Mohl, Raymond A. 2004. "Stop the Road Freeway Revolts in American Cities." *Journal of Urban History* 30 (5): 674–706.

Mollenkopf, John H. 1983. *The Contested City.* Princeton, N.J.: Princeton University Press.

Moody, Kim. 2007. *From Welfare State to Real Estate: Regime Change in New York City, 1974 to the Present.* New York: New Press.

Moore, Deborah Dash. 1988. "Reconsidering the Rosenbergs: Symbol and Substance in Second Generation American Jewish Consciousness." *Journal of American Ethnic History* 8 (1): 21–37.

Moretti, Franco. 1987. *The Way of the World: The Bildungsroman in European Culture.* London: Verso.

Morris, R. B. 2009. "I Am No Doctor." In *Naked Lunch@50: Anniversary Essays,* edited by Oliver Harris and Ian MacFadyen. Carbondale: Southern Illinois University Press.

Moses, Robert. 1951. *The United Nations and the City of New York: [Report to Mayor Impellitteri and the Board of Estimate].* New York: Office of the City Construction Co-ordinator.

Moynihan, Daniel Patrick. 1965. *The Negro Family: The Case for National Action*. Washington, D.C.: Office of Policy Planning and Research, Department of Labor.

Mullins, Greg A. 2002. *Colonial Affairs: Bowles, Burroughs, and Chester Write Tangier*. Madison: University of Wisconsin Press.

Mumford, Lewis. 1956a. "Magic with Mirrors." In *From the Ground Up: Observations on Contemporary Architecture, Housing, Highway Building, and Civic Design*. New York: Harcourt, Brace.

———. 1956b. "UN Model and Model UN." In *From the Ground Up: Observations on Contemporary Architecture, Housing, Highway Building, and Civic Design*. New York: Harcourt, Brace.

Murch, Donna Jean. 2010. *Living for the City: Migration, Education, and the Rise of the Black Panther Party in Oakland, California*. Chapel Hill: University of North Carolina Press.

Murison, Justine. 2011. *The Politics of Anxiety in Nineteenth-Century American Literature*. Cambridge: Cambridge University Press.

Musto, David. 1999. *The American Disease: Origins of Narcotic Control*. Oxford: Oxford University Press.

Nadel, Alan. 1995. *Containment Culture: American Narrative, Postmodernism, and the Atomic Age*. Durham, N.C.: Duke University Press.

Naison, Mark. 1983. *Communists in Harlem during the Depression*. Urbana: University of Illinois Press.

New York City Committee on Slum Clearance. 1949. *Preliminary Report on Initial New York City Projects under Title I of the Housing Act of 1949*. July 14, 1949. New York.

———. 1950. *Second Report to Mayor William O'Dwyer from the Mayor's Committee on Slum Clearance by Private Capital*. January 23, 1950. New York.

———. 1951. *North Harlem. Slum Clearance Plan under Title 1 of the Housing Act of 1949*. New York.

———. 1956. *Lincoln Square: Slum Clearance Plan under Title I of the 1949 Housing Act*. New York.

Newton, Huey P. 1995. "The Women's Liberation and Gay Liberation Movements: August 15, 1970." In *The Huey P. Newton Reader*, edited by David Hilliard and David Weise. New York: Seven Stories.

Ngô, Fiona I. 2014. *Imperial Blues: Geographies of Race and Sex in Jazz Age New York*. Durham, N.C.: Duke University Press.

Nwaubani, Ebere. 2003. "The United States and the Liquidation of European Colonial Rule in Tropical Africa, 1941–1963." *Cahiers D'études Africaines*, no. 3, 505–51.

Oberlander, H. P., and Eva M. Newbrun. 2011. *Houser: The Life and Work of Catherine Bauer, 1905–64*. Vancouver: UBC Press.

O'Connor, Alice. 2008. "The Privatized City: The Manhattan Institute, the Urban Crisis, and the Conservative Counterrevolution in New York." *Journal of Urban History* 34 (2): 333–53.

O'Donohue, Kathleen. 2012. *Liberty and Justice for All? Rethinking Politics in Cold War America.* Boston: University of Massachusetts Press.

Olster, Stacey. 1997. "Something Old, Something New, Something Borrowed, Something (Red, White, and) Blue: Ayn Rand's *Atlas Shrugged* and Objectivist Ideology." In *The Other Fifties: Interrogating Midcentury American Icons*, edited by Joel Foreman. Urbana: University of Illinois Press.

O'Meally, Robert. 1988. *New Essays on "Invisible Man."* Cambridge: Cambridge University Press.

Oppenheimer, Gerald M. 1991. "To Build a Bridge: The Use of Foreign Models by Domestic Critics of U.S. Drug Policy." In "Confronting Drug Policy: Part 1," special issue, *Milbank Quarterly* 69 (3): 495–526.

Orleck, Annelise, and Lisa G. Hazirjian. 2011. *The War on Poverty: A Grassroots History.* Athens: University of Georgia Press.

Orr, Stanley. 2010. *Darkly Perfect World: Colonial Adventure, Postmodernism, and American Noir.* Columbus: Ohio State University Press.

Ottley, Roi. 1943. *"New World A-Coming": Inside Black America.* New York: Houghton Mifflin.

Panitch, Leo, and Sam Gindin. 2013. *The Making of Global Capitalism: The Political Economy of American Empire.* New York: Verso.

Parenti, Christian. 1999. *Lockdown America: Police and Prisons in the Age of Crisis.* London: Verso.

Paton, Fiona. 2010. "Monstrous Rhetoric: *Naked Lunch*, National Insecurity, and the Gothic Fifties." *Texas Studies in Literature and Language* 52 (1): 48–69.

Peck, Jamie. *Constructions of Neoliberal Reason.* 2010. Oxford: Oxford University Press.

Pepper, Andrew. 2010. "The 'Hard-Boiled' Genre." In *A Companion to Crime Fiction*, edited by Charles J. Rzepka and Lee Horsley. Hoboken, N.J.: Wiley-Blackwell.

Perkins Gilman, Charlotte. 1972. *The Living of Charlotte Perkins Gilman.* New York: Arno.

———. 2013. *The Yellow Wallpaper and Other Writings.* New York: Bantam Classics.

Perrin, Tom. 2011. "Rebuilding Bildung: The Middlebrow Novel of Aesthetic Education in the Mid-Twentieth-Century United States." *Novel* 44 (3): 382–401.

Pfeil, Fred. 1995. "White Guys." In *Studies in Postmodern Domination and Difference.* London: Verso.

Pizer, Donald. 1984. *Realism and Naturalism in Nineteenth-Century American Literature*. Carbondale: Southern Illinois University Press.

Plath, Sylva. *The Bell Jar*. London: Faber and Faber, 1963.

Porter, Dennis. 1981. *The Pursuit of Crime: Art and Ideology in Detective Fiction*. New Haven: Yale University Press.

Pritchett, Wendell E. 2003. "The 'Public Menace' of Blight: Urban Renewal and the Private Uses of Eminent Domain." *Yale Law & Policy Review* 21 (1): 1–52.

"Private Financing Sought to Replace 7 City Slum Areas." 1951. *New York Times (1923–Current File)*.

Provine, Doris M. 2008. *Unequal under Law: Race in the War on Drugs*. Chicago: University of Chicago Press.

Puar, Jasbir. 2007. *Terrorist Assemblages: Homonationalism in Queer Times*. Durham, N.C.: Duke University Press.

Puar, Jasbir K., and Amit Rai. 2002. "Monster, Terrorist, Fag: The War on Terrorism and the Production of Docile Patriots." *Social Text* 20 (3): 117–48.

Purcell, Richard. 2013. "An Integrative Vernacular: Ellison, Dante, and Social Cohesion in the Post–Civil Rights Era." *ELH* 80 (3): 917–44.

Queer Kids of Queer Parents Against Gay Marriage! 2009. "Resist the Gay Marriage Agenda!" https://queerkidssaynomarriage.wordpress.com/.

Rabinowitz, Paula. 1991. *Labor & Desire: Women's Revolutionary Fiction in Depression America*. Chapel Hill: University of North Carolina Press.

———. 2014. *American Pulp: How Paperbacks Brought Modernism to Main Street*. Princeton N.J.: Princeton University Press.

Radford, Gail. 2008. *Modern Housing for America: Policy Struggles in the New Deal Era*. Chicago: University of Chicago Press.

Rand, Ayn. (1969) 1975. *The Romantic Manifesto: A Philosophy of Literature*. New York: Signet.

———. 1992. *Atlas Shrugged*. New York: Signet.

———. 1997. *Letters of Ayn Rand*. New York: Penguin.

Raskin, A. H. 1953. "Story of the Rosenbergs: Two Links in Atomic Conspiracy." *New York Times (1923–Current File)*.

Reddy, Chandan. 2011. *Freedom with Violence: Race, Sexuality, and the US State*. Durham, N.C.: Duke University Press.

Reiss, Suzanna. 2014. *We Sell Drugs: The Alchemy of US Empire*. Berkeley: University of California Press.

Richardson, Michael, and Krzysztof Fijałkowski. 1996. *Refusal of the Shadow: Surrealism and the Caribbean*. Translated by Fijałkowski and Richardson. London: Verso.

Ricoeur, Paul. 1990. *Time and Narrative, Volume 1*. Translated by Kathleen McLaughlin and David Pellauer. Chicago: University of Chicago Press.

Rideout, Walter B. 1992. *The Radical Novel in the United States, 1900–1954: Some Interrelations of Literature and Society*. New York: Columbia University Press.

Riesman, David, Nathan Glazer, and Reuel Denney. 1961. *The Lonely Crowd*. New Haven: Yale University Press.

Riis, Jacob A. 2004. *How the Other Half Lives: Studies among the Tenements of New York*. New York: Barnes and Noble.

Rose, Mark H., and Raymond A. Mohl. 2012. *Interstate: Highway Politics and Policy since 1939*. Knoxville: University of Tennessee Press.

Rosemont, Franklin, and Robin D. G. Kelley. 2009. *Black, Brown, & Beige: Surrealist Writings from Africa and the Diaspora*. Austin: University of Texas Press.

Ross, Andrew. 1988. "Intellectuals and Ordinary People: Reading the Rosenberg Letters." *Cultural Critique*, no. 9, 55–86.

Ross, Kristin. 1988. *The Emergence of Social Space: Rimbaud and the Paris Commune*. Minneapolis: University of Minnesota Press.

———. 1996. *Fast Cars, Clean Bodies: Decolonization and the Reordering of French Culture*. Cambridge: MIT Press.

———. 2016. *Communal Luxury: The Political Imaginary of the Paris Commune*. New York: Verso.

Rotella, Carlo. 1998. *October Cities: The Redevelopment of Urban Literature*. Berkeley: University of California Press.

Saldaña-Portillo, María J. 2003. *The Revolutionary Imagination in the Americas and the Age of Development*. Durham, N.C.: Duke University Press.

Schaub, Thomas. *American Fiction in the Cold War*. 1991. Madison: University of Wisconsin Press.

Schneiderman, Davis. 2009. "'Gentlemen I Will Slop a Pearl': The (Non) Meaning of *Naked Lunch*." In *Naked Lunch@50: Anniversary Essays*, edited by Oliver Harris and Ian MacFadyen. Carbondale: Southern Illinois University Press.

Schwartz, Joel. 1993. *The New York Approach: Robert Moses, Urban Liberals, and Redevelopment of the Inner City*. Columbus: Ohio State University Press.

Schwartz, Lawrence H. 1988. *Creating Faulkner's Reputation*. Knoxville: University of Tennessee Press.

Scott, James C. 1998. *Seeing Like a State: How Certain Schemes to Improve the Human Condition Have Failed*. New Haven: Yale University Press.

Sedgwick, Eve Kosofsky. 1993. "Queer Performativity: Henry James's *The Art of the Novel*." *Gay and Lesbian Quarterly* 1 (1): 1–16.

Self, Robert O. 2005. *American Babylon: Race and the Struggle for Postwar Oakland: Race and the Struggle for Postwar Oakland*. Princeton, N.J.: Princeton University Press.

Server, Lee. 1994. *Over My Dead Body: The Sensational Age of the American Paperback, 1945–1955*. San Francisco: Chronicle.

Shack, William. 2001. *Harlem in Montmartre*. Berkeley: University of California Press.

Shakur, Assata. 1987. *Assata: An Autobiography*. London: Zed.

Shannon, Joshua A. 2004. "Claes Oldenburg's 'The Street' and Urban Renewal in Greenwich Village, 1960." *Art Bulletin* 86 (1): 136–61.

Sheehan, Stephen. 2004. "The Written Off Beat: The Rewritten Text of William Burroughs' *Naked Lunch*." *Philament: A Journal of Literature, Arts, and Culture* 3. http://www.philamentjournal.com/issue3/.

Shelley, Mary Wollstonecraft. 1999. *Frankenstein*, or, the Modern Prometheus. Ware, Hertfordshire: Wordsworth Editions.

Shepherd, P. D. W., and D. C. Watt. 1949. "Curare-Modified Electric Convulsion Therapy." *British Medical Journal* 1 (4610): 752–56.

Singer, Katherine. 2009. "Stoned Shelley: Revolutionary Tactics and Women under the Influence." *Studies in Romanticism* 48 (4): 687–707.

Singh, Nikhil P. 1998. "The Black Panthers and the 'Undeveloped Country' of the Left." In *The Black Panther Party Reconsidered*, edited by Charles E. Jones. Baltimore: Black Classic Press.

———. 2004. *Black Is a Country: Race and the Unfinished Struggle for Democracy*. Cambridge: Harvard University Press.

Slotkin, Richard. 1988. "The Hard-Boiled Detective Story: From the Open Range to the Mean Streets." In *The Sleuth and the Scholar: Origins, Evolution, and Current Trends in Detective Fiction*, edited by Barbara A. Rader and Howard G. Zettler. Westport, Conn.: Greenwood.

Smith, Erin A. 2000. *Hard-Boiled: Working-Class Readers and Pulp Magazines*. Philadelphia: Temple University Press.

Smith, Neil. 1979. "Toward a Theory of Gentrification: A Back to the City Movement by Capital, Not People." *Journal of the American Planning Association* 45 (4): 538–48.

———. 1987. "Gentrification and the Rent Gap." *Annals of the Association of American Geographers* 77 (3): 462–65.

———. 1996. *The New Urban Frontier: Gentrification and the Revanchist City*. New York: Routledge.

———. 2002. "New Globalism, New Urbanism: Gentrification as Global Urban Strategy." *Antipode* 34 (3): 427–50.

———. 2011. "The Evolution of Gentrification." In *Houses in Transformation: Interventions in European Gentrification*, edited by Jaap Jan Berg et al., 15–26. Rotterdam: naio1o Publishers.

Spade, Dean. 2009. "Trans Law and Politics on a Neoliberal Landscape." *Temple Political & Civil Rights Law Review* 18:353–73.

———. 2015. *Normal Life: Administrative Life, Critical Trans Politics, and the Limits of the Law*. Durham, N.C.: Duke University Press.

Spillane, Mickey. 2001. *The Mike Hammer Collection*. Vol. 2, *One Lonely Night, The Big Kill, Kiss Me Deadly*. New York: New American Library.

Spira, Tamara. 2012. "Neoliberal Captivities: Pisagua Prison and the Low Intensity Form." *Radical History Review*, no. 112, 127–46.

Stanley, Fred L., and Louise H. Pratt. 1989. *Conversations with James Baldwin*. Jackson: University of Mississippi Press.

Stansell, Amanda. 2003. "Surrealist Racial Politics at the Borders of 'Reason': Whiteness, Primitivism, and *Négritude*." In *Surrealism, Politics, and Culture*, edited by Raymond Spiteri and Donald LaCross. Farnham, UK: Ashgate.

Steadman Jones, Daniel. 2012. *Masters of the Universe: Hayek, Friedman and the Birth of Neoliberal Politics*. Princeton, N.J.: Princeton University Press.

Stieglitz, Joseph. 2002. *Globalization and Its Discontents*. New York: Penguin.

Stryker, Susan. 2001. *Queer Pulp: Perverted Passions from the Golden Age of the Paperback*. San Francisco: Chronicle.

Sudan, Rajani. 2013. *Fair Exotics: Xenophobic Subjects in English Literature, 1720–1850*. Philadelphia: University of Pennsylvania Press.

Stuelke, Patricia. 2013. "The Making of the Affective Turn: US Imperialism and the Privatization of Dissent in the 1980s." Ph.D. diss., Boston University.

Sugrue, Thomas J. 2005. *The Origins of the Urban Crisis: Race and Inequality in Postwar Detroit*. Princeton, N.J.: Princeton University Press.

Stevens, Margaret. 2017. *Red International and Black Caribbean: Communists in New York City, Mexico and the West Indies, 1919–1939*. London: Pluto.

Szalay, Michael. 2000. *New Deal Modernism: American Literature and the Invention of the Welfare State*. Durham, N.C.: Duke University Press.

———. 2011. "Ralph Ellison's Unfinished Second Skin." *American Literary History* 23 (4): 795–827.

———. 2012. *Hip Figures: A Literary History of the Democratic Party*. Stanford: Stanford University Press.

Tabb, William. 1982. *The Long Default: New York City and the Urban Fiscal Crisis*. New York: Monthly Review.

Teaford, Jon C. 1990. *The Rough Road to Renaissance: Urban Revitalization in America, 1940–1985*. Baltimore: Johns Hopkins University Press.

Truman, Harry. 1949a. "Inaugural Address." January 20, 1949.

———. 1949b. "Letter to the Chairman of the House Judiciary Committee on the Problem of Concentration of Economic Power." July 9, 1949.

Tucker-Abramson, Myka. 2017. "States of Salvation: *Wise Blood* and the Rise of the New Right." *PMLA* 132 (5): 1166–80.

Tyler May, Elaine. 2008. *Homeward Bound: American Families in the Cold War Era*. New York: Basic.

Vaidon, Lawdom. 1977. *Tangier: A Different Way*. Lanham, Md.: Scarecrow.

Vail, Ken. 1999. *Duke's Diary: The Life of Duke Ellington, 1950–1974*. Lanham, Md.: Scarecrow.

Von Eschen, Penny. 2009. *Satchmo Blows up the World: Jazz Ambassadors Play the Cold War*. Cambridge: Harvard University Press.

Wacquant, Loïc. 2009a. *Prisons of Poverty*. Minneapolis: University of Minnesota Press.

———. 2009b. *Punishing the Poor: The Neoliberal Government of Social Insecurity*. Durham, N.C.: Duke University Press.

Wagner-Martin, Linda. 1992. *"The Bell Jar," a Novel of the Fifties*. New York: Twayne.

Wald, Alan M. 1994. *Writing from the Left: New Essays on Radical Culture and Politics*. New York: Verso.

Walker, Dick. 1981. "A Theory of Suburbanization: Capitalism and the Construction of Urban Space in the United States." In *Urbanization and Urban Planning under Advanced Capitalist Societies*, edited by Michael J. Dear and Allen J. Scott, 383–430. New York: Methuen, 1981.

Walker, Mabel L. 1938. *Urban Blight and Slums: Economic and Legal Factors in their Origin, Reclamation, and Prevention*. Cambridge: Harvard University Press.

Wallace, Michelle. 1990. *Black Macho and the Myth of the Superwoman*. New York: Verso.

Walonen, Michael K. 2011. *Writing Tangier in the Postcolonial Transition: Space and Power in Expatriate and North African Literature*. Farnham, U.K.: Ashgate, 2011.

Warren, Kenneth. 2012. *What Was African American Literature?* Cambridge: Harvard University Press.

Warwick Research Collective. 2015. *Combined and Uneven Development: Towards a New Theory of World-Literature*. Liverpool: Liverpool University Press.

Wechsberg, Joseph. 1952. "Anything Goes." *New Yorker*, April 12, 1952, 62–70.

Weiss, Marc A. 1980. "The Origins and Legacy of Urban Renewal." In *Federal Housing Policy and Programs: Past and Present*, edited by J. P. Mitchell. New Brunswick, N.J.: Rutgers University Press.

Wharton, Edith. 2012. *House of Mirth*. London: Penguin Classics.

White, E. B. 2002. "Here Is New York." In *Empire City: New York through the Centuries*, edited by Kenneth Jackson. New York: Columbia University Press.

Whiting, Frederick. 2006. "Monstrosity on Trial: The Case of *Naked Lunch*." *Twentieth Century Literature* 52 (2): 145–74. http://www.jstor.org.proxy .lib.sfu.ca/stable/20479763.

Whyte, William H. 1956. *The Organization Man*. New York: Simon and Schuster.

———. 1968. *The Last Landscape*. Philadelphia: University of Pennsylvania Press.

Will, Barbara. 1998. "The Nervous Origins of the American Western." *American Literature* 70 (2): 293–316.

Wolfe, Jesse. 2000. "'Ambivalent Man': Ellison's Rejection of Communism." *African American Review* 34 (4): 621–37.

Wood, Edith E. 1935. *Introduction to Housing: Slum and Blighted Areas in the United States*. Washington, D.C.: US Government Printing Office.

"Work Nearing End at U.N. Plaza Site." 1952. *New York Times (1923–Current File)*.

Yu, Timothy. 2008. "Oriental Cities, Postmodern Futures: *Naked Lunch*, *Blade Runner*, and *Neuromancer*." *MELUS* 33 (4): 45–71.

Zieger, Susan. 2007. "Pioneers of Inner Space: Drug Autobiography and Manifest Destiny." *PMLA* 122 (5): 1531–47.

Zimet, Jaye. 1999. *Strange Sisters: The Art of Lesbian Pulp Fiction, 1949–1969*. New York: Penguin Putnam.

Zipp, Samuel. 2012. *Manhattan Projects: The Rise and Fall of Urban Renewal in Cold War New York*. New York: Oxford University Press.

———. 2013. "The Roots and Routes of Urban Renewal." *Journal of Urban History* 39 (3): 366–91.

Zisenwine, Daniel. 2010. *Emergence of Nationalist Politics in Morocco: The Rise of the Independence Party and the Struggle against Colonialism after World War II*. London: I. B. Tauris.

Žižek, Slavoj. 2002. "The Actuality of Ayn Rand." *Journal of Ayn Rand Studies* 3 (2) 215–27.

Zukin, Sharon. 2006. "Jane Jacobs: the Struggle Continues." *City & Community* 5, no. 3 (September): 223–26.

———. 2009. *Naked City: The Death and Life of Authentic Urban Places*. New York: Oxford University Press.

Abrams, Charles, 15, 64, 92
Adorno, Theodor, 18, 20
Al-Bakr, Ahmad Hassan, 145n12
American Disease, The (Musto 1973), 154n13
American Pulp (Rabinowitz 2014), 51
Anderson, Martin, 158n8
Another Country (Baldwin 1962): blight of urban dehumanization, 2, 4; experience vs. urban renewal, 3; NYC foreign, 1; racial liberalism breakdown, 9–10; urban decay, 10; urban shock, 1, 2; urban shock transformed, 4, 16
Arabic desert as frontier West, 66, 152n6
Armstrong, Louis, 145n12
Arrighi, Giovanni, 67–68
art and shock, 18–20
Ashe, Marie, 106–7, 121
Atlas Shrugged (Rand 1957): blight and renewal racialized, 87–88; blight of NYC, 84, 87, 88–89, 100; capital from public to private, 89–93, 102–3, 157n4; cities as frontier, 92–93, 100; conclusion of, 100–3, 159n11; creative destruction, 84, 85, 87, 92, 99–100; naturalism escape, 93 96, 101; naturalism's shock and uncanny, 84–85, 95; self-making, 85, 94, 96, 101–3, 158n10; shock as revitalizing, 85, 86, 92–93, 99, 102–3; shock as welfare state destructions, 97–100; shock theme overview, 16–17; suburban subject formation, 22; suburbs as frontier, 15, 89–90; unshockable men of mind, 98–100; urban shock transformed, 4, 16, 85, 92–93, 102–3; as white flight novel, 86, 89; as white flight to frontier, 89–91
Avila, Eric: blight as people of color, 3; Jacobs as mother of neoconservatism,

127; promiscuous black city, 111; white flight and urban decay, 10; world of urban strangers, 63–64

Baldwin, James: *Another Country* author, 1; urban renewal as "negro removal," 3, 9. See also *Another Country*
Baldwin, Kate, 110, 112–13, 118
Banks, Ann, 26–27
barricades: Harlem perspectives, 135; Paris 68 unrest, 126; *Siege* commodities, 132–33, 134–35
Baudelaire, Charles, 18
Bauer, Catherine, 5, 39, 87, 143n5
Beard, George Miller, 150n4
Beaumont, Matthew, 162n7
Bell Jar, The (Plath 1963): capital respatialized, 21; corpse after shock therapy, 115–17, 160n9; corpse of Joan, 107, 122, 123; corpse of suburban femininity, 116–17; "corpses" of ptomaine, 110; corpses of Rosenbergs, 107, 110–11, 115, 121–22, 123; domestication of women, 106–7, 110–11, 116, 160n10; *Feminine Mystique* as paratext, 105, 106, 123; foreignness of renewed New York, 111–14; foreignness of Rosenbergs, 109–10, 111, 113; frontier into urbanization, 16; hunger and consumption, 110, 120–21, 160n9; imprisonment, 115, 118, 123, 160n10; mental breakdown, 105, 117–20; promiscuous black city, 111–14; rest cure vs. West Cure, 114–21; shock and suburban sexual liberation, 123; shock as tool of critical disruption, 106; shock theme overview, 16; shock therapy as commodification, 105, 106, 115–17, 120; shock therapy as erasure, 118–23; slums and Rosenbergs, 109, 111; subject formation

Bell Jar, The (Plath 1963) (*continued*)
racial violence, 104, 105, 106, 107,
122–24; transformations, 104; UN
Building as NYC renewed, 104–5,
107–8, 109, 159n3; urban shock transformed, 4, 16, 118–19; women holding
cultural power, 22, 119. *See also* white
middle-class women

Benjamin, Walter: commodification of
labor, 116; shock and modern art, 18;
shock as urban norm, 3, 18, 20; striking of a match, 99

Berman, Marshall, 41

Berman v. Parker (1954), 157n4

Bewes, Timothy, 42–43

Beyond the Pleasure Principle (Freud 1921),
17, 30–31

black nationalism, 130, 131

Black Panther Party, 128, 162n4

blight: "blight" as term, 87–88; dehumanization of urban dwellers, 2, 4;
homonormativity at others' expense,
62; Housing Act (1949), 1, 2, 6; *Invisible Man* coffin tenements, 38–40;
medical solutions to, 33–34; *Naked
Lunch* urban decay, 63–64, 69–70;
"people of color," 3; as seeds of new
civilization, 92–93; "slums" versus, 87;
urban factories as, 33; urban renewal
perspective, 3, 5, 6, 40, 87

Boggs, James, and Grace Lee: "The City
Is the Black Man's Land," 130–31;
as foundational urban thinkers, 128;
National Organization for Black Power
inspiring, 162n6; readers of Marx, 132;
urban deindustrialization, 37, 131

Boggs Act (1951), 156n25

Bold, Christine, 90

Boston obscenity trial, 67, 153n8

Bowles, Paul, 65–66

Breton, André, 74

Bretton Woods, 11, 12

British imperialism and opium, 68

Britzolakis, Christina, 160n7

Brown, Edgar, 144n9

Brown v. Board of Education (1954), 157n4

Burroughs, William: *Naked Lunch* a "cut-
up" novel, 73, 155n17; *Naked Lunch*
author, 4; obscenity trials, 67, 153n8;
surrealists and Beats meet, 155n18. See
also *Naked Lunch*

Cameron, Ewen, 120

"camp cure." *See* "West Cures"

capitalism: accumulation by dispossession, 30, 160n10; alienation of
workers, 49–50; *Atlas Shrugged* capital
from public to private, 89–93, 102–3,
157n4; "blight" and "redevelopment
front," 87–88; cities as frontiers of
capital, 90, 92–93, 100, 137; city wage
slave, 47, 52–54, 58–59; commodification of masses, 160n9; deindustrialization shift, 136; dolls as workers
commodified, 36, 52–53; domesticity
of white women, 116, 160n10; economically productive bodies, 72–73;
gendered division of labor, 6, 110,
160n10; Goodwill Jazz Ambassadors,
9, 147n1; hygiene and race, 71; Marx
cycle of money, 67–68; new frontiers required, 15–16, 92; *Price of Salt*
subject formation, 49; property values
and ethnic groups, 88, 90–91; Rand's
romanticism genre, 93; Rockefeller
and UN Building, 160n4; self as frontier for capital, 16–21; shock normalizing privatization, 21; shock treatment
to purify, 17; suburbs as triumph of,
5–6, 8, 47, 56, 61, 90, 110; Third
World masculinity, 79–80; US anti-
imperialist imperialism, 65, 67, 71–72,
133–34; US postwar role, 13–14; urban anticapitalist vision, 127–28, 129;
urban war against imperialism, 131,
134–37; urbanization for restabilization, 7–9; women shopping downtown,
6, 58, 109. *See also* commodification;
gentrification; US hegemony

Caro, Robert, 143n8

Carpentier, Alejo, 65

Césaire, Aimé, 71–72

China, 68, 154n14

cities. *See* urban entries

"City Is the Black Man's Land, The"
(Boggs and Boggs 1966), 130–31; cities as sites of revolution, 131–32, 137,
162n6

Civil War against capitalist imperialism,
131, 134–37

Clover, Joshua, 136

cocaine: Industrial Revolution and,
68; *Naked Lunch* surplus population,

69–70; for nervous exhaustion, 68–69; as nonaddicting drug of content, 67; racial fears in the South, 154n13; US hegemony and, 153n10

Cold War: communist containment, 11–13, 146n19; drugs and US hegemony, 66–73, 78, 153n10; Goodwill Jazz Ambassadors, 145n12, 147n1; Housing Act (1949) ideology, 2; Jim Crow undermining hegemony, 32; "kitchen debate" in *Bell Jar*, 110; loyalty into "national character," 147n23; "military-psychology combination," 70–71, 77–78, 80, 154n14; racial liberalism strategy, 34; Red Scare and Lavender Scare, 150n2; Red Scare vs. white middle-class women, 106; Rosenbergs and slums, 109–10; shock therapy as brainwashing, 119; suburbs as triumph of capitalism, 5–6, 8, 47, 56, 61, 90, 110; Tangier challenging tenets, 75; UN Building as safety, 108–9; US systems of control, 72–73; urban renewal and capitalism, 7–9

Cole, Albert, 144n9

Coleridge, Samuel, 76–77

colonialism: decolonizing countries as frontiers, 66; gendered division of labor, 160n10; ghetto as alien land, 109, 130; International Zone history, 65, 152n4; Latahs, 78, 79, 156n22; postcolonialism as more colonialism, 65, 67, 71–72, 133–34; revolutionary intercommunalism, 134; shock normalizing colonization, 21; South embodying, 156n23; surrealism and postcolonial struggles, 32, 75; Third World masculinity, 79–80; urban renewal contradictions, 8–9

Columbia University in *Siege*, 135

commodification: accumulation by dispossession, 30, 160n10; *Bell Jar* consumption, 116, 160n9; *Bell Jar* suburban locus, 116–17; corpse of suburban commodified domesticity, 110–11; cycle of money/drugs, 67–68; "dolls" in *Bell Jar*, 115–17; dolls in *Invisible Man*, 35–38, 115–16; dolls in *Price of Salt*, 49, 52–53, 115–16; economically productive bodies, 72–73; novels escaping from, 65–66; shock as

tool of, 106, 115–17; *Siege* barricades, 132–33, 134–35

Communal Luxury (Ross 2016), 162n7

Commune: barricades and slogans, 132–33; destruction of statehood, 131–32; internationalism, 128, 133, 162n7; revolutionary intercommunalism, 134; riots against accumulation, 136; *Siege* heralding resurgence, 130, 162n5

communism: Communist Party supporting urban struggles, 126, 127–28; containment strategy, 11–13, 146n19; Ellison's rejection of social organizing, 41; Lavender Scare and, 47, 150n2; slums linked to via Rosenbergs, 109–10; technical assistance to vulnerable countries, 71–72

Congress for Cultural Freedom (CCF), 26

Conrad, Joseph, 43

Containment Culture (Nadel 1995), 146n19

Cool World, The (Miller 1957), 130

Corber, Robert, 150n2

corporations. *See* multinational corporations

Courtwright, David, 153n10

Crabgrass Frontier (Jackson 1987), 158n5

criminalization: being within city, 82; of drug addicts, 156n25; *Invisible Man* puppeteer, 35–36; *Naked Lunch* surplus, 63, 65, 69–70; neoliberalism and, 6, 10, 26; postwar global capitalism, 62. *See also* racialized criminality

curare, 76, 155n20

Dalla Costa, Mariarosa, 160n10

Death and Life of Great American Cities, The (Jacobs 1961), 127

deindustrialization of cities: black workers into surplus, 37, 131; blight as, 87; capitalism shift from production to circulation, 136; dolls in *Invisible Man*, 37–38; urban factories as blight, 33

Deleuze, Gilles, 70

Depression. *See* Great Depression

desegregation: Lafargue Clinic, 19, 27; public spaces made black, 44. *See also* segregation

Discourse on Colonialism (Césaire 1950), 71–72

dispossession: accumulation by dispossession, 30, 160n10; dispossess notices, 29; disruptive power of dispossessed, 32–33; exorcized from society, 30; hospitals' veneer of good amid, 33; *Invisible Man* pile of "junk," 28–32; *Naked Lunch* surplus, 63, 65, 69; private becoming public, 29; white flight identification with capital, 91–92. *See also* surplus

dolls: *Bell Jar* shock therapy dummy, 115–17; *Invisible Man* commodification and criminalization, 35–38, 115–16; *Naked Lunch* devil doll, 63; *Price of Salt* commodity fetishism, 49, 52–53, 115–16; *Price of Salt* positive subject making, 55

Dowbnia, Renée, 110, 160n9

drugs: "control societies" using, 70, 76–77, 78; criminalization of addicts, 156n25; curare, 76, 155n20; hegemonic regimes and, 68, 70, 153n10, 154n14; Industrial Revolution and, 68; Marx formula of capital and, 67–73; *Naked Lunch* surplus population, 69–70; for nervous exhaustion, 68–69; obscenity and, 153n8; "pantopon" of opium alkaloids, 69; prosecution for and lynching, 69–70; psychoactive, 70, 154n14; racial anxieties and, 154n13; Romanticism, imperialism, and, 74–75; US hegemony and, 66–73

Du Bois, W. E. B., 31; WEBDuBois Radio, 135

Duggan, Lisa, 46

Dunayevskaya, Raya, 162n5

Dyer-Witherford, Nick, 162n8

"ecological approach" to urban renewal, 87

Edelman, Lee, 61

Edwards, Brian, 75

Ellington, Duke, 145n12, 147n1

Ellison, Ralph: Congress for Cultural Freedom, 26; Great Depression effect on blacks, 27; housing, segregation, and urban policy, 26–28; *Invisible Man* author, 4; mental health as social issue, 27; reification, 41, 42–43; return of the repressed, 27, 30, 32; social organizing rejected, 41–42; surrealism of writing, 19, 27–28. See also *Invisible Man*

Emergence of Social Space, The (Ross 1988), 132

eminent domain: racial policy shift after *Brown*, 157n4; Title I of Housing Act (1949), 143n8; UN Building, 159n2

entrepreneurial subject: *Atlas Shrugged*'s escape from naturalism, 93–96, 101; *Bell Jar* Cold War state versus, 119; *Bell Jar* collateral damage in formation, 107, 122–24; *Bell Jar* protagonist attaining, 21, 105–6, 119–24; definition, 4; hard-boiled genre failure, 82–83; *Invisible Man* white entrepreneurialism, 26, 28, 38, 41, 44; *Price of Salt* subject formation, 49, 55, 60, 62; privatization of frontier, 4, 89–93, 102–3, 157n4; racial violence in formation, 104; remaking subject and metropolitan space, 47, 59, 62, 104; shock as tool of formation, 28, 86, 92–93, 99, 103, 106; subject-shaping in *Naked Lunch*, 70, 73, 77–78, 81; suburban homemakers as, 6, 21, 105–6, 119–24; Third World masculinity, 79; US anti-imperialist imperialism, 72; US deterritorial global empire, 65, 71–72. *See also* self-making

equality politics: definition, 46; global capitalism's inclusion and exclusion, 62; heteronormative domestic arrangements, 75; homonationalism, 61–62; homosexual respectability politics, 46–47, 49, 61–62

Eubank, Balph, 94–95

experience: hunger for, 110; shock as urban norm, 18; shock blunting, 3, 18, 69

Fair Employment Practices Committee, 7

Fantastic Art, Data, Surrealism (MoMA exhibit), 19, 148n4

Faulkner, William, 155n16

Federal Bulldozer, The (Anderson 1964), 158n8

Federal Highway Act (1956), 2

Federal Housing Administration (FHA): Housing Act (1949) segregation, 144n9; mortgage insurance "red" lines, 158n5

Federal Housing Authority on property values, 88

federal housing policy: low-cost mortgage racism, 143n6, 158n5; New Deal
of Roosevelt, 5, 6; segregation via
Federal funding, 6–8. *See also* Housing
Act (1949)

Federal Writer's Project: Ellison oral
histories, 26–27; "The Little Man at
Chehaw Station," 44–45

Federici, Sylvia, 160n10

Feldman, Stanley, 155n20

Feminine Mystique, The (Friedan 1963),
105, 106, 123

Fleissner, Jennifer, 94

Foley, Raymond, 7, 42

Forces of Habit (Courtwright 2001),
153n10

Foster, Hal: dolls in *Bell Jar*, 115–16;
dolls in *Invisible Man*, 36, 115–16; dolls
in *Price of Salt*, 52, 115–16; surrealism,
148n4

Foucault, Michel, 4, 70

Frankenstein (Shelley 1818), 84, 85, 87,
99–100

Freeman, Joseph, 54

Freud, Sigmund: cocaine for workers, 68,
69; compulsive repetition, 17, 20, 30–
31, 53, 95; death drive, 17, 20, 53, 69,
95, 97; *Naked Lunch* dream references,
74; negation, 98; into popular culture,
147n23; protective shield penetrated,
3, 17, 20, 30–31, 69, 95; uncanny, 95;
uncanny and shock, 31; uncanny and
surrealism, 148n4; unconscious not yet
colonized, 21

Freund, David, 90–91

Friedan, Betty, 105, 106, 123

Friedman, Milton, 17

Frontier Club, The (Bold 2013), 90

frontier imagery. *See* Western genre

Fundamentals of Real Estate Practice
(National Association of Real Estate
Boards 1943), 88

Geidel, Molly, 72, 79, 80

gender ideologies: *Feminine Mystique* as
Bell Jar paratext, 105, 106; gendered
division of labor, 160n10; suburban
gender spheres, 6, 110

gentrification: Battle of Washington
Square, 63–65, 125; frontier imagery shaping, 4, 14; Jacobs leading to,

126–27; rent gap, 8, 126, 144n10;
sovereignty of consumer choice,
144n10; urban renewal as precursor,
6–8, 126–27, 136–37

ghetto. *See* slums

Gillespie, Dizzy, 145n12, 147n1

Gindin, Sam, 13, 65, 71, 146n18

Goodwill Jazz Ambassadors, 9, 145n12,
147n1; Belgian Congo and Louis
Armstrong, 145n12; Iraq and Duke
Ellington, 145n12; Syria and Dizzy
Gillespie, 145n12

Goonewardena, Kanishka, 21

gothic genre in *Naked Lunch*, 74

Great Depression: *Bell Jar* hunger, 110,
160n6; city growth halted, 4–5, 27;
dispossess notices, 29; Ellison on effects on blacks, 27; slum creation, 5;
into urban renewal and suburbanization, 7, 28

Greeson, Jennifer Rae, 156n23

hard-boiled genre in *Naked Lunch*, 80–83

Harlem: Ellison oral histories, 26–27;
Ellison's "Harlem Is Nowhere," 19,
27, 31, 34; Harlem Hellfighters, 31;
"Harlem is ours!," 162n6; Lafargue
Clinic, 19, 27; Lincoln Center, 44, 45;
as Paris, 19, 132; *Siege of Harlem* overview, 22–23, 128, 129; Title I project
and funeral parade, 40. See also *Siege
of Harlem*

*Harlem Document: Photographs, 1932–
1940* (Banks and Siskind 1981), 27

Harvey, David: accumulation by dispossession, 30; capitalism requiring new
frontiers, 15, 92; Paris pre-Commune,
132

Haussmann, Baron, 2, 3, 18

Hayek, Frederich, 146n17

Heart of Darkness (Conrad 1899), 43

Herman, Ellen, 147n23

Hesford, Victoria, 56

heteronormative domestic arrangements,
75

Highsmith, Patricia: *Price of Salt* author,
4; on *Price of Salt* ending, 60. See also
Price of Salt, The

highway system: for downtown shoppers,
56, 58; Federal Highway Act, 2; *Price of
Salt*, 22, 56–57; for slum clearance, 56

historicism framework of postwar novels, 11–13
Hoberek, Andrew, 11, 89–90
Hoffman, Julius, 153n8
"Hog Pawn" (Faulkner 1955), 155n16
Home Owners Loan Corporation "red" neighborhoods, 158n5
homeowners instead of renters, 6. *See also* privatization
homology method of criticism, 12, 13
homonationalism, 61–62
homonormativity, 46–47, 49, 61–62
hooks, bell, 106
Horne, Frank, 6–7
hospitals in urban renewal, 33–34
House of Mirth (Wharton 1905), 53
Houseman, Gerald, 94
Housing Act (1937), 5
Housing Act (1949): "Demonstration of Slum Conditions," 40; first policy on blight, 1, 2, 6; gentrification origins, 6–8, 126–27, 136–37; Harlem Title I project, 40; ideology of, 2; Robert Moses origins, 25; NYC as ground zero, 1, 2, 143n2; public-private partnerships, 39, 108; racial segregation, 6–8; shocks cleared away, 20; slum clearance delinked from public housing, 144n9; Title I eminent domain, 143n8; Title I funding segregation, 144n9; Title I project blueprint, 143n2; Title I psychological clearing, 20; Title I UN Building, 108, 159nn2,3
Housing and Home Finance Agency (HHFA): Housing Act (1949) segregation, 6–7; slum clearance, 143n8
Huber, Matthew, 4, 103
Humphrey, Hubert, 137
hygiene and global capitalism, 71, 154n15

Impellitteri, Vincent R., 159n3
Industrial Revolution and drugs, 68
International Congress for Modern Architecture Athens Charter (1933), 89
International Zone (Tangier), 65, 80
Invisible Man (Ellison 1952): dispossession, 16, 28–32; "disruptions" aiding urban renewal, 32–34; dolls as commodification and criminalization, 35–38; explosive scenes as slum clearance, 33; funeral parade and

Harlem Title I project, 40; personal responsibility, 28, 39, 43; plans and planning, 25–26, 27, 28, 32–34, 41; public black and private white, 22; reification, 42–43, 44; shock for subject formation, 28; shock of systemic and racialized violence, 30–32; surplus, 28–29, 31–32, 37–38; urban shock transformed, 4, 16, 35
Isenberg, Alison, 58, 109

Jackson, Kenneth, 158n5
Jackson, Thomas H., 153n8
Jacobs, Jane, 64, 125–27
James, Selma, 160n10
Jameson, Fredric: always historicize, 13; fear of class slippage, 101; homology method, 12; Marx and human nature, 134; textual utopia, 129
Jim Crow: *Invisible Man*'s new racial regime, 26; shock of systemic violence, 31–32; from South to black mind, 43–44; as Southern inequality, 4, 8; undermining US hegemony, 32; violence and segregation of North, 27, 147n3. *See also* segregation
Jiménez, José, 128
Johnson, Lyndon, 92
"Judge Lynch in New York" (Ellison; 1939), 147n3
jungle city. *See* urban jungle
Junky (Burroughs 1952), 153n8
Jurca, Catherine, 14, 15, 86, 102

Kennan, George, 12
Kerouac, Jack, 66
Keynesianism and neoliberalism, 11, 146n18
Khrushchev, Nikita, 110, 128
Klein, Naomi, 17
Kruse, Kevin, 44

Lafargue Clinic (Harlem), 19, 27
Larson, Scott, 126
Last Landscape, The (Whyte 1968), 14
Lavender Scare: definition, 47; happy ending against, 61; linked to national weakness, 47, 61, 150n2; Red Scare defense of lesbianism, 49, 61; Red Scare structure of, 150n2; urban anxieties, 55–56
Le Corbusier, 25

Lebel, Jean-Jacques, 155n18
Lefebvre, Henri, 6
Let It Come Down (Bowles 1952), 65–66
Levenson, Jacob, 6
LGBT landscape: from anti-police more policing, 46, 150n1; homonationalism, 61–62; homosexual respectability politics, 46–47, 49; Lavender Scare, 47, 49, 55–56, 61, 150n2; lesbian pulp novel sites, 51, 55; lesbianism for national renewal, 49, 61; novel with happy ending, 60–61; queer politics, 61; young woman/old woman in fiction, 55, 151n7
"Little Man at Chehaw Station, The" (Ellison 1978), 44–45
Living for the City (Murch 2010), 162n4
Lonely Crowd, The (Riesman 1950), 15
Long Twentieth Century, The (Arrighi 1994), 67–68
Lost Steps, The (Carpentier 2001), 65
Lumumba, Patrice, 145n12
lynchings: black on black, 41; cocaine and Southern racial fears, 154n13; *Naked Lunch* Interzone, 73; *Naked Lunch* surplus, 69–70; white mannequins in *Invisible Man*, 35

Maghreb Desert (North Africa), 66, 152n6
Making of Global Capitalism (Panitch and Gindin 2013), 13, 65, 71, 146n18
Malcolm X, 162n6
Man in the Gray Flannel Suit, The (Wilson 1956), 14
Marx, Karl: alienation of workers, 50; circuit of capital formula, 67–68; commodity fetishism, 36, 52, Commune, 131–32, 133; human nature variability, 134; surplus population, 37
Matthew Shepard Law Enforcement Enhancement (2009), 150n1
May, Elaine Tyler, 61
McCann, Sean, 12, 81–82
medical solutions to blight, 33–34
Melamed, Jodi, 9–10, 34
Melley, Timothy, 78, 119, 123
Michaels, Walter Benn, 12
Mies, Maria, 160n10
Miller, Warren: liberal integrationism, 130; *Siege of Harlem* author, 22–23, 128. See also *Siege of Harlem*

Mitchell, Clarence, 7
Mitchell, Silas Weir, 16, 48, 121
modern art and shock, 18–20
Modern Housing (Bauer 1934), 143n5
Modern Housing movement, 5, 6
Mont Pèlerin and neoliberalism, 11, 146n17
Moretti, Franco, 61
Morocco, independence of, 65, 75, 80, 152n4. See also Tangier
morphine. See opium
Moses, Robert: Battle of Washington Square, 64–65, 125; blight per urban renewal, 3; Committee on Slum Clearance, 2, 25, 40, 64, 143n2, 149n9; ideology of urban renewal, 2; Jacobs versus, 125–26; modern planning in *Invisible Man*, 25; UN Building, 108, 159nn2,3
Moynihan, Daniel Patrick, 134
Moynihan Report (1965), 134, 135
multinational corporations: "Islam Inc." of *Naked Lunch*, 70, 71; *Naked Lunch* penetration by, 72, 79–80
Mumford, Lewis: Modern Housing movement, 5; public housing, 39, 87; UN Building, 160n4
Murch, Donna Jean, 162n4
Museum of Modern Art (MoMA), 19, 148n4
Musto, David, 154n13, 156n25

Nadel, Alan, 146n19
Naked Lunch (Burroughs 1959): criminalization of drug addicts, 156n25; criminalization of surplus, 63, 65, 69–70; drugs and capital, 67–68; drugs and imperialism, 74–76, 78–79; drugs and surplus population, 69–70; drugs and US hegemony, 66–73; Freudian dream references, 74; Freudian language of shock, 69; gentrification, 63–65; gothic genre, 74; hard-boiled genre, 80–83; hygiene and freedom, 71; International Zone history, 65, 80, 152n4; Interzone dream structure, 73–80; miscegenation, 76, 78; noir genre, 63–64, 80; obscenity, 67, 153n8; penetrations, 72, 78–80; racist, southern whites, 156n23; Reconditioning Center historical equivalent, 72–73; Romantic genre, 66, 74–78; suburbs as frontier,

Naked Lunch (Burroughs 1959) (*continued*)
15; surrealist genre, 74, 75, 78; US
hegemony formation, 22, 65, 66; urban
shock transformed, 4, 16, 69–70, 78;
Western genre, 65–66, 80
Napoleon III and urbanization, 3
Narcotics Control Act (1956), 156n25
National Association of Real Estate
Boards, 88
national character: Cold War loyalty into,
147n23; hygiene and race, 71; Lavender Scare threat to, 47, 61, 150n2
National Highway Act (1944), 5
National Housing Act (1937), 5. *See also*
Housing Act (1949)
National Negro Council, 144n9
National Organization for Black Power,
162n6
national security and Lavender Scare, 47,
61, 150n2
naturalist genre: *Atlas Shrugged* escape
from, 93–96, 101; *Atlas Shrugged*
shock and uncanny, 84–85, 95; *Bell Jar*
protagonist transforming from, 105–6;
Burroughs's *Junky*, 153n8; Ellison
shifting away from, 27; *Invisible Man's*
critiques of, 33; modern woman, 53; as
older shock-based modernism, 4; *Price
of Salt* moving west from, 57, 60; *Price
of Salt* shift from, 48, 53; *Price of Salt*
urban decline, 47
Negro Family, The (Moynihan 1965), 134,
135
neoliberalism: "entrepreneurial subject"
of, 4, 21, 103; "equality" politics,
46–47; homosexual respectability
politics, 46–47, 49, 61–62; Keynesianism and, 11, 146n18; Mont Pèlerin
and, 11, 146n17; novels leading to
neoliberal hegemony, 10–16; racial
liberalism breakdown, 10; racialized
criminality origins, 6, 10, 26; shock
and self-making, 16–21, 28; suburbanization and female liberation, 116–24;
suburban subject, urban handout, 91,
93, 100; urban colonization, 136–37;
urban crisis national discourse, 21–22;
urban renewal as profitable failure,
158n8; urbanism origins, 4–10; white
private, racialized public, 7, 22, 39,
44, 91, 118; white suburban and black

urban roots, 3, 4–10. *See also* criminalization; entrepreneurial subject
nervous exhaustion and drugs, 68–69
neurasthenic strain, 48, 57, 150n4. *See
also* "West Cures"
New Masses (periodical), 27, 54
New York City (NYC): *Atlas Shrugged*
blighted city, 84, 87, 88–89, 100;
Battle of Washington Square, 63–65,
125; *Bell Jar* hunger in city of desires,
110; Committee on Slum Clearance, 2,
25, 40, 64, 143n2, 149n9; foreignization of renewal, 1, 111–14; Jacobs
and gentrification, 126–27; Jacobs vs.
Moses myth, 125–26; novels escaping
for authentic cultures, 65–66; postwar
novels, 14; transformation in *Bell Jar*,
104; transformation in *Price of Salt*,
47; urban renewal ground zero, 1, 2,
143n2; white femininity rescued from,
118–119. *See also* Harlem; United Nations (UN) Building
Newton, Huey P., 128, 131–32, 134
Ngô, Fiona, 66, 152n6
Nixon, Richard, 110
Nkrumah, Kwame, 133–34

Obama, Barack, 150n1
obscenity trials, 67, 153n8
O'Dwyer, William, 108, 143n2
O'Meally, Robert, 38
"On Some Motifs in Baudelaire" (Benjamin 1999), 3, 99
On the Road (Kerouac 1957), 66
opium: hegemony and, 68, 153n10;
Naked Lunch surplus population,
69–70; for nervous exhaustion, 68–69;
"pantopon" of opium alkaloids, 69;
profane and quantitative like money,
67–68; Romanticism, imperialism,
and, 74–75
Oppenheimer, Gerald M., 156n25
Ottley, Roi, 19

Panitch, Leo, 13, 65, 71, 146n18
"pantopon" of opium alkaloids, 69
Paris: Benjamin on shock, 3, 18; "blud-
geoned into modernity," 2; Commune,
130, 131–32, 133, 162nn5,7; Harlem
as, 19, 132
Paton, Fiona, 74

Patriarchy and Accumulation on a World Scale (Mies 1999), 160n10
Peace Corp Fantasies (Geidel 2015), 72
perception. *See* experience
Perkins Gilman, Charlotte, 115
Perrin, Tom, 54, 62
Philosophy and Revolution (Dunayevskaya 1982), 162n5
plans and planning in *Invisible Man*, 25–26, 27, 28, 32–34, 41
Plath, Sylvia: *Bell Jar* author, 4; female liberation erasures, 106; hunger and consumption, 110–11; New York renewed, 105; Rosenbergs, 109–10; UN Building, 107–8; woman as figure of US dominance, 22, 119. See also *Bell Jar, The*
Point Four, platform of Truman, 71–72
Poison Arrows (Feldman 2005), 155n20
Political Unconscious, The (Jameson 1981), 13
postcolonialism as more colonialism, 65, 67, 71–72, 133–34
postwar novels: containment/subversion framework, 11–13; experience despite urban shock, 3; global not national, 14; neoliberal hegemony result, 10–16; neoliberal shock imagery, 17; US West and frontier, 14–16; urban shock transformed, 4, 16. *See also* road novels; Western genre
Powell, Adam Clayton, 39–40
Price of Salt, The (Highsmith 1952): alienation of workers, 49–50; bohemianism, 50–51, 54, 56, 58, 61; distancing and identification dance, 50–52, 53; doll as positive subject making, 55, dolls as commodity fetishism, 49, 52–53, 115–16; happy ending, 60–61; highway as structure and transformation, 22, 48; Lavender Scare, 47, 49, 61, 150n2; lesbianism for national renewal, 49; the price of salt sacrifices, 60–61; self-making, 47, 53–55, 58–59, 60; slums breeding perversion, 47, 62; suburbs as frontier, 15, 47–48; urban shock transformed, 4, 16
prison industrial complex, 46
Pritchett, Wendell, 157n4
privatization: capital from public to private, 4, 89–93, 102–3, 157n4;

desegregation making public black, 44; dispossession making private public, 29; "entrepreneurial subject" of neoliberalism, 4; Housing Act (1949) public-private partnerships, 39, 108; *Price of Salt*, 49; *Price of Salt* suburbs, 56; public of New Deal vs. postwar private, 82; shock normalizing, 21; *Siege* abolishing private property, 129, 135; *Siege* seductions by Privileged People, 134–35; suburbs creating, 6; white power, black slum-shock, 34; white private, black public, 7, 22, 39, 44, 91, 118
proletariat, 134, 162n8
property values: blight as opportunity, 93; decline as blight, 87, 93; ethnic groups reducing, 88, 90–91; as race-neutral arguments, 7; UN Building raising, 159n3
psychology: as anxiety and battle, 147n23; Cold War "military-psychology combination," 70–71, 77–78, 80, 154n14
Puar, Jasbir, 61
public black, private white, 7, 22, 39, 44, 91, 118. *See also* privatization
public housing projects: New Deal housing bills, 5, 82; shift to public-private regime, 39, 108; slum clearance link, 144n9
"'Public Menace' of Blight, The" (Pritchett 2003), 157n4
Public Works Administration housing program, 5
Purcell, Richard, 45

Rabinowitz, Paula, 51
racial anger: erased by "therapeutic" shock, 34; failure of racial liberalism, 9–10; medical solution to, 33 34; NYC in *Another Country*, 9
racial liberalism: breakdown in *Another Country*, 9–10; as Cold War strategy of harmony, 34–35; "The Little Man at Chehaw Station," 45; whites escaping urban decay, 42
racialized criminality: dolls in *Invisible Man*, 35–38; entrepreneurism denied, 28; *Naked Lunch* surplus, 63, 65, 69–70; origins, 6, 10, 26; public of New Deal vs. postwar private, 82;

racialized criminality (*continued*)
  public-private regime of housing, 39.
  See also criminalization
racism: "blight" and "redevelopment,"
  88, 157n4; "colored man of means,"
  88; drugs and racial anxieties, 154n13;
  gendered division of labor, 160n10;
  hygiene and, 71; *Invisible Man* in
  North, 33; low-cost mortgage ranking
  systems, 143n6, 158n5; *Naked Lunch*
  racist, southern whites, 156n23; New
  Deal housing bills, 5–6; property value
  loss justification, 88, 90–91; "racial
  liberalism," 9–10, 34–35, 42, 45;
  redlining, 143n6, 144n9, 158n5; *Siege
  of Harlem* not race war, 134–36; US
  hegemony and, 8–9, 32; urban renewal
  as segregation policy, 6–8, 144n9,
  157n4, 158n5; white power, black
  slum-shock, 34; white private, black
  public, 7, 22, 39, 44, 91, 118. *See also*
  racial anger; racialized criminality
Rand, Ayn: *Atlas Shrugged* author, 4; on
  conclusion of *Atlas Shrugged*, , 159n11;
  romanticism genre of, 93–96; urban
  renewal versus, 158n8. See also *Atlas
  Shrugged*
real estate: "colored man of means," 88;
  segregation via federal funding, 6–8,
  144n9, 157n4, 158n5; UN Building
  raising values, 159n3; urban colonization, 136–37. *See also* redlining
Red Scare: Communist Party despite,
  128; defense by white middle-class
  women, 106; defense of lesbianism, 49,
  61; Lavender Scare structure, 150n2
redlining: Housing Act (1949), 144n9;
  low-cost mortgage ranking systems,
  143n6; "red" neighborhoods, 158n5
rent gap, 8, 126, 144n10
return of the repressed: Ellison's surrealism, 27; *Invisible Man*'s dispossessed,
  30, 32; modernism haunted, 32; *Naked
  Lunch* surplus, 69–70, 78
revolutionary intercommunalism, 134
Ricoeur, Paul, 12
Riesman, David, 15
Riis, Jacob, 87
"Rime of the Ancient Mariner"
  (Coleridge 1798), 76–77
Riot. Strike. Riot. (Clover 2016), 136

riots: as Civil War, 131, 134–36; ending
  urban renewal, 10; *Invisible Man* riot
  part of "the plan," 28, 32–33, 40–41;
  Invisible Man veterans' riot, 30, 32–33;
  Siege of Harlem anticipating, 128, 134;
  struggles against accumulation, 136–37
road novels: commodity culture escape,
  65–66; development of self, 16; *Price of
  Salt* mobility, 48, 55, 56–57; Western
  frontier shifted to road, 15, 56. *See also*
  "West Cures"
Rockefeller, John D., 108, 160n4
Romantic genre, 66, 74–78
Romantic Manifesto, The (Rand 1969), 93
romanticism genre of Ayn Rand, 93–96
Ronell, Avital, 67, 153n8
Roosevelt, Franklin Delano, 5, 158n5
"Roots and Routes of Urban Renewal,
  The" (Zipp 2013), 143n3
Rosenberg, Julius and Ethel: execution
  and shock therapy, 106, 115; foreign-
  ness of, 109–10, 111, 113; slums
  symbol, 109, 111
Ross, Kristin, 71, 132, 162n7
Rotella, Carlo: postcolonialism as more
  colonialism, 133–34; *Siege* anticipating
  riots, 128, 133; *Siege* as black nationalism satire, 129–30; urban crisis narrative formation, 21–22

Saldaña-Portillo, María Josefina, 79, 80
Satchmo Blows up the World (Von Eschen
  2004), 145n12
Schwartz, Joel, 33, 64
Scott, James C., 126
Sedgwick, Eve Kosofsky, 62
segregation: cocaine and racial fears,
  154n13; desegregation of public spaces,
  44; Ellison on effects on democracy,
  27; international urbanism versus,
  129; lunacy as social condition of,
  27; private white, public racialized, 7,
  22, 39, 44, 91, 118; redlining, 143n6,
  144n9, 158n5; suburban subject, urban
  handout, 91; urban renewal as policy
  of, 6–8, 144n9, 157n4, 158n5; West as
  white, 58, 90. *See also* Jim Crow
self-making: *Atlas Shrugged* men of mind,
  85, 94, 96, 101–3, 158n10; drugs and
  poisonous status quo, 75; Ellison's
  agony and transcendence, 19; as

genre of hard-boiled, 81; *Price of Salt* transformations, 47, 54–55, 58–59, 60; road novel self development, 16; shock and modern art, 18; shock as modernist refiguring of, 16–21, 102–3, 111; shocks of urban decay as therapeutic, 86, 92–93, 99; suburban subject, urban handout, 91, 93. *See also* entrepreneurial subject; "West Cures"

Servicemen's Readjustment Act (1944), 5

Shelley, Mary Wollstonecraft, 85

Sheltering Sky, The (Bowles 1949), 65–66

shock: absence of in *Siege*, 125; *Atlas Shrugged* men of mind unshockable, 98–100, 102–3; *Atlas Shrugged* welfare state destructions, 97–100; *Bell Jar* erasure, 118–24; *Bell Jar* female commodification, 105, 106, 115–17, 120; *Bell Jar* transformations of, 106; Benjamin on urbanization, 3, 18, 20; Ellison surrealism on lunacy, 27; Freud's protective shield penetrated, 3, 17, 20, 30–31, 69, 95; Freud's uncanny and, 31; inflicted to protect society, 34; modern art and, 18–20; modernist refiguring into self-making, 16–21, 102–3, 111; as obscenity, 153n8; shell shocked, slum shocked, 19, 34; subject formation tool, 28, 86, 92–93, 99, 103, 106; subject-shaping in *Naked Lunch*, 70; surplus of *Naked Lunch*, 69–70, 78; of systemic and racialized violence, 30–32; transformation of urban shock, 4, 16, 35, 102–3; from transformative to capitalist tool, 19–21, 35–38, 40–41; women's liberation privatized, 123

Shock Doctrine, The (Klein 2007), 17

Siege of Harlem (Miller 1965): barricades, 132–33, 134–35; black nationalism satire, 130; Commune, 130, 162n5; freedom of Harlem, 135; Harlem's "internal colony" seceding, 22–23, 128, 129; internationalism, 133–34; liberal integrationism, 130; Privileged People, 129, 134–35; proletariat vs. capitalist imperialism, 128, 134–37; riots as Civil War, 131, 134–37; slogans, 133, 135; textual utopia genre, 129–30

Simkhovitch, Mary, 87

Singer, Katherine, 75

Siskind, Aaron, 27

Situationists, 6

slogans: from rallying cry to marketing, 126, 132; *Siege of Harlem*, 133, 135

slums: Battle of Washington Square, 64; "blight" versus, 87; breeding perversions, 47, 62; clearance–public housing link, 144n9; creation of, 5, 6; ghetto as alien land, 109, 130; highway system for clearance, 56; National Housing Act, 5; New Deal housing bills, 5–6; racist populism behind tolerance, 64; Rosenbergs and, 109, 111; shell shocked, slum shocked, 19, 34

Slums and Blighted Areas in the United States (Wood; 1939), 157n3

Smith, Neil, 8, 14, 92

Soviet Union: Cold War "military-psychology combination," 154n14; Iraq and Duke Ellington, 145n12; US segregation, 8. *See also* Cold War

Spade, Dean, 150n1

Stansell, Amanda, 75

State Committee for Anti-Discrimination (New York), 9

subject formation. *See* entrepreneurial subject

suburbs: *Atlas Shrugged* as white-flight novel, 22, 89, 102; Cold War triumph of capitalism, 5–6, 8, 47, 56, 61, 90, 110; as frontier, 14–15, 89–90, 92, 119; gender spheres, 6, 110; highway system for shopping downtown, 56, 58; Housing Act (1949) cities mirroring, 6, 143n8; *Invisible Man* as critique of, 26, 42; "kitchen debate" in *Bell Jar*, 110; low-cost mortgage ranking systems, 143n6, 158n5; New Deal housing bills, 5, 6; *Price of Salt*, 47–48, 55, 56, 61; as prison, 114–17; private white, public racialized, 7, 91, 118; public of New Deal vs. postwar private, 82; sexual veneer of city, 123; shocks cleared away, 20; *Siege* seductions by Privileged People, 134–35; suburban tax revolts, 10, 11; threat to American way of life, 47–48; women commodified, 106, 116–17; women holding cultural power, 22, 119; women shopping downtown, 6, 58, 109; women's disorders rest cure, 114–17

surplus: black workers in deindustrialization, 37, 131; *Invisible Man*, 28–29,
31–32, 37–38; *Naked Lunch* dispossession, 63, 65, 69; *Naked Lunch* drugs,
69–70; *Naked Lunch* Reconditioning
Center, 72; unwaged surplus, 69, 134;
valuable as test subjects, 72
surrealism: Beats and surrealists meet,
155n18; defined by Hal Foster, 148n4;
drug-induced Romanticism, 75; Ellison and MoMA exhibit, 19, 148n4;
Ellison writing style, 19, 27–28; *Naked
Lunch* Interzone dream, 74; postcolonial struggles and, 32, 75; rejected by
postwar novels, 4; shock and modern
art, 18
Szalay, Michael, 12, 41

Tangier (Morocco): Cold War tenets
challenged, 75, 79; as free markets and
moral permissiveness, 66, 75, 80; heading west to, 65, 66; history of International Zone, 65, 80, 152n4; *Naked
Lunch* Interzone, 75–76, 78–79; Third
World masculinity, 79–80
Teaford, Jon, 143n8
tenements. *See* slums
Title I of Housing Act (1949): eminent
domain, 143n8; funding segregation,
144n9; project blueprint, 143n2; psychological clearing, 20; United Nations
Building, 108, 159nn2,3
"Toward a Theory of Gentrification"
(Smith 1979), 144n10
Truman, Harry, 71–72, 128

United Nations (UN) Building: as
Cold War and urban security, 108–9;
criticism of, 160n4; foreignness of
renewed New York, 111; as New York
renewed, 105, 107–8, 109, 159n3; *Siege
of Harlem* internationalism, 133; *Siege
of Harlem* secession, 129, 135; Title I
project, 108, 159nn2,3
US hegemony: drugs of *Naked Lunch*,
66–73, 78, 153n10; formation in *Naked
Lunch*, 22, 65, 66; International Zone
history, 65, 152n4; Jim Crow undermining, 32; modern suburban woman
leading, 22, 119; novels leading to
neoliberal hegemony, 10–16; postwar
role of global empire, 13–14; "self-

proclaimed policeman," 66; suburban
domesticity fueling, 61; UN Building,
108–9, 160n4; US anti-imperialist
imperialism, 65, 67, 71–72, 133–34;
urban crisis national discourse, 21–22;
urban renewal importance, 8–9; urban
war against imperialism, 131, 134–37
US Narcotic Farm / Prison, 72
US Public Health Service, 72
Urban Blight and Slums (Walker; 1938),
157n3
urban crisis: blight of white flight, 87;
as crisis of shopping, 58; national
discourse on, 21–22
urban decline: *Another Country*'s Rufus,
10; communal living, 6; deindustrialization, 1, 6, 37–38; deindustrialization
and black workers, 37, 131; migrations
in and out, 1, 4–5, 6; *Naked Lunch*,
63–64, 69–70; *Price of Salt*, 47–48,
55, 56; racialized criminality origins,
6; shell shocked, slum shocked, 19,
34; shock as subject formation, 86;
Tangier, 80; white escape, 42
urban jungle: *Atlas Shrugged* New York,
89; *Bell Jar* New York, 107, 112; *Siege
Harlem*, 135
urban renewal: Battle of Washington
Square, 63–65, 125; blight, 3, 5, 6, 40,
87; "blight" as term, 87–88; cities as
frontiers of capital, 90, 92–93, 100,
137; Civil War against imperialism,
131, 134–37; disruption actually
aiding, 32–34; "ecological approach,"
87; end of, 10, 126; as foreignization
threat, 1, 111–13; as gentrification precursor, 6–8, 126–27, 136–37; highway
system and slum clearance, 56;
homonormativity at others' expense,
62; hospitals' role, 33–34; Housing
Act (1949) creating, 6; hygiene and,
154n15; as ideological, 2; *Invisible
Man* as critique of, 26; *Invisible Man*
"disruptions" aiding, 32–34; lesbianism
as tool for, 49, 61; "negro removal,"
3, 9, 126; "neoliberal urbanism," 8;
NYC as ground zero, 1, 2, 143n2; *Price
of Salt* transformations, 47, 59, 62;
"racial liberalism," 9–10; Rand versus,
158n8; rent gap, 7–8, 126, 144n10; as
segregation policy, 6–8, 144n9, 157n4,
158n5; UN Building, 108, 159nn2,3;

urban factories as blights, 33; urban shock transformed, 4, 16, 35; women shopping downtown, 6, 58, 109. *See also* gentrification

"urban sensorium" engagement, 21

utopia, textual genre, 129–30

Virginian, The (Wister 1902), 48

Von Eschen, Penny, 145n12

Wacquant, Loïc, 66

wages: cast-off surplus, 69, 134; city wage slave, 47, 52–54; city wage slave West Cure, 58–59

Wagner-Martin, Linda, 119

Walker, Mabel, 157n3

Warwick Research Collective, 13–14

Washington, Booker T., 38, 44

"West Cures": Arabic desert for, 152n6; *Atlas Shrugged* shocks of urban decay, 86, 92–93; *Bell Jar* rest cure, 114–17, 119; *Bell Jar* West Cure, 117–21; hard-boiled failure, 81–83; *Naked Lunch* return to the city, 80, 81; "neurasthenic strain," 48, 57, 150n4; *Price of Salt* women triumphing, 57–59; of road novels, 16, 48, 57

Western genre: *Bell Jar* transformation, 105–6; capitalism requiring frontiers, 15–16, 92; cities as frontier, 4, 14–16, 57, 59, 66, 111–12; cities as frontiers of capital, 90, 92–93, 100, 137; frontier as commodification escape, 65–66; frontier privatized, 4, 89–93, 102–3, 157n4; hard-boiled failure, 81–83; Maghreb Desert as frontier, 66, 152n6; *Naked Lunch* domestic imperialism, 66, *Naked Lunch* heading west, 65, 66, "neurasthenic strain," 48, 83, 150n4; outdoors for self mastery, 48, 58–59; *Price of Salt* mobility, 48, 55; *Price of Salt* moving west, 57, 60; road narratives from, 15, 56; self as frontier for capital, 16–21; suburbs as frontier, 14–15, 89–90, 92, 117–18; suburbs stripping frontier spirits, 48; West as classless whiteness, 58; West as free markets and moral permissiveness, 66, 75, 80; West as white, 58, 90; western frontier and the East, 66, 152n6. *See also* road novels; "West Cures"

Wharton, Edith, 53

White, E. B., 108, 129

White Diaspora (Jurca 2011), 14, 15, 86, 102

white entrepreneurialism, 26, 28, 38, 41, 44. *See also* entrepreneurial subject

white flight: *Atlas Shrugged* as, 86, 89; *Atlas Shrugged* as frontier-Western, 90–91; blight created by, 87; capital vs. shell-shocked middle class, 92–93, 102–3; as flight from inadequacy, 114; suburban subjects, urban handouts, 91, 100; white diaspora novels, 14, 15, 86, 102; white femininity rescued from urban decay, 118–19; worker-turned-shopper to domesticity, 116. *See also* suburbs

White Flight (Kruse 2005), 44

white middle-class women: assumed value of whiteness, 113–14, 121; collateral damage in formation, 107; corpse of suburban commodified domesticity, 110–11; *Feminine Mystique* oppression, 106; holding cultural power, 22, 119; inadequacy, 113–14, 121; infected by foreignness, 111–14; protecting US from threats, 106; sexuality controlled, 120–22; shopping downtown, 6, 58, 109; suburbanization and female liberation, 117–24

Whiting, Frederick, 67, 74, 153n8

Whyte, William, 14, 92

Wilson, Sloan, 14

Wister, Owen, 48

Wood, Edith Elmer, 87, 157n3

working class vs. proletariat, 162n8

Worthing, Keith, 94–95

Wright, Henry, 39, 87

Wright, Richard, 27

X, Malcolm. *See* Malcolm X

Yellow Wallpaper, The (Perkins Gilman 2013), 115

Yu, Timothy, 76, 78

Zeckendorf, William, 108

Zipp, Samuel, 143n3

Žižek, Slavoj, 158n10

Zukin, Sharon, 127

Lightning Source UK Ltd.
Milton Keynes UK
UKHW01f0003261018
331237UK00001B/35/P